CAMBRIDGE
UNIVERSITY PRESS

Physics

for Cambridge International AS & A Level

WORKBOOK

David Sang & Graham Jones

DEDICATED TEACHER AWARDS

Teachers play an important part in shaping futures. Our Dedicated Teacher Awards recognise the hard work that teachers put in every day.

Thank you to everyone who nominated this year, we have been inspired and moved by all of your stories. Well done to all of our nominees for your dedication to learning and for inspiring the next generation of thinkers, leaders and innovators.

Congratulations to our incredible winner and finalists

WINNER

Ahmed Saya
Cordoba School for A-Level,
Pakistan

Sharon Kong Foong
Sunway College,
Malaysia

Abhinandan Bhattacharya
JBCN International School Oshiwara,
India

Anthony Chelliah
Gateway College,
Sri Lanka

Candice Green
St Augustine's College,
Australia

Jimrey Buntas Dapin
University of San Jose-Recoletos,
Philippines

For more information about our dedicated teachers and their stories, go to

dedicatedteacher.cambridge.org

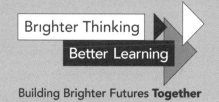

Brighter Thinking
Better Learning

Building Brighter Futures **Together**

CAMBRIDGE
UNIVERSITY PRESS

Shaftesbury Road, Cambridge CB2 8EA, United Kingdom

One Liberty Plaza, 20th Floor, New York, NY 10006, USA

477 Williamstown Road, Port Melbourne, VIC 3207, Australia

314–321, 3rd Floor, Plot 3, Splendor Forum, Jasola District Centre, New Delhi – 110025, India

103 Penang Road, #05-06/07, Visioncrest Commercial, Singapore 238467

Cambridge University Press is part of the University of Cambridge.

It furthers the University's mission by disseminating knowledge in the pursuit of
education, learning and research at the highest international levels of excellence.

www.cambridge.org
Information on this title: www.cambridge.org/9781108859110

© Cambridge University Press & Assessment 2020

First published 2016
Second edition 2020

20 19 18 17 16 15 14 13 12 11 10 9 8

Printed in the Netherlands by Wilco BV

A catalogue record for this publication is available from the British Library

ISBN 978-1-108-85911-0 Workbook with Digital Access

Additional resources for this publication at www.cambridge.org/9781108859110

....

> Contents

> Introduction

This Workbook has been written to help you develop the skills you need to succeed in your AS & A Level Physics course. The exercises in this Workbook will provide opportunities for you to practise the following skills:

- showing understanding of the scientific phenomena and theories that you are studying

- solving numerical and other problems

- thinking critically about experimental techniques and data

- making predictions and using scientific reasons to support your predictions.

This Workbook is designed to support the Coursebook, with specially selected topics where students would benefit from further opportunities to apply skills, such as application, analysis and evaluation in addition to developing knowledge and understanding. (The Workbook does not cover all topics in the Cambridge International AS & A Level Physics syllabus (9702)). An introduction at the start of each exercise tells you which skills you will be working with as you answer the questions. The exercises are arranged in the same order as the chapters in your Coursebook. At the end of each chapter a set of exam-style questions are provided to further support the skills you have practised in that chapter.

We hope that this book not only supports you to succeed in your future studies and career, but will also stimulate your interest and your curiosity in physics.

> How to use this series

This suite of resources supports students and teachers following the Cambridge International AS & A Level Physics syllabus (9702). All of the books in the series work together to help students develop the necessary knowledge and scientific skills required for this subject. With clear language and style, they are designed for international learners.

The coursebook provides comprehensive support for the full Cambridge International AS & A Level Physics syllabus (9702). It clearly explains facts, concepts and practical techniques, and uses real-world examples of scientific principles. Two chapters provide full guidance to help students develop investigative skills. Questions within each chapter help them to develop their understanding, while exam-style questions provide essential practice.

The workbook contains over 100 exercises and exam-style questions, carefully constructed to help learners develop the skills that they need as they progress through their Physics course. The exercises also help students develop understanding of the meaning of various command words used in questions, and provide practice in responding appropriately to these.

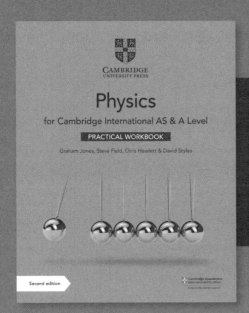

This write-in book provides students with a wealth of hands-on practical work, giving them full guidance and support that will help them to develop all of the essential investigative skills. These skills include planning investigations, selecting and handling apparatus, creating hypotheses, recording and displaying results, and analysing and evaluating data.

The teacher's resource supports and enhances the questions and practical activities in the coursebook. This resource includes detailed lesson ideas, as well as answers and exemplar data for all questions and activities in the coursebook and workbook. The practical teacher's guide, included with this resource, provides support for the practical activities and experiments in the practical workbook.

Teaching notes for each topic area include a suggested teaching plan, ideas for active learning and formative assessment, links to resources, ideas for lesson starters and plenaries, differentiation, lists of common misconceptions and suggestions for homework activities. Answers are included for every question and exercise in the coursebook, workbook and practical workbook. Detailed support is provided for preparing and carrying out for all the investigations in the practical workbook, including tips for getting things to work well, and a set of sample results that can be used if students cannot do the experiment, or fail to collect results.

> How to use this book

Throughout this book, you will notice lots of different features that will help your learning. These are explained here.

CHAPTER OUTLINE

These appear at the start of every chapter to introduce the learning aims and help you navigate the content.

TIP

The information in these boxes will help you complete the exercises, and give you support in areas that you might find difficult.

Exercises

Appearing throughout this book, these help you to practise skills that are important for studying AS & A Level Physics.

EXAM-STYLE QUESTIONS

Questions at the end of each chapter are more demanding exam-style questions, some of which may require use of knowledge from previous chapters. Answers to these questions can be found in the digital version of the Workbook.

KEY EQUATIONS

A list of equations which will help you to complete the exercises appears at the start of every chapter.

KEY WORDS

Key vocabulary is highlighted in the text when it is first introduced. Definitions are then given in the margin, which explain the meanings of these words and phrases.

You will also find definitions of these words in the Glossary at the back of this book.

COMMAND WORDS

Command words that appear in the syllabus and might be used in exams are highlighted in the exam-style questions when they are first introduced. In the margin, you will find the Cambridge International definition.

You will also find the same definitions in the Glossary at the back of this book. *

* The information in this section is taken from the Cambridge International syllabus for examination from 2022. You should always refer to the appropriate syllabus document for the year of your examination to confirm the details and for more information. The syllabus document is available on the Cambridge International website at www.cambridgeinternational.org.

Chapter 1

Kinematics: describing motion

CHAPTER OUTLINE

- define and use distance, displacement, speed and velocity

- draw and interpret displacement–time graphs

- describe laboratory methods for determining speed

- understand the differences between scalar and vector quantities, and give examples of each

- use vector addition to add and subtract vector quantities that are in the same plane

KEY EQUATIONS

$$\text{average speed} = \frac{\text{distance travelled}}{\text{time taken}}$$

$$\text{average speed} = \frac{\Delta d}{\Delta t}$$

$$\text{velocity} = \frac{\text{change in displacement}}{\text{time taken}}$$

$$\text{velocity} = \frac{\Delta s}{\Delta t}$$

Exercise 1.1 Speed calculations

These questions will help you to revise calculations involving speed, distance and time. You will also practise converting units. The SI unit of time is the second (s). It is usually best to work in seconds and convert to minutes or hours as the last step in a calculation. The correct scientific notation for metres per second is $m\,s^{-1}$.

1   A train travels 4000 m in 125 s. The measurement of the time is not exact and the uncertainty in the time is ±1 s. The uncertainty in the distance is negligible.

   a   Calculate the average speed of the train.

   b   Calculate the percentage uncertainty in the time.

   c   Using the time as 125 − 1 = 124 s, calculate the maximum value of the average speed given by these values. Give your answer to a sensible number of significant figures.

   d   Using your answers to parts c and a, calculate the percentage uncertainty in the average speed of the train.

> **TIP**
>
> When multiplying or dividing quantities, the percentage uncertainty in the final result is found by adding together the percentage uncertainty in each of the quantities.
>
> This means your answer to **d** should be the same as the answer to **b** to one significant figure.

2   A spacecraft is orbiting the Earth with a constant speed of $8100 \, \text{m s}^{-1}$. The radius of its orbit is 6750 km.

    a   Explain what is meant by the term *constant speed*.

    b   Calculate how far it will travel in 1.0 hour.

    c   Calculate how long it will take to complete one orbit of the Earth. Give your answer in minutes.

3   A police patrol driver sees a car that seems to be travelling too fast on a motorway (freeway). He times the car over a distance of 3.0 km. The car takes 96 s to travel this distance.

    a   The speed limit on the motorway is $120 \, \text{km h}^{-1}$. Calculate the distance a car would travel at $120 \, \text{km h}^{-1}$ in one minute.

    b   Calculate the distance a car would travel at $120 \, \text{km h}^{-1}$ in 1 s.

    c   Calculate the average speed of the car, in m s^{-1}.

    d   Compare the car's actual speed with the speed limit. Was the car travelling above or below the speed limit?

4   It is useful to be able to compare the speeds of different objects. To do this, the speeds must all be given in the same units.

    a   Calculate the speed, in m s^{-1}, of the objects in each scenario, **i**–**vi**. Give your answers in standard form (also known as *scientific notation*), with one figure before the decimal point.

        i   Light travels at $300\,000\,000 \, \text{m s}^{-1}$ in empty space.

        ii   A spacecraft travelling to the Moon moves at $11 \, \text{km s}^{-1}$.

        iii An athlete runs 100 m in 10.41 s.

        iv   An alpha-particle travels 5.0 cm in $0.043 \times 10^{-6} \, \text{s}$.

        v   The Earth's speed in its orbit around the Sun is $107\,000 \, \text{km h}^{-1}$.

        vi   A truck travels 150 km along a motorway in 1.75 h.

    b   List the objects in order, from slowest to fastest.

Exercise 1.2 Measuring speed in the laboratory

You can measure the speed of a moving trolley in the laboratory using a ruler and a stopwatch. However, you are likely to get better results using light gates and an electronic timer. In this exercise, you will compare data from these different methods and practise analysing data.

1   A student used a stopwatch to measure the time taken by a trolley to travel a measured distance of 1.0 m.

    a   Explain why it can be difficult to obtain an accurate measurement of time in this way.

    b   Explain why the problem is more likely to be greater if the trolley is moving more quickly.

2 This diagram shows how the speed of a trolley can be measured using two light gates connected to an electronic timer. An interrupt card is fixed to the trolley:

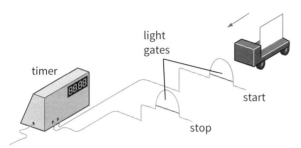

Figure 1.1: For Question 2. Determining acceleration using two light gates.

  a Describe what happens as the trolley passes through the light gates.

  b Name the quantity shown on the timer.

  c What other measurement must be made to determine the trolley's speed? Describe how you would make this measurement.

  d Explain how you would calculate the trolley's speed from these measurements.

  e Explain why this method gives the trolley's *average* speed.

3 It is possible to determine the average speed of a trolley using a single light gate.

  a Draw a diagram to show how you would do this.

  b Describe what happens as the trolley passes through the light gate.

  c Explain how you would find the trolley's average speed using this arrangement.

4 A ticker-timer can be used to record the movement of a trolley. The ticker-timer makes marks (dots) on paper tape at equal intervals of time.

  a Sketch the pattern of dots you would expect to see for a trolley travelling at constant speed.

  b A ticker-timer makes 50 dots each second on a paper tape. State the time interval between consecutive dots.

  c A student measures a section of tape. The distance from the first dot to the sixth dot is 12 cm. Calculate the trolley's average speed in this time interval. Give your answer in $m\,s^{-1}$.

> **TIP**
>
> When using ticker-timers, think about whether to count the dots or the spaces between the dots.

Exercise 1.3 Displacement–time graphs

A **displacement**–time graph is used to represent an object's motion. The gradient of the graph is the object's velocity. These questions provide practice in drawing, interpreting and using data from displacement–time graphs.

1 Velocity is defined by the equation:

$$\text{velocity} = \frac{\Delta s}{\Delta t}$$

  a State what the symbols s and t stand for.

  b State what the symbols Δs and Δt stand for.

  c Sketch a straight-line displacement–time graph and indicate how you would find Δs and Δt from this graph.

> **KEY WORD**
>
> **displacement:** the distance travelled in a particular direction

> **TIP**
>
> Remember to label your graph axes with the correct quantities.

2 This sketch graph represents the motion of a car:

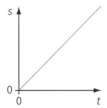

Figure 1.2: For Question 2. Distance–time graph of a car in motion.

a Explain how you can tell that the car was moving with constant velocity.

b Copy the sketch graph and add a second line to the graph representing the motion of a car moving with a higher constant velocity. Label this 'faster'.

c On your graph, add a third line representing the motion of a car which is stationary. Label this 'not moving'.

3 This graph represents the motion of a runner in a race along a long, straight road:

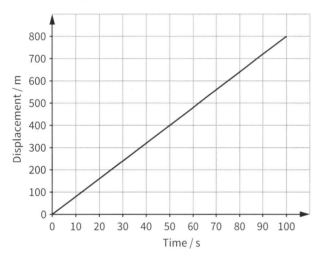

Figure 1.3: For Question 3. Displacement–time graph for a runner.

Use the graph to deduce:

a the displacement of the runner after 75 s

b the time taken by the runner to complete the first 200 m of the race

c the runner's velocity.

4 This table gives values of displacement and time during a short cycle journey:

Displacement / m	0	80	240	400	560	680
Time / s	0	10	20	30	40	50

Table 1.1: Data for a cyclist.

a Draw a displacement–time graph for the journey.

b From your graph, deduce the cyclist's greatest speed during the journey.

Exercise 1.4 Adding and subtracting vectors

These questions involve thinking about displacement and velocity. These are vector quantities – they have direction as well as magnitude. Every quantity in physics can be classified as either a **scalar** or a **vector** quantity. A vector quantity can be represented by an arrow.

1   A scalar quantity has magnitude only.

   a   Name the scalar quantity that corresponds to displacement.

   b   Name the scalar quantity that corresponds to velocity.

   c   For each of the following quantities, state whether it is a scalar or a vector quantity: mass, force, acceleration, density, energy, weight.

2   This drawing shows a piece of squared paper. Each square measures 1 cm × 1 cm. The track shows the movement of a spider that ran around on the paper for a short while:

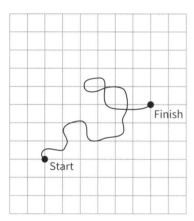

Figure 1.4: For Question 2. Movement of a spider.

   a   How many squares did the spider move *to the right*, from start to finish?

   b   How many squares did the spider move *up the paper*?

   c   Calculate the spider's displacement between start and finish.

      Make sure that you give the distance (in cm) and the angle of its displacement relative to the horizontal.

   d   Estimate the distance travelled by the spider. Describe your method.

3   A yacht sails 20 km due north. It then turns 45° to the west and travels a further 12 km.

   a   Calculate the distance, in km, travelled by the yacht.

   b   Draw a scale diagram of the yacht's journey. Include a note of the scale you are using.

   c   By measuring the diagram, determine the yacht's displacement relative to its starting point.

4   A passenger jet aircraft can fly at 950 km h⁻¹ relative to the air it is flying through. In still air it will therefore fly at 950 km h⁻¹ relative to the ground.

   a   A wind of speed 100 km h⁻¹ blows head-on to the aircraft, slowing it down. What will its speed relative to the ground be?

   b   If the aircraft was flying in the opposite direction, what would its speed be relative to the ground?

   c   The aircraft flies in a direction such that the wind is blowing at it sideways (in other words, at 90°).

      i   Draw a diagram to show how these two velocities add together to give the resultant velocity of the aircraft.

      ii   Calculate the aircraft's speed relative to the ground.

5   Subtract a displacement of 5.0 m in a direction 030° (N30°E) from a displacement of 10 m in a northerly direction.

TIP

To subtract a vector, add on a vector equal in size but in the opposite direction, i.e. add on a 5.0 m vector at 210°.

EXAM-STYLE QUESTIONS

1   a   **Define** speed.   [1]

      This diagram shows a laboratory trolley with an interrupt card mounted on it. The trolley will pass through a single light gate:

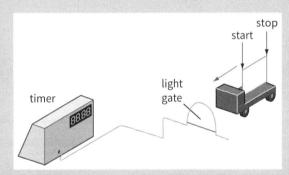

Figure 1.5

   b   **Explain** how the card causes the timer to start and stop.   [3]

   c   The card is 10 cm wide. The timer indicates a time of 0.76 s. **Calculate** the average speed of the trolley.   [2]

   d   Explain why the speed you calculated in **c** is the trolley's *average* speed.   [1]

[Total: 7]

2   A slow goods train is travelling at a speed of 50 km h⁻¹ along a track. A passenger express train that travels at 120 km h⁻¹ sets off along the same track two hours after the goods train.

   a   Draw a displacement–time graph to represent the motion of the two trains.   [4]

   b   Use your graph to **determine** the time at which the express train will catch up with the goods train.   [1]

[Total: 5]

COMMAND WORDS

Define: give precise meaning

Explain: set out purpose or reasons / make the relationships between things evident / provide why and/or how and support with relevant evidence

Calculate: work out from given facts, figures or information

Determine: establish an answer using the information available

CONTINUED

3 This graph represents the motion of a car along a straight road:

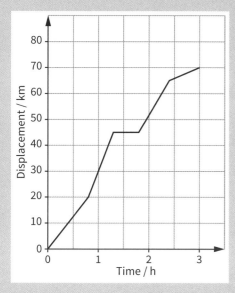

Figure 1.6

From the graph, deduce the following:

a the time taken for the car's journey [1]

b the distance travelled by the car during its journey [1]

c the car's average speed during its journey [1]

d the car's greatest speed during its journey [1]

e the amount of time the car spent travelling at the speed you calculated in **d** [1]

f the distance it travelled at this speed. [1]

[Total: 6]

4 A physical quantity can be described as either 'scalar' or 'vector'.

a **State** the difference between a *scalar quantity* and a *vector quantity*. [2]

b Define *displacement*. [1]

A light aircraft flies due east at $80 \, \text{km h}^{-1}$ for $1.5 \, \text{h}$. It then flies due north at $90 \, \text{km h}^{-1}$ for $0.8 \, \text{h}$.

c Calculate the distance travelled by the aircraft in each stage of its journey. [2]

d Draw a scale diagram to represent the aircraft's journey. [2]

e Use your diagram to determine the aircraft's final displacement relative to its starting point. [2]

[Total: 9]

COMMAND WORD

State: express in clear terms

Chapter 2

Accelerated motion

CHAPTER OUTLINE

- define and use acceleration
- draw velocity–time graphs and use them to determine acceleration and displacement
- derive and use the four equations of motion for uniformly accelerated motion in a straight line
- solve problems involving motion under gravity, including free fall and the motion of projectiles
- describe an experiment to determine the acceleration of free fall

KEY EQUATIONS

$$\text{acceleration} = \frac{\text{change in velocity}}{\text{time taken}}$$

$$a = \frac{v - u}{t} = \frac{\Delta v}{\Delta t}$$

acceleration = gradient of velocity–time graph

displacement = area under velocity–time graph

For a velocity v at an angle θ to the x-direction the components are:

x-direction: $v\cos\theta$

y-direction: $v\sin\theta$

Equations of motion for constant acceleration:

equation 1: $v = u + at$

equation 2: $s = \dfrac{(u + v)}{2} \times t$

equation 3: $s = ut + \dfrac{1}{2}at^2$

equation 4: $v^2 = u^2 + 2as$

Exercise 2.1 Velocity–time graphs

This exercise provides practice in drawing, using and interpreting velocity–time graphs. Remember that **acceleration** is the gradient of a velocity–time graph; displacement is the area under a velocity–time graph.

KEY WORD

acceleration: rate of change of velocity of an object

1   This graph represents the motion of a vehicle:

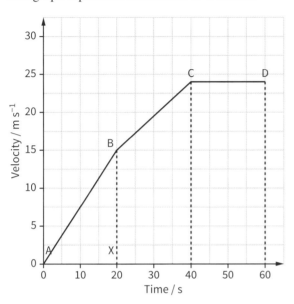

Figure 2.1: For Question 1. Velocity–time graph representing the motion of a vehicle.

a   How can you tell from the graph that the vehicle started from rest?

b   After what time did the vehicle stop accelerating? Explain how you can tell.

c   The vehicle is accelerating in the section **AB**. Use the triangle **ABX** to calculate the time for which the vehicle accelerated in this section.

d   Determine the increase in the vehicle's velocity in this time.

e   Use your answers to **c** and **d** to calculate the vehicle's acceleration in the section **AB**.

f   Now consider section **BC** of the graph. Follow the same steps as in parts **c** to **e** to calculate the vehicle's acceleration in the section **BC**.

g   Calculate the area of the triangle **ABX**. What does this area represent?

h   Calculate the total distance travelled by the vehicle in its journey **ABCD**.

2   This table shows how the velocity of a car changed as it moved along a straight road:

Velocity / m s⁻¹	10	10	17	24	28	28	28
Time / s	0	20	40	60	80	100	120

Table 2.1: Data for the velocity of a car.

   a   Draw a velocity–time graph to represent the car's journey.

   b   Between which two times was the car's acceleration greatest? Calculate its acceleration between these times.

   c   Calculate the distance travelled by the car during its journey. You will need to divide the area under the graph into rectangles and triangles.

3   A car is approaching traffic lights. The driver brakes so that the car's velocity decreases from $22\,\mathrm{m\,s^{-1}}$ to $7\,\mathrm{m\,s^{-1}}$ in a time of $10\,\mathrm{s}$.

   a   Sketch a velocity–time graph to represent this section of the car's journey.

   b   Calculate the car's acceleration.

   c   State how the graph shows that the car is decelerating. Remember that 'decelerating' means that the car's velocity is decreasing; its acceleration is *negative*.

   d   On your graph, shade the area which represents the car's displacement as it is braking.

   e   Calculate the displacement of the car as it is braking.

4   A moving train decelerates at a rate of $0.2\,\mathrm{m\,s^{-2}}$ for a time of $50\,\mathrm{s}$. In this time, it travels a distance of $2000\,\mathrm{m}$. Deduce the train's velocity just before it started to decelerate. Start by sketching a velocity–time graph and mark on it the information given in the question.

Exercise 2.2 Deriving the equations of motion

There are four equations of motion, sometimes known as the 'suvat equations'. This exercise will help you to understand their derivation.

Equation 1: $v = u + at$

Equation 2: $s = \dfrac{(u+v)}{2} \times t$

Equation 3: $s = ut + \dfrac{1}{2}at^2$

Equation 4: $v^2 = u^2 + 2as$

1   a   Which quantities do the symbols s, u, v, a and t represent?

     b   The equations only apply to an object moving with **uniform acceleration** in a straight line. What is meant by the phrase *uniform acceleration*? Remember that acceleration is a vector quantity.

2   Equation 1 can be deduced from the definition of acceleration.

   a   Acceleration can be defined as:

     $\dfrac{\text{(final velocity} - \text{initial velocity)}}{\text{time}}$

     Write this equation in symbols.

b   Rearrange the equation to give the first of the equations of motion.

c   Which of the five quantities from question **1a** is not involved in this equation?

3   Equation 2 can be found by imagining that an object moves at a constant velocity equal to its average velocity.

a   Write an equation (in words and then in symbols) for the object's average velocity, in terms of its initial and final velocities.

b   Use your answer to part **a** to write down the equation for displacement. To find the object's displacement, multiply the average velocity by the time taken.

c   Which of the five quantities from question **1a** is not involved in this equation?

4   To deduce the equations 3 and 4, we start from a simple velocity–time graph:

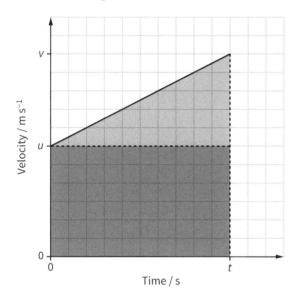

Figure 2.2: For Question 4. Velocity–time graph.

a   Describe the motion represented by this graph.

We have to deduce an equation for displacement. This is represented by the area under the graph. We can divide this area into two parts:

displacement = area of rectangle + area of triangle

b   The area of the rectangle represents the displacement if the object had moved at a steady speed u for time t. What is the value of this area?

c   The area of the triangle represents the object's *additional* displacement resulting from its acceleration. The height of this triangle is $v - u$. Rearrange the equation that defines acceleration to find the height of the triangle in terms of a and t.

d   The area of a triangle = $\frac{1}{2} \times$ base $\times$ height. Use your answer from **c** to write down the area of the triangle in terms of a and t.

e   Write down the complete equation for displacement s in terms of the two areas.

f   Which of the five quantities from question **1ba** is not involved in this equation?

> **TIP**
>
> Equation 1 defines acceleration.

5   Equation 4 has to be deduced from equations 1 and 2, using algebra.

   a   Write out equation 1. Rearrange it so that time t is its subject.

   b   Write out equation 2. Substitute for t using your answer to part **a**.

   c   Rearrange the equation to give an expression which has the form of 'the difference of two squares'.

   d   Make v^2 the subject of the equation.

   e   Which of the five quantities from question **1a** is not involved in this equation?

Exercise 2.3 Using the equations of motion

When using the equations of motion, you need to identify the 'suvat' quantities involved and the equation that links them.

1   A truck is moving at $12\,\text{m s}^{-1}$. It accelerates uniformly at $0.75\,\text{m s}^{-2}$ for $20\,\text{s}$.

   a   Calculate the velocity of the truck after this time.

   b   Calculate the average velocity of the truck while it is accelerating.

   c   Use your answers to **a** and **b** to calculate the distance the truck travels while it is accelerating.

   d   Check that you get the same answer to **c** using the equation:

$$s = ut + \frac{1}{2}at^2$$

2   A moving train decelerates at a rate of $0.2\,\text{m s}^{-2}$ for a time of $50\,\text{s}$. In this time, it travels a distance of $2000\,\text{m}$. Use one of the equations of motion to deduce the train's velocity just before it started to accelerate. (This is question **4** from Exercise 2.1 but now you can solve it more directly using one of the equations of motion.)

3   A car is stationary. It accelerates at $0.8\,\text{m s}^{-2}$ for $10\,\text{s}$ and then at $0.4\,\text{m s}^{-2}$ for a further $10\,\text{s}$. Use the equations of motion to deduce the car's final displacement. You will have to split the journey into two parts, since the acceleration changes after $10\,\text{s}$.

4   A car is being tested on a track. The driver approaches the test section at a speed of $28\,\text{m s}^{-1}$. He then accelerates at a uniform rate between two markers separated by $100\,\text{m}$. The car reaches a speed of $41\,\text{m s}^{-1}$.

   a   Calculate the car's acceleration.

   b   Calculate the time during which the car is accelerating.

> **TIP**
>
> Because the four *suvat* equations are connected to each other, you can usually find a way of using an alternative equation to check an answer.

Exercise 2.4 Motion under gravity

When an object moves in **free fall** under gravity, the only force acting on it is its weight, which acts vertically downwards. Near the surface of the Earth, the acceleration due to gravity is $g = 9.81\,\text{m}\,\text{s}^{-2}$ (approximately) vertically downwards. You can use the equations of motion to solve problems involving motion under gravity.

1   Give the sign, positive or negative, of the force on an object due to gravity near the surface of the Earth.

2   A stone is thrown vertically upwards. Eventually it falls to the ground.

   a   Copy and complete this table to show the signs, positive or negative, of the quantities shown.

Quantity	Displacement	Velocity	Acceleration
stone moving upwards			
stone at highest position			
stone falling downwards			

   Table 2.2: For Question 2a.

   b   Which of these velocity–time graphs represents the motion of the stone? Explain your choice.

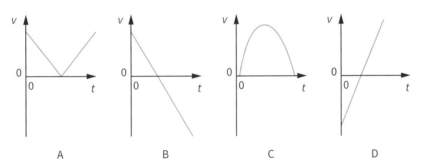

   Figure 2.3: For Question 2b. Four velocity–time graphs.

3   A child throws a ball vertically upwards and catches it when it returns to the ground. The ball's initial upward velocity is $6.5\,\text{m}\,\text{s}^{-1}$.

   a   Calculate the height to which the ball rises. Think about the ball's velocity at its highest point.

   b   Calculate the time the ball spends in the air. Think about the ball's final velocity.

   The child is standing on the edge of a cliff 55 m high when she throws the ball upwards. She allows the ball to fall to the bottom of the cliff.

   c   Calculate the speed with which the ball reaches the ground at the foot of the cliff.

   d   Calculate the time the ball spends in the air. Remember to consider both the upward and downward parts of the ball's movement.

4   An object that is fired or thrown upwards at an angle is called a *projectile*. This diagram shows the path of a projectile – in this case, an arrow – fired at 45° to the horizontal with an initial velocity of 24 m s⁻¹. It then moves freely through the air, so that the only force acting on it is gravity. It lands some distance away on the level ground:

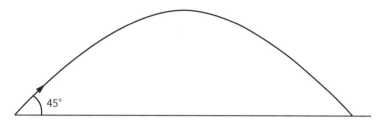

Figure 2.4: For Question 4. Diagram showing the motion of a projectile thrown upward at an angle.

TIP

A projectile in the absence of air resistance has constant acceleration vertically downwards and constant velocity horizontally.

To calculate the distance travelled by the arrow, we must first calculate the time it spends in the air. To do this, we consider its vertical motion.

a   Calculate the vertical (upward) **component** of the arrow's initial velocity.

b   What is the arrow's vertical displacement when it lands on the ground?

c   Calculate the time the arrow spends in the air.

Now we can consider the arrow's horizontal motion.

d   No horizontal forces act on the arrow. What is its horizontal acceleration?

e   Calculate the horizontal component of the arrow's initial velocity.

f   Calculate the distance travelled horizontally by the arrow.

5   A projectile travels the greatest horizontal distance on level ground if it is initially fired at 45° to the horizontal. Calculate the distance travelled by the arrow in question **4** if it was fired at 50° to the horizontal, at the same initial velocity as before. You can follow the same logical approach as in question **4**.

KEY WORD

component: the effect of a vector along a particular direction

TIP

For part **f**: you have calculated the time taken in part **c** and the arrow's horizontal velocity in part **e**.

EXAM-STYLE QUESTIONS

1 **a**   Define *acceleration*.   [1]

A train is travelling at 40 m s⁻¹ when the driver sees a red signal at a distance of 2.2 km ahead. The driver applies the brakes so that the train slows down with **uniform acceleration** and stops as it reaches the signal.

   b   Calculate the train's acceleration as it is braking.   [3]

   c   Calculate the time taken for the train to come to a halt.   [2]

   d   **Sketch** a velocity–time graph for this part of the train's journey. State how your graph shows that the train's acceleration is *uniform*.   [2]

   e   Indicate on your graph the area that represents the distance travelled by the train.   [1]

                                                                        [Total: 9]

KEY WORDS

uniform acceleration: when the change in velocity of an object is the same in the same time period; sometimes called constant acceleration

COMMAND WORD

Sketch: make a simple freehand drawing showing the key features

CONTINUED

2   In an experiment to determine *g*, the acceleration of free fall, a ball-bearing
is released so that it falls through a trapdoor, as shown in Figure 2.5:

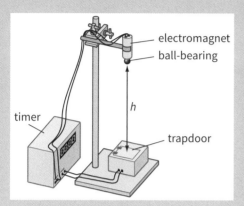

Figure 2.5

The timer starts when the ball is released and stops when the ball reaches the
trapdoor.

a   Explain how you would determine *g* from the height *h* and the
time taken *t*.   [3]

b   In practice, the timer may start slightly *before* the ball begins to fall,
because the electromagnetic force does not drop to zero instantaneously.
This means that the time *t* will be slightly greater than if the ball falls
completely freely. Will the value of *g* calculated be greater than expected,
or less? Explain your answer.   [2]

In an attempt to determine *g* using projectile motion, a student fires a
metal ball with an initial velocity of $12.0\,\text{m s}^{-1}$ and at an angle of 45° to the
horizontal, as shown in Figure 2.6. The ball lands at a distance of 14.7 m on
level ground. (You may assume air resistance is negligible.)

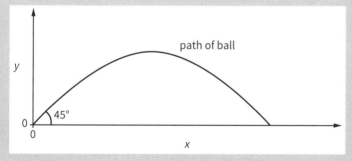

Figure 2.6

c   By considering the ball's horizontal motion, calculate the time
taken for the ball to travel this distance.   [2]

d   By considering the ball's vertical motion, calculate a value
for the acceleration of free fall.   [2]

[Total: 9]

Chapter 3

Dynamics: explaining motion

CHAPTER OUTLINE

- identify the forces acting on a body and represent them on a free body diagram
- calculate the resultant of several forces
- use the relationship force = mass × acceleration
- use the concept of weight as the effect of a gravitational field on a mass
- describe the motion of objects falling in a uniform gravitational field with air resistance
- understand that the weight of an object may be taken as acting at its centre of gravity

KEY EQUATIONS

force = mass × acceleration; $F = ma$

weight = mass × gravitational field strength; $W = mg$

Exercise 3.1 Identifying forces

You can determine how an object will move by considering all the forces acting on it. But first you must be able to identify the forces acting on an object and represent them on a free body diagram.

1   This diagram shows a man pushing a car to start it moving:

    a   To represent the car as a free body diagram, draw a rectangle. Add arrows to represent each of these forces:

- the pushing force provided by the man
- the weight of the car
- the upward **normal contact force** of the ground on the car. (Although there is a contact force on each wheel, you can represent these by a single upward force.)

Figure 3.1: For Question 1. Diagram of a man pushing a car.

KEY WORDS

normal contact force: the force at right angles to a surface when two objects are in contact

b Now imagine that the car is travelling at a steady speed. The forwards force on the car is provided by the engine; a backwards **resistive force** is provided by air resistance. Draw a second free body diagram to represent this situation.

c The car presses down on the road. Explain why this force is not included on the free body diagram.

2 This diagram shows a skier moving quickly down a slope:

Figure 3.2: For Question 2. Diagram of a woman skiing down a slope.

a Copy the diagram, drawing a rectangle to represent the skier. Add arrows to represent each of these forces acting on the skier:

- her weight; remember that weight acts vertically downwards
- the contact force of the ground; remember that the contact force acts at right angles to the surface
- air resistance and **friction** with the ground (these can be represented by a single arrow); remember that these resistive forces act in the opposite direction to an object's motion.

b Now imagine that the skier reaches level ground. Draw a free body diagram to show the forces acting on her.

3 When a fish moves through water, four forces act on it:

- its weight
- the **upthrust** of the water
- the forwards force produced by the movement of its body and fins
- the resistance of the water.

a Draw a free body diagram to represent these forces acting on a fish as it moves horizontally through water.

b Some fish leap out of the water to avoid predators. Think about the forces acting on the fish as it moves horizontally through the air. Draw a free body diagram for the fish in this situation. (Air resistance is negligible.)

Exercise 3.2 How forces affect motion

If the forces acting on a body are unbalanced, it will accelerate. Otherwise it will remain at rest or moving with constant velocity. This exercise gives you practice identifying resultant forces and the resultant accelerations.

1   These diagrams represent the forces acting on each of three objects, A, B and C:

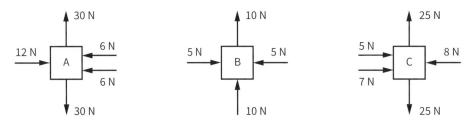

Figure 3.3: For Question 1. Force diagrams for three objects.

a   Determine the **resultant force** acting on each object. Which object has balanced forces acting on it?

b   For each of the other two objects, draw a diagram and add an arrow to represent the resultant force.

c   Describe how each of the objects will move as a result of the forces acting on it.

2   These free body diagrams represent the forces acting on two cars:

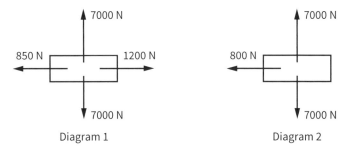

Diagram 1   Diagram 2

Figure 3.4: For Question 2. Force diagrams for forces acting on two cars.

a   Which diagram represents the forces acting on a car that is accelerating to the right?

b   Calculate the resultant force acting on this car.

The other diagram represents the forces on a car that is braking.

c   Name the forces acting on this car.

d   Calculate the resultant force acting on this car.

KEY WORDS
resultant force: the single force acting on a body that has the same effect as the sum of all the forces acting on it

Exercise 3.3 Force, mass and acceleration

Force, mass and acceleration are linked by the equation $F = ma$. In this equation, $\boldsymbol{F}$ represents the resultant force acting on mass m. This exercise gives you practice using and rearranging this equation and in using base units.

1   a   A truck of mass 40 000 kg accelerates at 1.20 m s^{-2}.

  Calculate the resultant force acting on the truck. Give your answer in kilonewtons (kN).

  b   Calculate the acceleration of a ball of mass 2.8 kg when a force of 48 N acts on it.

  c   A spacecraft accelerates at 0.40 m s^{-2} when a force of 200 N acts on it. Calculate the mass of the spacecraft.

2   A parachutist has a mass of 95 kg. She is acted on by an upward force of 1200 N caused by her parachute. (acceleration due to gravity $g = 9.81$ m s^{-2})

  a   Calculate the parachutist's weight.

  b   Calculate the resultant force acting on her and give its direction.

  c   Calculate her acceleration and give its direction.

> **TIP**
>
> To find the direction, it can help to draw a simple free body diagram.

3   A car of mass 680 kg is moving at 12 m s^{-1}. When the driver presses harder on the accelerator pedal, there is a resultant forwards force of 510 N on the car. This force acts for 20 s. Calculate:

  a   the car's speed after this time

  b   the distance travelled by the car in this time.

> **TIP**
>
> You may find it simplest to calculate the car's average speed.

4   An astronaut is on the Moon. He picks up a small rock. He carries out two simple experiments to determine its mass.

  a   He drops the rock from a height of 2.0 m and finds that it takes 1.6 s to reach the ground. Use this result to estimate the acceleration due to gravity on the Moon's surface.

  b   He hangs the rock from a newtonmeter and finds that its weight is 3.9 N. Use your answer to part **a** to estimate the mass of the rock.

  c   Calculate the weight of the rock on the surface of the Earth. Remember, the equation $W = mg$ is true everywhere, but g varies from place to place.

5   a   Write down the units of these quantities in terms of SI base units:

  speed, velocity, acceleration, force, kinetic energy (KE $= \frac{1}{2}mv^2$)

  b   A student writes down the formula $a = \frac{m}{F}$. Show that this formula must be incorrect as the equation is not **homogenous** (i.e. it has different base units on each side).

  c   Select the SI base units and the derived units from the list:

  speed, kilogram, force, mass, newton, mole, m s^{-1}

> **KEY WORD**
>
> **homogenous:** equations with the same base units on each side

Exercise 3.4 Terminal velocity

When an object moves through a fluid, such as air or water, it experiences a **drag** force. These questions are about how this force affects the body's motion.

1   This diagram shows a ship moving through water:

250 kN   500 kN

Figure 3.5: For Question 1. Diagram of a ship with thrust and drag forces.

Two horizontal forces act on the ship: the forwards thrust provided by its engines and the backwards drag force of the water.

a   Determine the resultant force acting on the ship. Remember to give both magnitude and direction.

b   The ship has a mass of 200 tonnes. Calculate its acceleration. (1 tonne = 10^3 kg)

The drag force on the ship increases as it moves faster. Eventually the ship's velocity is constant.

c   The ship has reached **terminal velocity**. Calculate the ship's acceleration at this point.

d   What can you say about the two horizontal forces acting on the ship?

e   Suggest two ways in which the ship's terminal velocity might be increased.

The ship leaves port and its engines are set to deliver constant maximum thrust.

f   Look at these graphs:

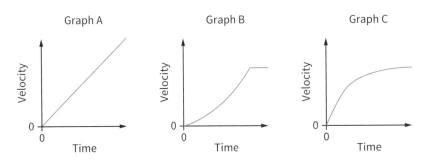

Figure 3.6: For Question 1f. Three velocity–time graphs.

Which of the graphs might represent how the ship's velocity changes? Explain your choice. Think about the gradient of the graphs.

g   Sketch a graph to show how the ship's acceleration changes up to the time when it reaches terminal velocity.

2 Figure 3.7 shows the forces acting on a parachutist at different points as he falls towards the ground. The lengths of the arrows represent the relative sizes of the forces.

a Name the two forces acting upwards and downwards on the parachutist.

b Which of the two diagrams represents the forces acting when the parachutist is moving more quickly through the air? Explain how you know.

c Which of the diagrams represents the forces acting as the parachutist falls at a slow, steady speed? Explain how you know.

d A parachutist falls freely through the air before opening his parachute. Explain why he decelerates when his parachute opens.

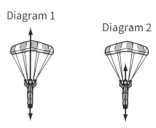

Figure 3.7: For Question 2. Two diagrams of forces acting on a parachutist.

EXAM-STYLE QUESTIONS

1 This diagram shows the forces acting on a body of mass 20.0 kg. The body is initially at rest.

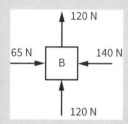

Figure 3.8

a Calculate the resultant force acting on the body. [2]

b State whether the forces on the body are balanced or unbalanced. [1]

c Calculate the body's acceleration. [2]

d Calculate the distance moved by the body in 10 s. [2]

[Total: 7]

2 A box of mass 12.0 kg is placed on a rough floor.

a Draw a free body diagram to represent the forces acting on the box. [2]

b Calculate the value of each force acting on the box. [3]

A girl pushes the box along the floor with a force of 35.0 N.
The box slides in a straight line with a constant velocity of 0.5 m s^{-1}.

c Are the forces on the box balanced or unbalanced? Explain how you know.
(acceleration due to gravity = 9.81 m s^{-2}) [2]

[Total: 7]

CONTINUED

3 A table tennis ball is thrown upwards. It rises through the air and then falls back to the ground, as shown in this diagram:

● Point A

Figure 3.9

For such a light-weight ball, air resistance is a significant force. Air resistance acts in the opposite direction to the ball's velocity and increases as its velocity increases.

a Draw a free body diagram to show the forces acting on the ball when it is moving upwards at point A. [2]

b State the direction of the ball's resultant acceleration when it is moving upwards at point A. [1]

c As the ball falls downwards, it passes again through point A. State whether its acceleration will be greater than, less than, or the same as when it was at point A moving upwards. Explain your answer. [2]

d State the ball's acceleration when it is at its highest point. Explain your answer. [2]

[Total: 7]

4 a Determine the SI base unit of force. [1]

b The resistive force F on a spherical ball as it moves through a fluid at speed v is given by the formula $F = k\rho v^2$, where k is a constant and ρ is the density of the fluid. Derive the base units of density (which equals $\frac{\text{mass}}{\text{volume}}$) and the base units of k. [2]

c A ball of weight 27 N falls through air with a terminal velocity of 30 m s^{-1}. Using the formula in **b** determine the resistive force when the ball has a speed of 10 m s^{-1}. [2]

d The speed v of ocean waves of wavelength λ is given by the formula $v = (g\lambda)^n$, where n is a constant and g is the acceleration of free fall. Determine the value of n. [2]

[Total: 7]

Chapter 4

Forces: vectors and moments

CHAPTER OUTLINE

- add two or more coplanar forces
- resolve a force into perpendicular components
- define and calculate the moment of a force
- state the conditions for a body to be in equilibrium
- use a vector triangle to represent coplanar forces in equilibrium
- state and apply the principle of moments
- define and use the concept of a 'couple' and calculate the torque of a couple

KEY EQUATIONS

moment = force × perpendicular distance from pivot

moment of a couple (torque) = one of the forces × perpendicular distance between the forces

Exercise 4.1 Adding forces

Chapter 3 included some problems in which a body was acted on by more than one force. This exercise includes situations where you need to use vector addition to find a resultant force.

1   This diagram shows an object with two forces acting on it. The forces are at 90° to each other:

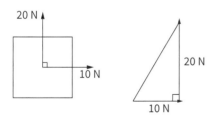

Figure 4.1: For Question 1. Diagram of forces acting on an object.

The diagram also shows the triangle we use to add these forces. In this case, it is sufficient to sketch the triangle.

a   Which side of the triangle represents the resultant force acting on the object?

b   Calculate the magnitude of the resultant force.

c   Use trigonometry to calculate the angle of the resultant force to the horizontal.

2   A falling stone is acted on by two forces:

- its weight, acting vertically downwards, of magnitude 15 N
- a force due to the wind, acting horizontally, of magnitude 3 N.

a   Draw a free body diagram to show the forces acting on the stone.

b   Sketch a triangle that will allow you to determine the resultant of the two forces.

c   In your triangle, the forces will have the same directions as in the free body diagram but they will be shown head-to-tail. Use Pythagoras' theorem to determine the magnitude of the resultant force on the stone.

d   Use trigonometry to calculate the angle of the resultant force to the horizontal.

> **TIP**
>
> If you see an angle of 90° in a question, you will probably have to use Pythagoras' theorem.

3   This diagram shows an object with two forces acting on it. In this case the two forces are not at 90° to each other:

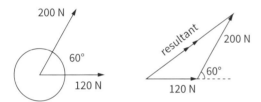

Figure 4.2: For Question 3. Diagram of an object with forces acting on it and triangle of forces.

The diagram also shows the triangle we use to add these forces. Note that the lines representing the two forces are joined head-to-tail.

a   Draw a scale diagram of the triangle. Use a scale of 20 N cm⁻¹ so that the 200 N force is represented by a line of length 10 cm.

b   Measure the length of the side of the triangle that represents the resultant force. State the value of the resultant force.

c   Measure the angle between the resultant force and the horizontal. State its value.

4   This free body diagram shows the two forces acting on a ship as its engine causes it to change direction:

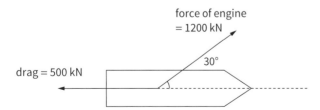

Figure 4.3: For Question 4. Diagram of forces acting on a ship.

a   Sketch a triangle that will allow you to determine the resultant force on the ship.

b   Now, following the same procedure as in question **3**, make a scale drawing and use it to deduce the magnitude and direction of the resultant force on the ship. Choose a scale that will give a large triangle covering, perhaps, half a page.

Exercise 4.2 Resolving forces

A single force can be broken down (resolved) into two **components** at right angles to each other.

1   Look at these diagrams:

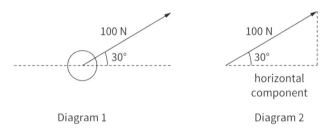

Diagram 1   Diagram 2

Figure 4.4: For Question 1. Diagram of force at an angle and diagram to show horizontal component.

Diagram 1 represents a force of 100 N acting at 30° to the horizontal.

Diagram 2 indicates how we would find the horizontal component of this force. We draw a right-angled triangle with the force vector as its hypotenuse. The horizontal component is then represented by the horizontal side of the triangle.

a   Use trigonometry to determine the horizontal component of the force.

b   Use a similar method to calculate the vertical component of the force. (You could draw a new triangle or use the one shown.)

c   Check your answers by using Pythagoras' theorem to show that the resultant of the two components is equal to the original force (100 N).

2   A force of 250 N acts at an angle of 45° to the vertical.

a   Determine the horizontal and vertical components of this force. Include a sketch to show these two components.

b   Explain why these two components are equal in magnitude.

3   This diagram represents the forces acting on a skier moving down a slope. The skier is accelerating down the slope:

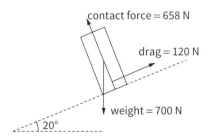

Figure 4.5: For Question 3. Diagram of forces on a skier moving downslope.

a   Calculate the component of the skier's weight down the slope.

b   Calculate the net force on the skier down the slope.

c   Explain why the contact force of the ground on the skier does not cause him to accelerate.

d   Show that the component of the skier's weight at right angles to the slope is equal to the contact force.

4   The idea of resolving a force to find its component in a particular direction can be extended to any other vector quantity. If an aircraft is flying NE at $300\,\text{m s}^{-1}$, calculate the component of its velocity in the direction due east.

Exercise 4.3 Moment of a force

There are two ways to increase the turning effect of a force (its **moment**):

- increase the force

- increase the distance of the force from the pivot.

This exercise provides practice in using this relationship and in using the **principle of moments**.

1   This diagram shows a beam that is acted on by four forces:

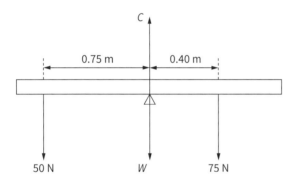

Figure 4.6: For Question 1. Forces acting on a beam.

The beam is balanced at its **centre of gravity**. This means that we can ignore two forces (the weight of the beam W and the upward contact force C of the pivot on the beam) because they pass through the pivot (distance = 0).

You have to decide whether the beam is in **equilibrium**.

a   Calculate the moment of the 50 N force about the pivot. State whether the moment acts clockwise or anticlockwise.

b   Repeat for the 75 N force.

c   Is the beam in equilibrium? Explain your answer.

2   This diagram shows a beam that is acted on by four forces. The weight of the beam and the contact force at the pivot are equal. Both act through the pivot and are not shown. It is in equilibrium:

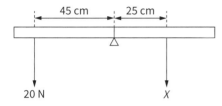

Figure 4.7: For Question 2. Forces acting on a beam.

You have to find the unknown force X.

a   Calculate the moment of the 20 N force about the pivot. State whether the moment acts clockwise or anticlockwise.

b   The beam is balanced so the unknown force X has an equal but opposite moment about the pivot. Use this fact to calculate the value of X.

3   This diagram shows a beam that is acted on by four forces. It is in equilibrium:

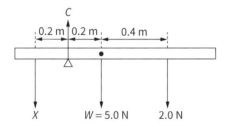

Figure 4.8: For Question 3. Forces acting on a beam.

The beam's weight does not act through the pivot and so it will have a turning effect that must be taken into account.

a   Two forces act clockwise about the pivot. Calculate the moment of each of these forces. Add the moments to find the total clockwise moment.

b   Calculate the unknown force X.

c   Knowing that the beam is balanced (in equilibrium), we can say that there is no resultant force acting on it. Use this idea to calculate the contact force C that acts on the beam at the pivot.

> **TIP**
>
> In calculating X, you can ignore the contact force C because it acts at the pivot, the point about which we are taking moments.

4   Two children are using a long, uniform plank balanced on a cylindrical oil drum as a seesaw. The plank has a mass of 40 kg. It is 5.0 m in length and it is pivoted at a point 2.0 m from one end.

Child A has a mass of 45 kg and sits at the end nearer to the pivot. Child B has a mass of 25 kg and sits at the other end.

a   Which one word in the question tells you that the plank's centre of gravity is at its midpoint?

b   Draw a diagram to represent this situation. Show the forces acting as multiples of g, the acceleration due to gravity.

c   Determine the resultant moment acting on the plank and indicate its direction on your diagram.

5 This diagram shows a box of length 25 cm acted on by four forces:

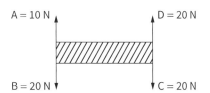

Figure 4.9: For Question 5. Forces acting on a box.

a Which two forces constitute a **couple** acting on the box? Explain your choice.

b Calculate the **torque of the couple**.

EXAM-STYLE QUESTIONS

1 A pendulum consists of a spherical mass (a bob) on the end of a light string. In this diagram, the bob is stationary. It is acted on by the horizontal force *F*. The bob has a weight of 1.8 N.

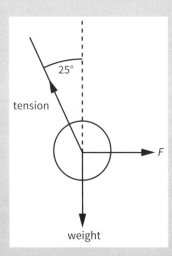

Figure 4.10

a The bob is acted on by three forces. State whether the bob is in equilibrium, and explain your answer. **[2]**

b Determine the vertical component of the tension in the string. **[2]**

c Determine the tension in the string. **[2]**

d Determine the value of the force *F*. **[2]**

e The bob is released by removing the force *F*. What will be the resultant force acting on the bob at this instant? **Give** its magnitude and direction. **[2]**

[Total: 10]

CONTINUED

2   This diagram represents a uniform rectangular block of weight 40 N. The block is stationary; it has been raised at one corner by a vertical force X:

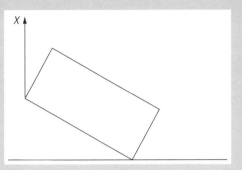

Figure 4.11

    a State the two conditions required for a body to be in equilibrium. **[2]**

    b Calculate the value of the force X. **[2]**

    c Calculate the value of the contact force that acts on the box at the point where the box touches the ground. Give the direction of this force. **[2]**

[Total: 6]

3   A flower basket is hung from the end of a uniform horizontal pole which projects from a wall, as shown. The pole is supported by a cable attached to a higher point on the wall:

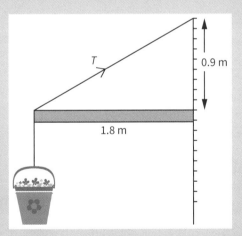

Figure 4.12

The pole has a mass of 10.0 kg; the flower basket has a mass of 14.0 kg.

    a By taking moments about the right-hand end of the pole, determine the value of the tension in the cable T. **[5]**

    b The wall exerts a force R on the pole. Deduce the horizontal component of R. **[3]**

[Total: 8]

Chapter 5

Work, energy and power

CHAPTER OUTLINE

- understand and use the concept of work

- apply the principle of conservation of energy

- understand and use the relationship between force and potential energy in a uniform field

- derive and use the formulae for kinetic energy (KE) and gravitational potential energy (GPE)

- use the equation for power

- understand what is meant by the efficiency of a system, and use this to solve problems

- describe how energy losses arise in practical devices

KEY EQUATIONS

work done = force × displacement $W = Fs$

change in g.p.e. $\Delta E_p = mg\Delta h$

kinetic energy $E_k = \dfrac{1}{2}mv^2$

efficiency $= \dfrac{\text{useful output energy}}{\text{total input energy}} \times 100\%$

power, $P = \dfrac{W}{t} = F \times v$

Exercise 5.1 The concept of work

When a force F acts on a body, the force may do work on the body. This exercise provides practice in calculating the work done in a number of different situations.

1   The **joule** is defined as the work done (or energy transferred) when a force of $1\,N$ moves a distance of $1\,m$ in the direction of the force. You should be able to answer the following questions using mental arithmetic.

Calculate the work done when:

a   a force of $1\,N$ moves a distance of $5\,m$ in the direction of the force

b   a force of $30\,N$ moves a distance of $1\,m$ in the direction of the force

c   a force of $30\,N$ moves a distance of $5\,m$ in the direction of the force.

KEY WORD

joule: the work done (or energy transferred) when a force of $1\,N$ moves a distance of $1\,m$ in the direction of the force

2   Imagine that you are trying to push a broken-down car along the road. You are not strong enough to make the car move.

   a   Four forces are acting on the car (its weight, the upward contact force from the road, your push and friction). Explain how you know that none of these forces does work on the car.

   b   A crane is used to lift the car upwards, off the road. Draw a free body diagram showing the forces that act on the car when it is above the ground.

   c   Which force has done work on the car when it has been lifted like this?

   d   The lifting force of the crane is 7500 N. Calculate the work done on the car when it has been raised 2.4 m above the road.

> **TIP**
>
> You can calculate the work done W using $W = Fs$. Take care! The displacements must be in the direction of the force.

3   A child sits at the top of a long, smooth slide, as shown. Her mass is 50 kg.

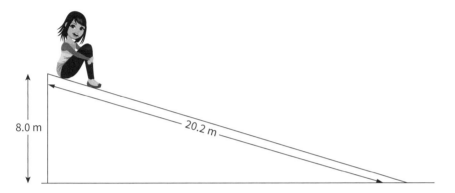

> **TIP**
>
> Look out for the 'code' word *smooth* in future questions during your course.

8.0 m   20.2 m

Figure 5.1: For Question 3. Diagram of a child on a slide.

   a   Calculate the child's weight.

   b   What does the word 'smooth' suggest to you about the frictional force on the child when she goes down the slide?

   c   Which force does work on the child as she goes down the slide?

   d   Calculate the work done on the child by this force as she moves from the top of the slide to the bottom. Remember that the distance moved must be in the direction of the force.

   e   Describe how the child's speed changes as she slides down.

4   When a force does work on a body, it transfers energy to the body. The amount of energy transferred to the body is equal to the work done on it by the force.

   Look back at question **2** to answer parts **a** and **b**.

   a   By how much does the energy of the car increase when the crane lifts it to a height of 2.4 m above the ground?

   b   What form does this increase in energy take?

   Look back at question **3** to answer part **c**.

   c   The child's **kinetic energy (KE)** increases as she moves down the slide. Determine the increase in her KE as she moves down the full length of the slide.

   Use the principle of conservation of energy to answer part **d**.

> **KEY WORDS**
>
> **kinetic energy (KE):** the energy of an object due to its motion

d In practice, no slide is perfectly smooth. Suppose that a frictional force of 80 N acts up the slide. Calculate the work done against this force as the child moves down the slide.

e Calculate the increase in the child's KE in this situation.

5 This diagram shows the orbits of two satellites around the Earth:

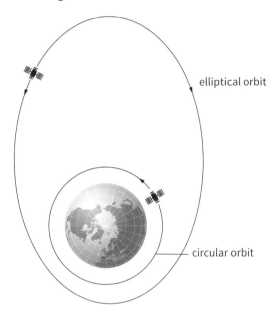

Figure 5.2: For Question 5. Orbits of two satellites around Earth.

One orbit is circular; the other is elliptical. In each case, the only force acting on the satellite is the pull of the Earth's gravity.

a Explain why the force of gravity does no work on the satellite that is in a circular orbit.

For the satellite in an elliptical orbit, its distance from the Earth changes. Some of the time it is closer to the Earth, and some of the time it is further away.

b At which point in its orbit does the satellite have its maximum **gravitational potential energy (GPE)**? Think about how GPE depends on height above the Earth's surface.

c Use the idea of 'work done by a force' to explain why the satellite's speed increases as it moves closer to the Earth.

d At which point in its orbit does the satellite have its maximum KE?

e Describe how the satellite's speed changes as it travels around its orbit.

6 The diagram shows a force of 70 N acting on an object at an angle of 30° to the horizontal direction.

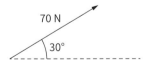

Figure 5.3: For Question 6.

> **KEY WORDS**
>
> **gravitational potential energy (GPE):** the energy of an object due to its position in a gravitational field

The force moves the object in the horizontal direction only. In a time of 4.0 s the distance moved is 5.0 m. Calculate:

a the component of the force in the horizontal direction

b the work done by the force

c the rate at which work is done by the force.

Exercise 5.2 Gravitational potential energy and kinetic energy

You can calculate the GPE and the KE of an object using these equations:

$E_\text{p} = mgh$

$E_\text{k} = \dfrac{1}{2}mv^2$

In this exercise you will look at the derivations of these equations. (The acceleration due to gravity at the surface of the Earth is 9.81 m s^{-2}.)

1 A ball of mass 0.35 kg was thrown upwards. It reached a height of 5.3 m above its starting position.

   a Calculate the weight of the ball.

   b Calculate the increase in its GPE when it is at its highest point.

   c Determine the decrease in the ball's GPE as it falls back down to its starting position.

2 The equation for GPE is $E_\text{p} = mgh$.

   a State the quantities represented by the symbols m, g and h.

   A body of mass m was raised at a steady speed in a gravitational field by a force F.

   b Explain how you know that the forces on the body were balanced.

   c Explain why it follows that $F = mg$.

   d The body was raised through a height h. Calculate the work done by the force F.

   e Determine the increase in the body's GPE.

3 The equation for KE is:

$E_\text{k} = \dfrac{1}{2}mv^2$

   a State the quantities represented by the symbols m and v.

   You can derive the KE equation starting from one of the equations of motion:

$v = u^2 + 2as$

   Imagine a body that is initially at rest. A force F acts on it to accelerate it to speed v.

   b Write down the body's initial velocity u.

   c Write down a modified equation of motion that takes your answer to part **a** into account.

d   Multiply both sides of the equation by $\frac{1}{2}m$.

e   On the right-hand side you now have the quantity *mas*. What is the quantity *ma* equal to? What is the quantity *mas* equal to?

4   This question involves calculating a *change* in KE. Take care when calculating a change in KE. You need to calculate the KE before and the KE after the change; do not be tempted to calculate using the change in *speed*.

    a   A boy of mass 54 kg is running at a speed of 5.0 m s⁻¹. Calculate his KE.

    b   The boy accelerates to a speed of 6.3 m s⁻¹. Calculate the change in his KE.

5   This diagram shows a simple pendulum:

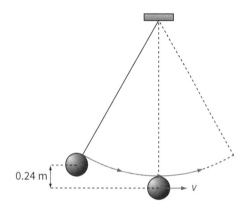

Figure 5.4: For Question 5. Diagram of a pendulum.

The pendulum bob has a mass of 25 g. When pulled to the left, it is 0.24 m above the lowest point in its swing.

    a   Determine the change in the bob's GPE when it swings from its starting point to the lowest point.

    b   Determine the speed *v* of the bob at its lowest point.

    c   Explain why the speed of the bob is greatest at the lowest point in its swing.

Exercise 5.3 Energy efficiency

Everything we do involves energy changes. We want to make the best use of our energy resources; we want to waste as little energy as possible – that's why it is important to understand the idea of **energy efficiency**.

KEY WORDS

energy efficiency:
the amount of useful energy as a fraction of the total energy

1   An electric lamp is supplied with 60 J of energy each second. It produces 2.4 J of light energy per second.

    a   Determine the amount of energy wasted as heat each second.

    b   Calculate the lamp's efficiency. Give your answer as a percentage. Remember that efficiency is the amount of useful energy as a fraction of the total energy.

2   This Sankey diagram represents the energy changes each second in a combined heat and power (CHP) station. CHP stations burn fuel to generate hot water and electricity:

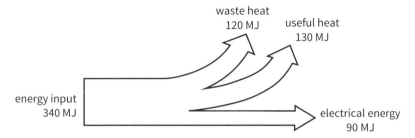

Figure 5.5: For Question 2. Sankey diagram representing the energy changes each second in a combined heat and power (CHP) station.

a   How much energy is supplied to the power station, by its fuel, each second?

To calculate efficiency, you need to identify all *useful* energy transfers. Wasted energy is usually heat, but not all heat is wasted energy.

b   How much useful energy does the power station supply each second?

c   How much energy is wasted by the power station each second?

d   Calculate the efficiency of the power station.

3   Imagine that you are lifting some heavy boxes onto a conveyor belt. Each box weighs 175 N and you have to lift it to a height of 1.2 m.

a   Calculate the work done in lifting each box.

b   After ten minutes, you have lifted 40 boxes. Calculate the work you have done.

c   In this time, your body has used 95 kJ of energy. How much of this energy is wasted?

d   Suggest the form taken by most of this wasted energy.

e   Calculate the efficiency of your body in this task. State whether you think the human body is efficient as a lifting machine.

4   A car of mass 650 kg accelerates from rest to a speed of 22 m s⁻¹.

a   Calculate the car's kinetic energy.

To achieve this acceleration, the car's engine burns 0.023 litre of petrol. Each litre of fuel stores 40 MJ of chemical energy.

b   Calculate the energy in the burned fuel.

c   Calculate the efficiency of the engine in accelerating the car.

Exercise 5.4 Power

Power is the rate at which work is done, or the rate at which energy is transferred per unit time. Its unit is the watt, W (1 W = 1 J s⁻¹).

1   You can apply the idea of power to any situation where energy is transferred. In these examples, divide energy by time to find power, or multiply power by time to find energy.

KEY WORD

power: the rate at which work is done (or energy is transferred) per unit time

    a   Calculate the power of an electric motor which transfers 180 000 J of energy in one minute. Give your answer in kW.

    b   A car has an engine rated at 45 kW. Calculate the energy transferred by the engine in one minute.

    c   A healthy, adult human requires about 10 MJ of energy from their food each day. Estimate their average power.

2   A lift in a shopping centre can transport 20 people to a height of 54 m in a time of 14 s. The lift compartment has a mass of 1420 kg and the average person has a mass of 60 kg.

    a   Calculate the combined mass of the compartment and the 20 people in it.

    b   Calculate the energy gained as the lift travels upwards. (Think about the lift as it rises. Which form of energy is increasing?)

    c   Calculate the rate at which energy is transferred by the lift motor to the compartment.

3   The power rating of an electric lamp tells you the rate at which it uses electrical energy.

    Lamp A has a power rating of 24 W, and a light output of 2.3 W.

    Lamp B has a power rating of 100 W, and a light output of 3.2 W.

    Which lamp is the more efficient? Show your calculation for each lamp.

> **TIP**
>
> Note that efficiency can be calculated using values of power instead of energy.

EXAM-STYLE QUESTIONS

1 **a**   Define the *joule*.   **[2]**

    b   A steel ball of mass 20 g is placed on a smooth, curved track as shown:

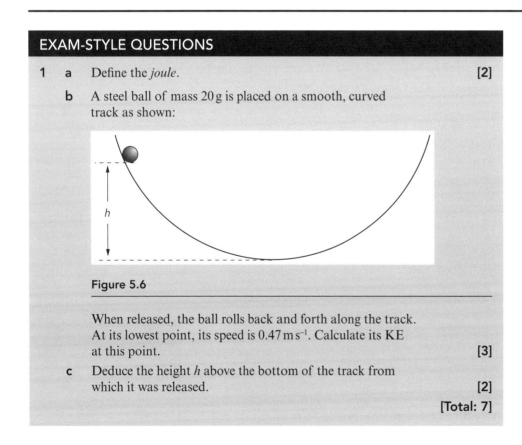

Figure 5.6

        When released, the ball rolls back and forth along the track. At its lowest point, its speed is 0.47 m s⁻¹. Calculate its KE at this point.   **[3]**

    c   Deduce the height h above the bottom of the track from which it was released.   **[2]**

                                      [Total: 7]

CONTINUED

2   This diagram shows a wooden block on a rough, 1.75 m long slope. It shows the four forces acting on the block as it is pulled, by a length of string, up the slope at a steady speed:

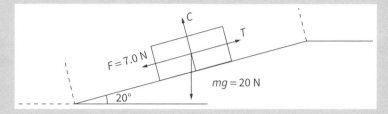

Figure 5.7

a   Explain why the contact force C does no work on the block as it moves.   [2]

b   Calculate the work done against the frictional force F by the block as it moves along the length of the slope.   [2]

c   Calculate the work done against the gravitational force mg by the block as it moves along the length of the slope. [2]

d   Calculate the work done by the pulling force T.   [2]

e   Calculate the value of T.   [2]

[Total: 10]

3   The diagram shows a car travelling up a slope at a constant speed of 20 m s⁻¹.

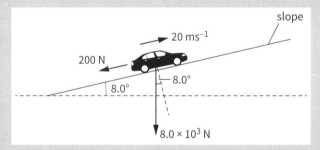

Figure 5.8

The weight of the car is 8000 N and there is a resistive force of 200 N acting down the slope, which is at 8.0° to the horizontal.

a   State what is meant by *work done*.   [1]

b   State the value of the resultant force acting on the car and explain your answer.   [2]

c   Calculate the increase in gravitational potential energy of the car per second.   [2]

d   Calculate the work done per second against the resistive force.   [2]

e   Calculate the power developed by the car as it travels up the slope.   [2]

[Total: 9]

Chapter 6

Momentum and Newton's laws

CHAPTER OUTLINE

- define linear momentum

- state and apply the principle of conservation of momentum

- relate force to the rate of change of momentum

- discuss energy changes and relative velocity of approach and separation in elastic and inelastic collisions

- state and apply Newton's three laws of motion

KEY EQUATIONS

momentum = mass × velocity; $p = mv$

force = rate of change of momentum; $F = \dfrac{\Delta p}{\Delta t}$

Exercise 6.1 Momentum calculations

The following exercise provides practice in rearranging and using the equation for **linear momentum**. Calculating the momentum of an object is not difficult, but remember that momentum is a vector quantity.

Always remember to check units and convert to scientific notation as needed.

1 Calculate the momentum of:

    a a lab trolley of mass 1.0 kg moving at 20 cm s^{-1}

    b a car of mass 650 kg moving at 24 m s^{-1}

    c the Earth, mass 6.0×10^{24} kg, moving at 29.8 km s^{-1} in its orbit around the Sun.

2 A runner of mass 74 kg is moving at 7.5 m s^{-1}. She accelerates to a speed of 8.8 m s^{-1}.

    a By how much has her momentum increased?

        You can use the change in velocity to calculate change in momentum.

    b By how much has her kinetic energy increased?

KEY WORDS

linear momentum: the product of an object's mass and velocity

TIP

Take care! You cannot use the change in velocity to calculate change in kinetic energy.

3   A spacecraft of mass 40 kg is in a circular orbit around the Earth. It moves at a constant speed of $8.1\,km\,s^{-1}$. It completes exactly half an orbit in a time of 46 minutes.

   a   By how much does its momentum change in this time? Remember that momentum is a vector quantity.

   b   By how much does its kinetic energy change in this time? Explain your answer.

   c   The force of gravity holds the spacecraft in its orbit. Calculate the work done by this force during one half-orbit.

Exercise 6.2 Getting a feel for momentum changes

You can use the principle of **conservation of momentum** to picture what happens when two objects collide head-on, or when two objects explode apart.

1   Picture a collision in which a moving object collides with a stationary object; they stick together. They must move after the collision if momentum is to be conserved, and their velocity must be less than that of the original moving object.

   a   A 1 kg mass moving at $6\,m\,s^{-1}$ collides with a stationary 2 kg mass. They stick together. Determine their speed after the collision.

   b   A 4 kg mass moving at $5\,m\,s^{-1}$ collides with a stationary 1 kg mass. They stick together. Determine their speed after the collision.

2   Now picture a collision in which the two objects do not stick together.

   a   A 1 kg mass moving at $6\,m\,s^{-1}$ collides with a stationary 1 kg mass. They do not stick together. After the collision, the first mass is stationary. What is the speed of the second mass?

   b   State whether kinetic energy is conserved in this collision.

3   Now picture an explosion in which a stationary object splits into two parts that move away from each other in opposite directions.

   a   An object explodes into two parts of equal mass. What can you say about their velocities?

   b   An object explodes into two parts, of masses 2 kg and 5 kg. The 2 kg mass moves at $30\,cm\,s^{-1}$. Calculate the speed of the 5 kg mass.

4   Trolley A has a mass of 5 kg and is moving at $2.0\,m\,s^{-1}$. Trolley B has a mass of 2.5 kg and is moving at $4.0\,m\,s^{-1}$ in the opposite direction. They collide and they stick together.

   a   Calculate the momentum of each trolley before the collision.

   b   What will be their velocity after the collision? Explain your answer.

   c   Explain why this is like an explosion in reverse.

> **KEY WORDS**
>
> **conservation of momentum:** within a closed system the total momentum in any direction is constant

Exercise 6.3 Momentum conservation calculations

Because momentum is always conserved when two or more objects interact, we can calculate unknown values of velocity. For two objects, we can represent the conservation of momentum as an equation:

$$m_1u_1 + m_2u_2 = m_1v_1 + m_2v_2$$

This exercise provides practice in using this equation.

1   A stationary mass explodes into two parts with masses 3.0 kg and 4.5 kg. The smaller mass flies off with a speed of 12 m s^{-1}.

   a   Determine the values of m_1u_1 and m_2u_2.

   b   Calculate the speed of the larger mass after the explosion.

   c   What can you say about the directions in which the two masses move?

2   A ball of mass 0.35 kg rolls along the ground at 0.60 m s^{-1}. It collides with a second, stationary ball of mass 0.70 kg and, after the collision, moves with a speed of 0.40 m s^{-1} in the same direction as before. The second ball moves off with speed 0.10 m s^{-1}.

   a   Calculate the momentum of the moving ball before the collision.

   b   Calculate the momentum of each ball after the collision.

   c   Show that momentum is conserved in this collision.

   d   In a perfectly elastic collision, kinetic energy is conserved. Calculate the kinetic energy of each mass before and after the collision. Is this a perfectly elastic collision?

3   A child throws a ball of mass 0.30 kg at a wall. It strikes the wall with a speed of 5.0 m s^{-1} and bounces off with the same speed in the opposite direction.

   a   Calculate the change in the ball's momentum.

   b   The ball collides with the wall, but the wall is attached to the Earth. This means that the momentum of the Earth has been changed by the collision. The mass of the Earth is 6.0×10^{24} kg. Estimate the change in the Earth's velocity caused by the collision with the ball.

Exercise 6.4 Force and momentum

When a force acts on a body and there is a displacement, work is done by the force on the body. The body accelerates, so its momentum changes. The force and the rate of change of momentum it produces are related by force = rate of change of momentum. For a constant force, we can write this as:

$$\text{force} = \frac{\text{change of momentum}}{\text{time taken}}$$

1 A car of mass 750 kg accelerates from 10 m s⁻¹ to 25 m s⁻¹ in a time of 22.5 s.

    a   Calculate the change in momentum of the car.

    b   Use your answer to part **a** to calculate the force causing the car to accelerate.

You can calculate the force in another way:

    c   Calculate the car's acceleration.

    d   Calculate the force using $F = ma$. Do you get the same answer as in part **b**?

2 A spacecraft is orbiting the Earth, as shown. Its velocity is shown at opposite points in its circular orbit:

Figure 6.1: For Question 2. Diagram showing spacecraft orbiting Earth with velocities.

    a   The spacecraft has a mass of 420 kg. Calculate the change in its momentum as it travels half-way around its orbit.

    b   The force on the spacecraft keeping it in orbit is its weight. Calculate its weight, if the gravitational field strength is 8.9 N kg⁻¹.

3 Your friend is running down the street and bumps into someone, who falls to the ground. The person complains, 'You really hurt me!' Your friend replies, 'But you hit me with exactly the same force as I hit you!'

Is your friend correct? Explain your answer.

Exercise 6.5 Newton's laws of motion

Newton's laws summarise much of the material covered in the first six chapters of this book. This exercise is designed to check your understanding of these important laws.

1 This question is about **Newton's first law of motion**.

    a   An object is stationary. No force acts on it. What does Newton's first law say about its motion?

    b   An object is moving. No force acts on it. What does Newton's first law say about its motion?

    c   An object is moving. It is acted on by four forces whose resultant force is zero. What does Newton's first law say about its motion?

    d   An object is moving with constant velocity. What does Newton's first law say about the forces acting on it?

    e   An object is moving at a steady speed along a curved path. What does Newton's first law say about the forces acting on it?

KEY WORDS

Newton's first law of motion: an object will remain at rest or keep travelling at constant velocity unless it is acted on by a resultant external force

2   This question is about **Newton's second law of motion**.

    a   An object is moving in a straight line with constant acceleration.

        i   What can you say about the rate of change of the object's momentum?

        ii   What does Newton's second law say about the forces acting on the object?

    b   A skydiver is falling towards the Earth. Her velocity is increasing but her acceleration is decreasing.

        i   What does Newton's second law say about the forces acting on the skydiver? Think about the skydiver's momentum and the rate at which it is changing.

        ii   Two forces act on the skydiver as she falls. Referring to these forces, explain how her velocity can be increasing while her acceleration is decreasing.

3   We can write Newton's second law using SI units:

resultant force = rate of change of momentum

    a   Explain why we have to say 'in SI units'.

    b   Use the equation to express the newton (N) in terms of SI base units.

4   This question is about **Newton's third law of motion**.

    a   Two bar magnets are placed close to one another with their north poles facing each other.

        i   State whether the magnets attract or repel each other.

        ii   What does Newton's third law tell you about the force each magnet exerts on the other?

    b   If you stand on the floor, two forces act on you: your weight and the upward contact force of the floor.

        i   Explain why these two forces are not an 'equal and opposite pair' in the sense of Newton's third law.

        ii   For each of the two forces, state the force that is equal and opposite to it, as described by Newton's third law. Remember that 'weight' is the Earth's gravitational pull on an object.

KEY WORDS

Newton's second law of motion: the net force acting on an object is equal to the rate of change of its momentum. The net force and the change in momentum are in the same direction

Newton's third law of motion: when two bodies interact, the forces they exert on each other are equal and opposite

EXAM-STYLE QUESTIONS

1   A bullet of mass 25 g is travelling at 450 m s^{-1} when it strikes the armour plating of a tank. It bounces back along the same path with a speed of 390 m s^{-1}.

    a   Calculate the change in momentum of the bullet.   **[3]**

    b   The time of impact of the bullet on the tank is 0.040 s.
Calculate the average force that acts on the bullet in this time.   **[2]**

    c   State whether the impact is elastic or inelastic.   **[2]**

    d   **Comment** on how the principles of conservation of energy and momentum apply to this collision.   **[3]**

                                                [Total: 10]

COMMAND WORD

Comment: give an informed opinion

CONTINUED

2 In an experiment to measure the speed of a bee as it flies, a small ball is hung by a thread. When the bee lands on the ball, the ball swings upwards. Scientists record a video of the bee as it lands and analyse the video to determine the height to which the ball swings.

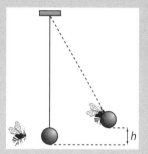

Figure 6.2

mass of bee = 0.25 g; mass of ball = 0.45 g

a The ball with the bee attached to it is found to rise to a vertical height *h* of 6.0 cm. Calculate its increase in gravitational potential energy. [2]

b Determine the speed of the ball + bee when it starts to swing upwards. [2]

c Determine the momentum of the ball + bee. [1]

d Determine the speed with which the bee lands on the ball. [2]

[Total: 7]

3 A ball P and a ball Q travel along the same line in the same horizontal direction.

Figure 6.3

Ball P has mass 200 g and a horizontal velocity of 0.64 m s⁻¹.

Ball Q has mass 300 g and a horizontal velocity of 0.42 m s⁻¹ in the same direction as P.

Ball P collides with ball Q. After the collision, ball P has a horizontal velocity of 0.45 m s⁻¹ and ball Q also moves in the same direction.

a **Identify** how the principle of conservation of momentum applies to the collision. [2]

b Calculate the final horizontal velocity of ball Q after the collision. [3]

c Use the relative velocity of the balls before and after the collision to decide whether the collision is elastic. [1]

d Use Newton's third law to explain why, during the collision, the change in momentum of ball P is equal and opposite to the change in momentum of ball Q. [2]

[Total: 8]

COMMAND WORD

Identify: name/select/recognise

Chapter 7

Matter and materials

CHAPTER OUTLINE

- define density and pressure

- derive and use the equation $\Delta p = \rho g \Delta h$

- understand how upthrust arises on a body in a fluid

- understand the effects of tensile and compressive forces, including Hooke's law

- define and use stress, strain and the Young modulus

- describe an experiment to determine the Young modulus

- distinguish between elastic and plastic deformation of a material

- understand and use force–extension graphs, including calculating work done and strain energy from the area under the graph

KEY EQUATIONS

$$\text{density} = \frac{\text{mass}}{\text{volume}}; \ \rho = \frac{M}{V}$$

$$\text{pressure} = \frac{\text{normal force}}{\text{area}}; \ P = \frac{F}{A}$$

change in pressure in a fluid = density × acceleration due to gravity × depth; $\Delta p = \rho g \Delta h$

$$\text{stress} = \frac{\text{force}}{\text{cross-sectional area}}; \ \sigma = \frac{F}{A}$$

$$\text{strain} = \frac{\text{extension}}{\text{original length}}; \ \varepsilon = \frac{X}{L}$$

$$\text{Young modulus} = \frac{\text{stress}}{\text{strain}}; \ E = \frac{\sigma}{\varepsilon}$$

elastic potential energy, $E = \frac{1}{2} Fx = \frac{1}{2} kx^2$

upthrust = $\rho g V$ (this equals the weight of liquid displaced)

$$\text{spring constant} = \frac{\text{force}}{\text{extension}}; \ k = \frac{F}{x}$$

Exercise 7.1 Density and pressure

A fluid exerts **pressure** on any surface with which it comes into contact. Pressure is the cause of the upthrust on any object immersed in a fluid. This exercise provides practice in calculations involving **density** and pressure.

Density calculations are not complicated but, in these examples, you will have to calculate the volume of a sphere and work with numbers in standard form (scientific notation).

1   Saturn is a gas giant planet – it consists mostly of a sphere of solidified hydrogen and helium.

Saturn's mass $= 5.7 \times 10^{26}$ kg; mean radius $= 58\,200$ km

   a   Calculate the mean density of Saturn.

   b   The mean density of the Earth is 5510 kg m^{-3}; its mean radius is 6371 km. Calculate the Earth's mass. Note: volume of a sphere $= \frac{4}{3}\pi r^3$

   c   What does this suggest about the composition of the Earth, compared with Saturn?

2   The pressure at a point in a fluid is caused by the weight of fluid above, pressing downwards. The pressure is given by $p = \rho g h$.

   a   State the quantity represented by each symbol in this equation and give its unit (name and symbol).

   b   Use the equation to find an expression for the pascal in terms of SI base units.

Figure 7.1 shows a tank containing a liquid of density 850 kg m^{-3}:

You can calculate the pressure on the base of the tank in steps which follow the derivation of the equation for pressure $p = \rho g h$.

   c   Calculate the volume, mass and weight of the liquid in the tank.

   d   Calculate the area of the base of the tank.

   e   Calculate the pressure on the base of the tank using pressure = force/area.

   f   Check your answer, using $p = \rho g h$.

In fact, the pressure at the surface of the liquid is atmospheric pressure, due to the atmosphere above.

   g   Atmospheric pressure is approximately 101 kPa. Calculate the total pressure on the base of the tank.

The *change* in pressure Δp if you move up or down in a fluid is given by:

$$\Delta p = \rho g \Delta h$$

where Δh is the change in depth.

   h   If you move upwards through the atmosphere, does atmospheric pressure increase or decrease?

   i   Calculate the change in pressure when a diver descends through a 5.0 m depth of water. (Assume the density of water $= 1000$ kg m^{-3} is constant over this depth.)

KEY WORDS

pressure: the force acting normally per unit area of a surface

density: the mass per unit volume of a material

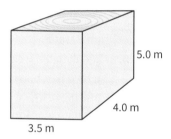

5.0 m

4.0 m

3.5 m

Figure 7.1: For Question 2c – g.

TIP

You can simply add the pressures in part g.

3   This diagram shows two identical wooden blocks A and B immersed in a tank of water:

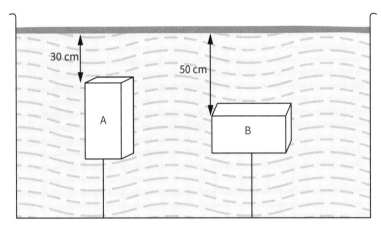

Figure 7.2: For Question 3. Diagram showing two identical wooden blocks A and B immersed in a tank of water.

Each block is held in position by a length of string attached to the bottom of the tank. Each block measures $20\,cm \times 20\,cm \times 50\,cm$. The density of the wood is $950\,kg\,m^{-3}$. The density of water is $1000\,kg\,m^{-3}$.

a   Use the idea of density to explain why the blocks tend to float upwards in the water.

b   Calculate the weight of a block.

c   Draw a free body diagram to show the forces acting on block A.

The upthrust of the water on the block arises because the pressure of the water produces a greater force on the lower surface of the block than on the upper surface.

d   Calculate the pressure of the water on the upper surface of block A.

e   Calculate the force exerted by the water on the upper surface of block A. State its direction.

f   Calculate the force exerted by the water on the lower surface of block A. State its direction.

g   Deduce the upthrust of the water on block A.

h   Calculate the tension in the string which holds block A in place.

i   Show that the upthrust of the water on block B is the same as on block A.

With more advanced maths, it can be shown that the upthrust on an object immersed in water is the same no matter how it is orientated.

Exercise 7.2 Stretching things

When considering the effect of tensile forces on a spring, we need only consider the load and extension. For a metal wire, we must take into account its physical dimensions by considering **stress** and **strain**.

1   The extension x of a spring is related to the load F by $F = kx$, where k is the **spring constant** (provided **Hooke's law** is obeyed).

a   Sketch a load–extension graph for a spring, indicating the region in which it obeys Hooke's law.

KEY WORDS

stress: the force per unit cross-sectional area in a wire

strain: the extension per unit length produced by tensile or compressive forces

spring constant: the force per unit extension

Hooke's law: provided the elastic limit is not exceeded, the extension of an object is proportional to the applied force

b A spring has a spring constant $k = 150\,\mathrm{N\,m^{-1}}$. Its un-stretched length is 30.0 cm.

   i Estimate the load required to increase its length to 35.0 cm.

   ii Explain why your answer to part **i** can only be an estimate.

2 A spring is stretched so that its length increases from 24.5 cm to 30.2 cm. The load producing this extension is 20.0 N.

   a Estimate the work done in stretching the spring. Remember that the load increases from 0 to 20 N as it stretches the spring.

   b Explain why this can only be an estimate.

3 A block of plastic foam is placed on firm ground. It is in the shape of a cube with sides of length 20.0 cm. A heavy weight is placed on top of the block, compressing it to a thickness of 17.4 cm.

   a Calculate the strain produced by the load.

   b The heavy weight consists of six masses, each of 5 kg. Determine the stress in the block. Give your answer in kPa.

4 You can think of the **Young modulus** of a material as a measure of its stiffness. This table shows the values of Young modulus for several metals:

Metal	copper	steel	aluminium	tin
Young modulus / GPa	130	210	70	50

Table 7.1: Data for the Young modulus of different metals.

   a Which of the metals shown in the table is the stiffest?

Wires of copper, steel and aluminium are compared in a test. Each wire is 1.0 m in length and has a cross-sectional area of 1.0 mm².

   b A tensile load of 100 N is applied to each wire. Which wire will extend the most? Explain your answer. There is no need for calculations here.

   c The Young modulus of steel is three times that of aluminium. If a particular load produces an extension of 0.20 mm in the steel wire, what extension will be produced in the aluminium wire? You can answer this by thinking in proportions.

   d Calculate the extension in the tin wire when a load of 200 N is applied.

5 This diagram shows a method for determining the Young modulus of a metal:

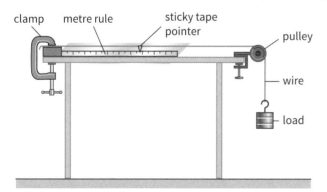

Figure 7.3: For Question 5. Diagram showing a method for determining the Young modulus of a metal.

KEY WORD

Young modulus: the ratio of stress to strain for a given material, provided Hooke's law is obeyed

---

TIP

You may need to calculate this in steps, starting by calculating the stress in the wire.

The length of the wire can be measured to the nearest 0.5 mm. To obtain satisfactory measurements of the extension of the wire, it should be several metres in length.

a   A thin steel wire is stretched so that its length increases from 4.539 m to 4.543 m. Calculate the strain in the wire.

b   The diameter of the wire is 1.20 mm. What instrument could be used to determine this?

c   Calculate the cross-sectional area of the wire.

d   The load on the wire is 200 N. Calculate the stress in the wire. Give your answer in MPa.

e   Deduce a value for the Young modulus of steel. Give your answer in GPa.

f   In practice, several measurements of load and extension would be made and a graph drawn. Sketch the graph you would expect to obtain and indicate how you would deduce the Young modulus from the graph.

> **TIP**
>
> Make sure you are familiar with the SI prefixes M and G.

EXAM-STYLE QUESTIONS

1   a   Define pressure.   [1]

b   Atmospheric pressure at the Earth's surface is 101 kPa. Calculate the force exerted by the atmosphere on a window pane of dimensions 60 cm by 125 cm.   [3]

c   Calculate the pressure on the base of a tank which contains water to a depth of 1.24 m. (density of water = 1000 kg m^{-3})   [3]

[Total: 7]

2   A spring is hung vertically and gradually loaded with masses suspended from its lower end. This table shows how the length of the spring changes as the load is increased:

Load / N	0	10	20	30	40
Length / cm	17.3	18.1	19.0	19.9	20.7

Table 7.2

a   Draw a load–extension graph based on the data in the table.   [3]

b   Use your graph to deduce a value for the spring constant of the spring.   [2]

c   Determine the elastic potential energy stored when a load of 25 N is applied to the spring.   [3]

[Total: 8]

CONTINUED

3 This diagram shows the load–extension graph for an aluminium wire:

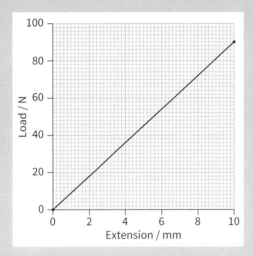

Figure 7.4

The wire is of length 2.00 m and cross-sectional area $2.5 \times 10^{-7}\,\text{m}^2$.

a Calculate the strain in the wire when a load of 50 N is applied. [3]

b Calculate the Young modulus of aluminium. [3]

c Calculate the work done on the wire when the load is increased from 25 N to 50 N. [4]

[Total: 10]

4 A wire of length 1.85 m and cross-sectional area $2.04 \times 10^{-7}\,\text{m}^2$ is stretched by a force of 13.9 N. The material of the wire has a Young modulus of $2.00 \times 10^{11}\,\text{Pa}$.

a Define *stress* and *strain*. [2]

b Calculate the extension of the wire. [2]

c A second wire is made from the same material and has the same volume. The second wire has twice the unstretched length of the original wire. Both wires are stretched by the same force.

Compare the extension of the second wire with the extension of the first wire, stating any assumptions that you make. [2]

[Total: 6]

COMMAND WORD

Compare: identify/ comment on similarities and/or differences

> Chapter 8

Current, potential difference and resistance

CHAPTER OUTLINE

- understand that electric current is a flow of charge carriers, with quantised charge

- use the equation $Q = It$

- use, for a current-carrying conductor, the expression $I = Anvq$

- define potential difference (p.d.), resistance and the volt

- recall and use $W = QV$, $V = IR$, $P = VI$, $P = I^2R$ and $P = \dfrac{V^2}{R}$

- draw and interpret circuit diagrams

- define electromotive force (e.m.f.) in terms of the energy transferred by a source in driving unit charge around a complete circuit

- distinguish between e.m.f. and p.d.

KEY EQUATIONS

charge = current × time; $Q = It$

potential difference = current × resistance; $V = IR$

power = potential different × current; $P = VI$

power = current² × resistance; $P = I^2R$

power = $\dfrac{\text{potential difference}^2}{\text{resistance}}$; $P = \dfrac{V^2}{R}$

energy (or energy transferred) = charge × potential difference = potential difference × current × time;
E (or W) = $QV = VIt$

current = area × number density × mean drift velocity × charge; $I = Anvq$

Exercise 8.1 Basic definitions and units, resistance, p.d. and e.m.f.

This exercise will help you understand and use basic definitions and their units. Rearranging units can be a challenge. If you are unsure, look up the definitions of the quantities first.

1   a   State one similarity between **potential difference** and **electromotive force**.

    b   State one difference between potential difference and electromotive force.

2   Match each quantity in the left column with a suitable unit from the right column:

electromotive force	A s
charge	V A⁻¹
resistance	J C⁻¹
power	J s⁻¹

3   State the quantity that can be described as:

    a   'the amount of energy transferred from a source to electrical energy per unit charge'

    b   'the amount of energy transferred from electrical energy to thermal energy per unit charge'

    c   'the rate of flow of electric charge'

    d   'one joule of energy per coulomb of charge'

    e   'one volt per amp'.

4   Four electrical quantities are:

    charge, current, potential difference, resistance

    State which quantity in the list:

    a   can be measured in joules per coulomb

    b   equals the product of two other quantities in the list

    c   equals the rate of change of another quantity in the list

    d   is a base quantity in the SI system

    e   is **quantised** (in other words, only occurs in multiples of a certain value).

5   Show that it is possible to express the Ω as $\mathrm{J\,s\,C^{-2}}$.

6   Four cells each of e.m.f. 1.5 V are connected together to make a 3.0 V battery connected to a filament lamp and a switch. Draw the circuit diagram. Make sure you use all four cells but that there is only a total e.m.f. of 3.0 V.

KEY WORDS

potential difference (p.d.): the energy transferred per unit charge as charge passes between two points

electromotive force (e.m.f.): the amount of energy changed from other forms into electrical energy per unit charge produced by an electrical supply

quantised: when a quantity has a definite minimum magnitude and always comes in multiples of that magnitude

7 You are provided with a resistor, a power supply, an ammeter and a voltmeter.

    a State what measurements must be made to find the **resistance** of the resistor.

    b Draw a circuit diagram of the apparatus.

    c State whether the voltmeter and the ammeter used in your circuit should have a low or a high resistance. The resistance of the resistor is a few ohms.

    d Explain why the voltmeter and ammeter should have the values of resistance you have chosen.

8 The current in a resistor is 0.80 A when the p.d. across it is 12 V.

    a Calculate the resistance of the resistor.

    b Calculate the p.d. which would be needed to produce a current of 1.2 A.

> **KEY WORD**
>
> **resistance:** ratio of the potential difference across the component to the current in the component

Exercise 8.2 Current and charge

This exercise offers practice in calculating current and the amount of charge.

Electrical current is often measured in mA (10^{-3} A) and µA (10^{-6} A). You need to use the correct power of 10 with the prefix given in the question. Some equations may include time, which should be measured in seconds. You will need to use the **elementary charge** $e = 1.6 \times 10^{-19}$ C. The charge on an electron is $-e$.

1 State the difference between the direction of electron flow in a circuit and the direction of the conventional current.

2 **a** Explain what is meant by the *electric current* in a conductor.

    b The charge passing through an electric drill in each minute is 360 C. Calculate the current.

    c A current of 250 µA passes through a lamp for three minutes. Calculate the charge that flows though the lamp in this time.

3 A current of 5.0 mA flows through a resistor for 12 minutes.

    a Calculate the amount of charge which passes through the resistor in this time.

    b Calculate the number of electrons which pass through the resistor in this time.

    c Calculate the time needed for a charge of 2.0 C to pass through the resistor.

4 In a time of 5.0×10^{-9} s, 100 electrons pass a point in a wire.

    a Calculate the charge that passes the point in this time.

    b Calculate the current in the wire.

    c Explain why the charge that passes the point is a multiple of 1.6×10^{-19} C.

5 Calculate the number of electrons in a beam hitting the screen of an oscilloscope each second when the beam current is 1.0 mA.

> **KEY WORDS**
>
> **elementary charge:** the smallest unit of charge that a particle or an object can have, $e = 1.6 \times 10^{-19}$ C

> **TIP**
>
> Make sure you know the prefixes µ (10^{-6}) and m (10^{-3})

Exercise 8.3 Electrical power and energy

This exercise provides practice in using several electrical formulae for power.
Remember also that power is $\dfrac{\text{work}}{\text{time}}$ or $\dfrac{\text{energy}}{\text{time}}$.
Power is sometimes measured in kW (10^3 W) or MW (10^6 W).

1   A lamp operates at a voltage of 8.0 V and has a power rating of 2.0 W.

   a   Calculate the current.

   b   Calculate the resistance of the lamp.

2   A 20 Ω resistor has a maximum power rating of 1.0 W. Calculate the maximum current in the resistor.

3   The battery in an electric car provides a steady power of 3.6 kW to the motor for a time of 2.0 hours. The e.m.f. of the battery is 180 V.

   a   Calculate the current in the motor.

   b   Calculate the charge the battery delivers.

   c   Calculate the energy delivered to the motor. Give your answer in MJ.

4   A battery provides a steady current of 0.25 A for 20 hours. In this time, the electrical energy produced by the battery is 9.6×10^4 J.

   a   Calculate the e.m.f. of the battery.

   b   Calculate the electrical power produced by the battery.

5   The generator in a power station has a power of 2.4 MW. The cable from the power station has a resistance of 4.0 Ω and carries a current of 20 A.

   a   Calculate the e.m.f. of the generator.

   b   Calculate the power wasted in the cable.

> **TIP**
>
> $P = VI = I^2R = \dfrac{V^2}{R}$
> Take care to use the correct formula. In **b**, V must be the voltage across the cable if you use a formula that involves V.

6   A student wants to obtain a large heating effect in a resistor connected to a laboratory power supply. He uses the formula $P = I^2R$, and decides to use a high resistance. Another student uses the formula $P = \dfrac{V^2}{R}$ and decides to use a low resistance. Explain which student is correct and why the other student is incorrect.

7   Discuss the energy transfer taking place within the battery of a mobile phone:

   a   when it is being used to make a call

   b   when it is being charged.

Exercise 8.4 Charge carriers

In this exercise, you will have to think about and use the equation $I = nAvq$. The elementary charge $e = 1.6 \times 10^{-19}$ C is usually the value for q.

1   The current I in a metal conductor of cross-sectional area A is given by the formula $I = nAvq$.

    a   Define the terms n, q and v.

    b   Using the symbols n, A, v and q find:

       i   the number of **charge carriers** in a wire of length l

       ii   the total charge on all the charge carriers in the wire

       iii   the time taken for a charge carrier in the wire to travel from one end to the other

       iv   the current in the wire.

    c   A piece of metal and a piece of plastic insulator each have the same dimensions and the same potential difference across them. Explain how the relative values of n for the metal and the plastic affect the current in each.

KEY WORDS
charge carrier: a charged particle which contributes to an electric current; may be an electron, a proton or an ion

2   Name the charge carriers responsible for the current in a:

    a   metal

    b   salt solution that conducts electricity.

3   When a current of $2.0\,A$ flows through a piece of wire that has a cross-sectional area of $1.0 \times 10^{-6}\,m^2$, the **mean drift velocity** of the electrons is $2.5 \times 10^{-4}\,m\,s^{-1}$.

    a   Calculate the number of free electrons per unit volume of the material. Be careful to give the unit of n correctly.

    b   State what happens to the drift velocity if the current is halved.

    c   State what happens to the drift velocity if the diameter of the wire is doubled and the current is unchanged. Think about what happens to the area if diameter is doubled. Then look at the equation.

KEY WORDS
mean drift velocity: the average speed of a collection of charged particles forming a current in a conductor

4   An aluminium wire, with cross-sectional area $1.2 \times 10^{-6}\,m^2$ and length $5.0\,m$, contains 3.6×10^{23} atoms. Each atom contributes three free electrons to the wire.

    a   Calculate the number of free electrons per unit volume in aluminium.

    b   The wire carries a current of $5.0\,A$. Calculate the mean drift velocity of the electrons.

5   A wire has a cross-sectional area of $1.8 \times 10^{-7}\,m^2$ and contains 8.0×10^{28} free electrons per m^3. The mean drift velocity of electrons in the wire is $8.7 \times 10^{-4}\,m\,s^{-1}$.

    a   Calculate the current in the wire.

    b   The wire is $5.0\,m$ long. Calculate the time it takes a free electron in the wire to travel from one end to the other.

    c   Calculate the number of free electrons in the wire.

    d   The wire carries current to a motor. Explain why there is no time delay in the motor starting when the current is switched on.

6   Two pieces of wire P and Q are made of the same material but have different diameters. They are connected in series with each other and a power supply.

    a   State which terms in the equation $I = Anvq$ are the same for both wires.

    b   The cross-sectional area of P is twice that of Q. Calculate the ratio $v_P : v_Q$.

EXAM-STYLE QUESTIONS

1 a Define the *e.m.f.* of a cell. [2]

b The current in a power cable from a power station is 300 A. Calculate the number of electrons passing through the cross-section of the wire in one second. ($e = 1.6 \times 10^{-19}$ C) [1]

c The cross-sectional area of the wire is 9.0×10^{-4} m^2 and the density of the free electrons is 1.6×10^{29} m^{-3}.

  i Calculate the mean drift velocity of the free electrons in the wire. [1]

  ii Explain the difference between the mean drift velocity and the mean speed. [1]

  iii One part of the wire has a smaller diameter than the rest. Explain why the mean drift velocity is different in this part of the wire. [2]

                                    [Total: 7]

2 a Define the *resistance* of a resistor. [2]

b An electric heater contains three identical heating elements, shown as resistors P, Q and R, in this diagram:

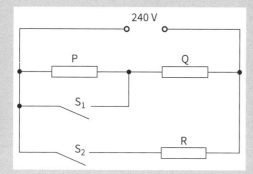

Figure 8.1

  Each heating element has a constant resistance and is designed to operate at a voltage of 240 V and a power of 1.2 kW.

  i Calculate the resistance of one of the elements. [3]

  ii Calculate the power developed in an element that operates on a voltage of 120 V. (You may assume its resistance is the same as in part **i**.) [2]

  iii The switches shown in the diagram are open. Copy and complete the table to show the total power output of the heater when the switches are closed as shown. [4]

S$_1$	S$_2$	Total power / kW
closed	closed	
closed	open	
open	closed	
open	open	

Table 8.1

                                      [Total: 11]

Chapter 9

Kirchhoff's laws

CHAPTER OUTLINE

- recall Kirchhoff's first and second laws and their links to conservation of charge and energy

- use Kirchhoff's laws to derive and apply a formula for the combined resistance of two or more resistors in series

- use Kirchhoff's laws to derive and apply a formula for the combined resistance of two or more resistors in parallel

- apply Kirchhoff's laws to solve simple circuit problems

KEY EQUATIONS

Kirchhoff's first law, $\Sigma I_{in} = \Sigma I_{out}$

Kirchhoff's second law, $\Sigma E = \Sigma IR$ (where Σ means 'sum of')

series resistors, $R = R_1 + R_2 + R_3 + \ldots$

parallel resistors, $\dfrac{1}{R} = \dfrac{1}{R_1} + \dfrac{1}{R_2} + \dfrac{1}{R_3} + \ldots$

charge = current × time; $Q = It$

potential difference = current × resistance; $V = IR$

power = potential different × current; $P = VI$

energy = charge × potential difference; $E = QV$

Exercise 9.1 Kirchhoff's laws and conservation

This exercise tests your understanding of Kirchhoff's laws and how they relate to **conservation of charge** and energy.

1   Write, in your own words, Kirchhoff's first and second laws. You may have to remind yourself of the laws from the Key Words box later in this exercise but do not just copy them out.

2   Look at these quantities:

   charge, e.m.f., energy, p.d., time

   State the quantity from the list that is conserved in:

   a   Kirchhoff's first law

   b   Kirchhoff's second law.

KEY WORDS

conservation of charge: electric charge can be neither created nor destroyed

---

3 Look at this circuit:

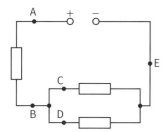

Figure 9.1: For Question 3. Circuit diagram.

The current at **A** is 6.0 A. The current at **C** is 1.0 A.

a Calculate the charge that flows through **A** in 10 s.

b Explain why the current at **B** is the same as at **A**.

c Using **Kirchhoff's first law**, calculate the current at **D**.

d Using Kirchhoff's first law, calculate the current at **E**.

e Explain why the current at **C** is different from the current at **D**.

4 In this circuit, the potential difference (p.d.) across the 40 Ω resistor is 8.0 V:

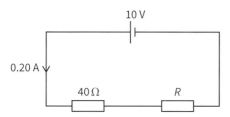

Figure 9.2: For Question 4. Circuit diagram.

The circuit operates for a time of 10 s.

a Calculate the charge that passes through the cell in this time.

b Calculate the energy produced by the cell.

c Calculate the thermal energy (heat) produced in the 40 Ω resistor.

d Using the idea of conservation of energy, calculate the thermal energy produced in the resistor R in 10 s.

e Using your answers to **a** and **d**, calculate the p.d. across the resistor R.

f Explain how **Kirchhoff's second law** is a consequence of the conservation of energy in this circuit. Use values for energy that you have calculated.

5 a Look at the diagram in Figure 9.3.

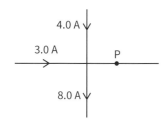

Figure 9.3: For Question 5. Diagram showing current into and out of point P.

KEY WORDS

Kirchhoff's first law: the sum of currents entering any point is equal to the sum of the currents leaving that same point. This law represents the conservation of charge

Kirchhoff's second law: the sum of the e.m.f.s around a closed loop is equal to the sum of the p.d.s in that same loop. This law represents the conservation of energy

Find the value of the current and the direction of the current at **P**.

b   Explain your answer to **a** in terms of the charges that flow in 1.0 s.

6   In this circuit, two batteries are connected as shown. They have negligible internal resistance:

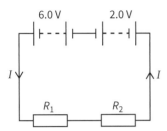

Figure 9.4: For Question 6. Circuit diagram.

Notice that the batteries are connected the opposite way around to each other.

a   State the sum of the e.m.f.s in the circuit.

b   The p.d. across R_1 is 1.0 V. Calculate the p.d. across R_2.

c   Explain why the current is in the direction shown.

d   1.0 C of charge passes around the circuit. State the energy change that occurs in:

   i   the 6.0 V battery

   ii   the 2.0 V battery

   iii R_1.

Exercise 9.2 Series and parallel circuits

In this exercise you will make calculations on circuits where resistors are connected in series and in parallel.

1   Four resistors of resistance R are connected as shown. There are no other connections:

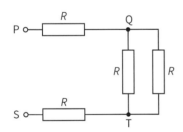

Figure 9.5: For Question 1. Circuit diagram.

Calculate the total resistance, in terms of R, between:

a   P and Q

b   Q and T

c   P and T

d   P and S.

2 Three resistors are connected to terminals A and B, as shown:

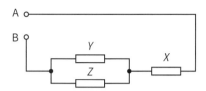

Figure 9.6: For Question 2. Circuit diagram.

a Complete this table to find the unknown values. Note: R_{AB} is the resistance of the circuit between terminals A and B.

X / Ω	Y / Ω	Z / Ω	R_{AB} / Ω
400	400	400	
20	400	400	
200	300		400
400		500	600

Table 9.1: For Question 2a.

b When *X*, *Y* and *Z* are each 400 Ω, a p.d. of 12 V is applied between A and B:

i Calculate the current in *X*. (12 V is not the voltage across *X* so $I \neq \dfrac{12}{400}$.)

ii Calculate the p.d. across *X*. (You can use $V = IR$ with the current from **i**.)

iii Calculate the p.d. across *Y*. (You can use Kirchhoff's second law.)

3 A student has three 6.0 Ω resistors. He uses two or three of the resistors in an electric circuit. Calculate the six possible values for the total resistance of the circuit and describe each combination of the resistors. The resistances may be connected in series, in parallel, or both in series and in parallel. Draw a circuit with two or three of the resistors before you start each calculation.

4 A battery of e.m.f. 6.0 V and no internal resistance is connected as shown:

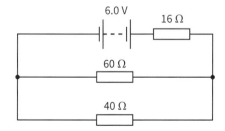

Figure 9.7: For Question 4. Circuit diagram.

a Calculate the total resistance of the circuit.

b Calculate the current in the 16 Ω resistor.

5 A student writes a proof that the total resistance of two resistors in series is $R_1 + R_2$. She uses the idea of two resistors connected to an e.m.f. V_t.

Her proof is:

$V_t = V_1 + V_2$

$IR_t = IR_1 + IR_2$

So, $R_t = R_1 + R_2$

a   State where Kirchhoff's first law is used in the proof.

b   State where Kirchhoff's second law is used in the proof.

c   Write out a proof that the total resistance of two resistors in parallel is
     $\dfrac{1}{R_t} = \dfrac{1}{R_1} + \dfrac{1}{R_2}$. Indicate where Kirchhoff's laws are used in your proof.

Exercise 9.3 Applying Kirchhoff's second law to more complex circuits

In this exercise, you will need to apply Kirchhoff's second law to more complex circuits. Make sure that you understand what is meant by the total e.m.f. in a closed loop. Sometimes you have to add and sometimes subtract e.m.f.s.

1   In this circuit there are three loops that can be drawn to apply Kirchhoff's second law. The cells have negligible internal resistance:

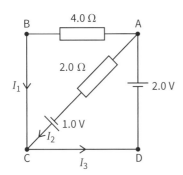

Figure 9.8: For Question 1. Circuit diagram.

a   One of the closed loops is ABCDA. State the other two closed loops.

b   Determine the total e.m.f. in each of the three closed loops:

Choose a direction to follow around a loop, in the direction of the current. If there are two cells in the loop, you either need to add or subtract their e.m.f.s. Add the e.m.f.s if both cells on their own produce a current in the direction of the loop. Subtract an e.m.f. if a cell produces a current in the *opposite* direction to the current you have drawn around the loop.

c   Write similar equations using Kirchhoff's second law for each of the other two loops.

Kirchhoff's second law for loop ABCDA gives the equation $2.0 = 4.0I_1$, where I_1 is the current in A.

d   Solve the equations for I_1 and I_2.

e   Write the formula that relates I_1, I_2 and I_3.

2 In this circuit, the cells have negligible internal resistance:

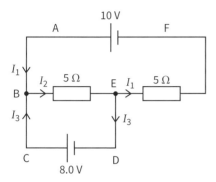

Figure 9.9: For Question 2. Circuit diagram.

a Write the formula that relates I_1, I_2 and I_3.

b Write an equation that uses Kirchhoff's second law in the closed loop CBEDC.

c Write an equation that uses Kirchhoff's second law in the closed loop ABEFA.

d Calculate I_1, I_2 and I_3.

e Write an equation that uses Kirchhoff's second law in the loop ABCDEFA.

3 A battery of e.m.f. 8.0 V and resistance 3.0 Ω is connected with a battery of e.m.f. 4.0 V and resistance 1.0 Ω. All the components are in series. One of the batteries can be reversed in direction.

a Calculate the maximum and minimum total e.m.f. in the circuit.

b Calculate the maximum and minimum current in the circuit.

4 Four resistors of resistance R are connected as shown. There are three closed loops. The top loop includes E_1 and three resistors, the bottom loop contains E_2 and two resistors.

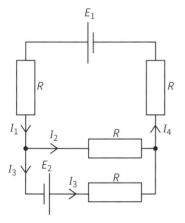

Figure 9.10: For Question 4. Circuit diagram.

a Write the formula that relates I_1, I_2 and I_3.

b Explain why $I_4 = I_1$.

c Write the formula that relates E_1, R, I_1, I_2 and I_4 using the top loop.

d Write the formula that relates E_2, R, I_2 and I_3 using the bottom loop. The positive direction for the e.m.f. is anticlockwise (the 'direction' of E_2) so, for a resistor where the current is clockwise, the 'IR' term will be negative.

e Write the formula that relates E_1, E_2, R, I_1 and I_3 using the outside loop. Take the positive direction as anticlockwise so that both E_1 and E_2 are positive in this direction.

EXAM-STYLE QUESTIONS

1 This diagram shows a 12 V power supply, with negligible internal resistance, connected to three resistors:

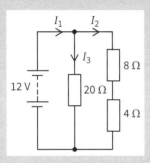

Figure 9.11

a Use Kirchhoff's first law to state the relationship between I_1, I_2 and I_3. [1]

b Use Kirchhoff's second law to calculate I_2. [2]

c Calculate I_3. [1]

d Explain how Kirchhoff's second law can be applied to the closed loop that contains just the three resistors. [2]

e Calculate the total resistance of the circuit. [2]

f Calculate the ratio: $\dfrac{\text{power provided by battery}}{\text{power in 20 }\Omega\text{ resistor}}$ [3]

[Total: 11]

2 **a** State Kirchhoff's first law. [1]

b State the quantity that is conserved in the first law. [1]

c Kirchhoff's second law shows that when a cell of e.m.f. E is connected to two resistors in series, the e.m.f. is equal to the sum of the p.d.s across the two resistors. Explain how this is a consequence of conservation of energy. [2]

d A car battery is charged using a battery charger with an e.m.f. of 16 V. The e.m.f. of the car battery at the start of the charging process is 8.0 V. The connections of the charger to the battery and the resistances in the circuit are shown in Figure 9.12.

CONTINUED

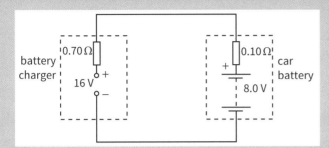

Figure 9.12

i   Calculate the total resistance of the circuit. [1]

ii   Calculate the current in the circuit. [2]

iii To reduce the current in the battery to 2.0 A, a resistor is placed in series in the circuit. Determine the resistance of this resistor. [2]

iv State two reasons why the positive terminal of the battery charger must *not* be connected to the negative terminal of the car battery. [2]

[Total: 11]

TIP

Take the whole circuit as a loop and remember to add the emfs of the cell taking note of their directions.

3 A current I enters a network of 16 identical resistors, as shown:

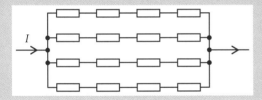

Figure 9.13

Each resistor has a resistance of 20 Ω.

a Calculate the total resistance of the network. [2]

b Describe how all 16 resistors can be connected together to have a total resistance of 80 Ω. [2]

c Explain one advantage of using many resistors in a network, rather than using a single resistor. [1]

[Total: 5]

4 A p.d. of 12 V is applied to the resistor network shown in Figure 9.14.

a Calculate the resistance of the circuit when the switch is closed. [2]

b Calculate the current at A when the switch is closed. [2]

c Calculate the p.d. between A and B when the switch is closed. [2]

d Describe what happens to the p.d. between A and B when the switch is opened. Explain your ideas. [2]

[Total: 8]

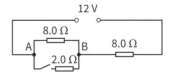

Figure 9.14

Chapter 10

Resistance and resistivity

CHAPTER OUTLINE

- sketch and discuss the I–V characteristics of a metallic conductor at constant temperature, a semiconductor diode and a filament lamp

- state Ohm's law

- recall and use $R = \dfrac{\rho l}{A}$

- understand that the resistance of a thermistor decreases as the temperature increases

KEY EQUATIONS

potential difference = current × resistance; $V = IR$

resistance = $\dfrac{\text{resistivity} \times \text{length}}{\text{area}}$; $R = \dfrac{\rho l}{A}$

power = potential difference × current = current² × resistance = $\dfrac{\text{potential difference}^2}{\text{resistance}}$; $P = VI = I^2R = \dfrac{V^2}{R}$

Exercise 10.1 Ohm's law

Ohm's law is both a relationship *and* a condition. Notice it does not mention the word resistance at all, even though the unit of resistance is the ohm. This exercise allows you to learn and think about the law.

1 **a** Explain why each of these statements is *not* a correct statement of Ohm's law:

    i The potential difference across a component is proportional to its resistance.

    ii The potential difference across a component is proportional to the current.

    iii The potential difference across a component equals the current multiplied by the resistance.

    iv The resistance of a wire is constant, provided the temperature is constant.

    b Suggest which statement is the best and rewrite it correctly.

KEY WORDS

Ohm's law: the current in a metallic conductor is directly proportional to the potential difference across its ends provided physical conditions, such as temperature, remain constant

2   This graph shows the variation with current of the p.d. across three components:

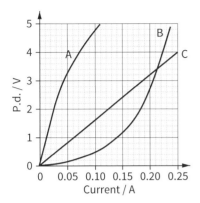

Figure 10.1: For Question 2. Graph showing the variation with current of the p.d. across three components A, B and C.

a   State which component obeys Ohm's law. Explain how you know.

b   State which line shows an increasing resistance at higher currents. Explain your ideas.

c   State, for each component, any range of voltages where the resistance is constant.

3   This table shows values of current and p.d. obtained for a metal wire:

Current / A	0	0.10	0.20	0.30	0.40	0.50
P.d. / V	0	0.20	0.40	0.60	1.00	1.80

Table 10.1: Data for Question 3.

a   Explain whether Ohm's law applies over the whole range of currents.

b   State the range of currents where the resistance is constant.

Exercise 10.2 Other components

For this exercise, you need to know the *I–V* characteristic graphs for a **diode** and for a filament lamp, and some reasons why these graphs are not straight lines. This exercise also contains practice in writing out an experiment and describing precautions for an electrical experiment, as well as looking at the **light-dependent resistor (LDR)** and **thermistor**.

1   You plan to carry out an experiment to obtain the (*I–V*) characteristic of a lamp.

a   Draw a suitable circuit diagram for your experiment.

b   Describe how to carry out the experiment.

c   Suggest one precaution that would enable accurate results to be obtained.

Your experiment needs to vary the voltage. Check that your experiment can do this. A simple series variable resistor may be used, but is not ideal as it cannot reduce the voltage down to 0 V. If you know about a potential divider, draw a circuit that can reduce the voltage down to 0 V.

> **KEY WORDS**
>
> **diode:** an electrical component that only conducts in one direction
>
> **light-dependent resistor (LDR):** a resistor whose resistance decreases as the brightness of the light falling on it increases
>
> **thermistor:** a resistor whose resistance decreases as the temperature increases

2   This graph shows the $(I–V)$ characteristic of a light-emitting diode (LED) in the forward direction:

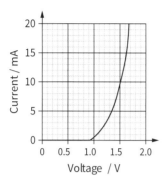

Figure 10.2: For Question 2. Graph showing the $(I–V)$ characteristic of a light-emitting diode in the forward direction.

a   Explain how the graph shows that the diode does not obey Ohm's law.

b   Name one other device that does not obey Ohm's law.

c   Calculate the resistance of the diode when the voltage is 1.5 V.

d   Describe how the resistance of the diode changes as the voltage increases from 0 to 1.6 V.

e   The voltage applied to the diode is reversed. State the resistance of the diode.

f   Describe the new current–voltage graph.

3   The light-emitting diode from question **2** operates with a current of 15 mA and a p.d. of 1.6 V. When a voltage larger than 1.6 V is applied to the diode it becomes too hot. A protective resistance R is placed in series with the diode and a 16 V supply, as shown:

Determine the value of R that allows the diode to operate at 15 mA.

4   A lamp is rated as 12 V, 48 W. The resistance of the lamp has a constant value of 0.50 Ω when the p.d. is between 0 and 1 V.

a   Calculate the current in the lamp at its working temperature. The working temperature is when the lamp is at the rated voltage. Use the formula for power, voltage and current.

b   Sketch a graph to show the current–voltage $(I–V)$ characteristic of the lamp. Draw an appropriate scale for current on the y-axis and a scale for voltage on the x-axis. Mark points on your graph where you can. You can find the current at 1 V and plot points at 0, 1 V and 12 V and then make the shape correct.

c   On your graph from part **b**, draw the current–voltage $(I–V)$ characteristic of a resistor of constant resistance 3.0 Ω.

d   State why the lamp does not have a constant resistance.

5   a   Draw the circuit symbol for a thermistor and for an LDR.

b   A graph of current against voltage (an $I–V$ characteristic) for a thermistor is not a straight line. Explain why.

c   Sketch a typical graph of the resistance variation with light intensity for an LDR. Suggest suitable values for the resistance of an LDR in the dark.

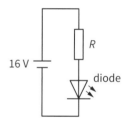

Figure 10.3: For Question 3. Circuit diagram with LED.

TIP

Use the p.d. across the diode to find the p.d. across the protective resistor and then find the value of R.

Exercise 10.3 Resistivity and resistance: the basics

This exercise helps you think about the relationship between resistance, length and area, and the difference between resistance and **resistivity**. Some simple calculations can be done just by recognising that resistance is proportional to length and inversely proportional to area. To help you use the correct unit for resistivity and other electrical units, you will gain practice in changing electrical and other units into the base SI units.

KEY WORD

resistivity: a measure of electrical resistance, defined as resistance × cross-sectional area / length

1   a   Write down a word equation that defines the resistivity of a material.

    b   Explain the difference between resistance and resistivity.

    c   Explain why resistivity is a property of the material from which a wire is made but the resistance per unit length of a wire is not.

2   A student incorrectly writes down the unit of resistivity as Ω/m.

    a   State the correct SI unit of resistivity.

    b   Express the unit of resistivity in terms of the SI units V, A and m. (You need to change Ω into a combination of V and A.)

    c   Express the unit of resistivity in terms of the SI base units kg, m, s and A.

TIP

First change V into JC^{-1}, then use $C = As$, and finally use $J = Nm$ and $N = kg\,m\,s^{-2}$.

3   Describe a method to determine, accurately, the resistivity of a metal wire. The available apparatus includes a battery, a switch, a variable resistor, an ammeter and a voltmeter.

Your method should involve readings of different lengths, plotting a graph and using its gradient.

Your description should include:

*   a circuit diagram
*   a statement of the quantities to be measured and the instruments used
*   the graph to plot
*   how the gradient is used
*   a statement of which measurement is likely to have the largest percentage uncertainty if ordinary school apparatus and a thin wire is used
*   one precaution to enable the temperature of the wire to be constant for all readings and one other precaution to increase the accuracy of the result.

4   A wire is 20 m long, has a cross-sectional area of $10^{-8}\,m^2$ and a resistance of $200\,\Omega$. Several other wires are made from the same material but with different dimensions. In each case, calculate the resistance of the wire.

    a   length = 40 m; cross-sectional area = $10^{-8}\,m^2$

    b   length = 20 m; cross-sectional area = $2 \times 10^{-8}\,m^2$

    c   length = 100 m; cross-sectional area = $5 \times 10^{-8}\,m^2$

5   Calculate the resistivity of a length of wire which has a resistance of $60\,\Omega$, cross-sectional area of $2.0 \times 10^{-8}\,m^2$ and length of 20 m.

6   Calculate the length of wire required to make a resistance of $1000\,\Omega$ if the wire has cross-sectional area of $1.0 \times 10^{-8}\,m^2$ and the material has resistivity of $1.0 \times 10^{-6}\,\Omega m$.

7 A wire is 2.0 m long and has a resistance of 50 Ω.

    a Calculate the cross-sectional area of the wire if it is made of a material of resistivity $5 \times 10^{-7}\,\Omega\,m$.

    b Calculate the radius of the wire.

Exercise 10.4 Resistivity and resistance: harder problems

This exercise gives you practice in some harder examples where you have to use $R = \frac{\rho l}{A}$.

The units are mixed – for example, resistivity in Ω m and length in cm – so make sure you convert them so they are consistent.

1 The cylindrical core of a pencil is made of material of resistivity $5.0 \times 10^{-3}\,\Omega\,m$. The core has a length of 15 cm and a diameter of 0.20 cm.

    a Calculate the resistance of the core. (As resistivity is given in Ω m, work throughout with metres. Convert the length and diameter to metres before using the equation.)

    b Outline how to use the resistivity of the core to find the thickness t of a line of width w and length l drawn by the pencil on a piece of paper. (Think about a thin pencil line. Write down the formula using w and t instead of A and rearrange the formula to find t.)

2 A sample of conducting putty is rolled into a cylinder which is 8 cm long and has a radius of 1.5 cm. The resistivity of the putty is $4.0 \times 10^{-3}\,\Omega\,m$.

    a Calculate the resistance between the ends of the cylinder.

    b The putty is rolled into a cylinder with half the radius and a length which is four times longer. Determine the new resistance.

3 A wire made from tin has a cross-sectional area of $7.8 \times 10^{-8}\,m^2$. The resistivity of tin is $1.2 \times 10^{-7}\,\Omega\,m$.

    a Calculate the minimum length of wire needed so that the current in the wire is smaller than 3.0 A when there is a p.d. of 2.0 V across the wire.

    b A second wire made from tin has the same volume as the first wire but is longer. The second wire also has a p.d. of 2.0 V across it. Complete this table, stating whether the given quantity is *smaller*, *bigger* or the *same* for this second wire:

Quantity	For the second wire the quantity is:
cross-sectional area	
resistance	
resistivity	
current	
power produced	

Table 10.2: For Question 2b.

> **TIP**
>
> These calculations can be performed simply using the idea that resistance is proportional to length and inversely proportional to area.

4   This diagram shows a thin film of carbon used as a resistor:

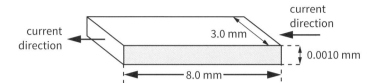

current
direction

current
direction

3.0 mm

0.0010 mm

8.0 mm

Figure 10.4: For Question 4. Diagram showing a thin film of carbon used as a resistor.

a   The resistivity of carbon is $5.0 \times 10^{-6}\,\Omega\,\text{m}$. Calculate the resistance of the thin film.

b   The current direction is changed so that current enters the top face of the film and leaves by the lower face. Calculate the resistance of the film.

5   The fuse fitted to a three-pin plug contains a piece of fuse wire with a resistance of $0.20\,\Omega$. The wire is $15\,\text{mm}$ long and has a resistivity of $1.45 \times 10^{-6}\,\Omega\,\text{m}$.

a   Calculate the diameter of the fuse wire.

b   Another fuse wire has the same power developed inside it, but has a smaller current. Explain how. (This is possible using a wire of the same length and of the same material.)

6   Wire A and wire B are connected in parallel. There is the same p.d. across each wire.

This table gives data about the two wires:

	Wire A	Wire B
resistivity of metal	ρ	2ρ
length	l	$\frac{1}{2}l$
radius	r	$2r$

Table 10.3: Data for Question 6.

> **TIP**
>
> Rewrite the formula, making ρ the subject, and then insert the numbers.

a   Using the formula area $= \pi r^2$, calculate this ratio:

cross-sectional area of wire A : cross-sectional area of wire B

b   Using the formula $R = \frac{\rho l}{A}$, calculate this ratio:

resistance of wire A : resistance of wire B

c   Calculate this ratio:

current in wire A : current in wire B

d   Calculate this ratio:

power dissipated in wire A : power dissipated in wire B

EXAM-STYLE QUESTIONS

1 This graph shows the (I–V) characteristic of a 350 mA, 6.0 V filament lamp:

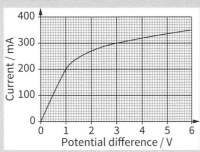

Figure 10.5

a State how the graph shows that the filament lamp does not obey Ohm's law. [1]

b Calculate the resistance of the lamp for currents between 0 and 200 mA. [2]

c State and explain what happens to the resistance of the lamp as the current increases. [2]

d Draw a sketch graph to show how the resistance of the filament lamp varies with current. [2]

e The filament of the lamp is a wire of constant radius 8.0×10^{-6} m, made from tungsten. The resistivity of tungsten is $3.5 \times 10^{-7}\,\Omega$ m. The current in the lamp is 350 mA. Calculate the length of the filament in the lamp. [2]

[Total: 9]

2 A semiconducting diode is an example of a non-ohmic component.

a State what is meant by a *non-ohmic component* and give one other example of such a component. [2]

b Sketch the (I–V) characteristic of a diode in both forwards bias (positive values of V) and negative bias (negative values of V). [3]

c Describe the significant features of the graph in terms of potential difference, current and resistance. [3]

[Total: 8]

3 a State Ohm's law. [2]

b State what can be said about the resistance of a material that obeys Ohm's law. [1]

c A cable consists of 12 strands of copper wire, each of diameter 1.2 mm, connected in parallel. The resistivity of copper is $1.7 \times 10^{-8}\,\Omega$ m.

i Calculate the cross-sectional area of one strand of the copper wire. [2]

ii Calculate the resistance of one strand of copper wire of length 10 m. [2]

iii Determine the combined resistance of all the 12 strands in the cable. [2]

[Total: 9]

> Chapter 11
Practical circuits

CHAPTER OUTLINE

- understand the effects of the internal resistance of a source of e.m.f. on the terminal potential difference (p.d.)

- understand the principle of a potential divider circuit as a source of variable p.d.

- recall and solve problems using the principle of the potentiometer as a means of comparing potential differences

- explain the use of thermistors and light-dependent resistors in potential dividers to provide a potential difference that is dependent on temperature and light intensity

KEY EQUATIONS

internal resistance $r = \dfrac{(E - V)}{I}$

voltage = current × resistance; $V = IR$

$E = \dfrac{I}{(R + r)}$

$P = VI$ for the external resistor

$P = EI$ for the source

$P = I^2 r$ for the internal resistance

$V_{out} = V_{in} \dfrac{R_2}{R_1 + R_2}$

In a potentiometer: $\dfrac{E_1}{E_2} = \dfrac{\text{balance length for e.m.f. 1}}{\text{balance length for e.m.f. 2}}$

Exercise 11.1 One cell, three voltages

This exercise develops your understanding of the differences and relationships between e.m.f., potential difference, current and **internal resistance**.

1   The equation $E = V + Ir$ applies to a cell of e.m.f. E and internal resistance r.

    a   Describe each quantity as a potential difference. One has been done for you in the following table.

E	The e.m.f. of a cell – the potential difference across the cell when there is no current
V	
Ir	

KEY WORDS

terminal potential difference: the p.d. across an external resistor connected across a source of e.m.f.

b Describe each quantity using ideas about energy. One has been done for you.

E	The electrical energy per unit charge produced in the cell
V	
Ir	

2 Real cells have internal resistance.

a State a situation where the e.m.f. E of a cell is equal to V, the **terminal potential difference.**

b In use, E is normally greater than V. Explain why.

c It is possible that $E = Ir$ and that $V = 0$. Explain how this is done.

3 A high-resistance voltmeter placed alone across the terminal of a battery reads 6.0 V. When a 12 Ω resistor is also placed across the terminals, the p.d. falls to 4.0 V.

a State the value of the e.m.f. of the battery.

b Explain why there is no p.d across the internal resistance of the battery when the reading is 6.0 V.

c State the value of the p.d across the internal resistance when the resistor is connected.

d A student finds the current using the formula $I = \frac{V}{R}$. The value of the resistance she uses is 12 Ω. State which value of voltage she should use. (Look to see the voltage across the resistor that you use in the equation.)

e Another student finds the internal resistance of the cell current using the formula $R = \frac{V}{I}$. State which value of voltage he should use.

4 This graph shows the variation of the potential difference across a cell with the current in it:

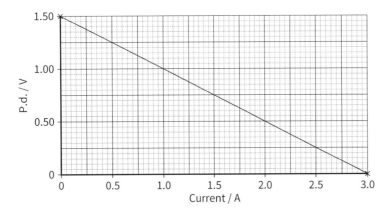

Figure 11.1: For Question 4. Graph showing the variation of the potential difference across a cell with the current in it.

a   The formula for the cell is $E = V + Ir$.

Using the graph, copy and complete this table to show the values of the three terms. One has been done for you:

Current / A	E / V	V / V	p.d. across the internal resistance (E − V) / V
0			
0.5	1.50	1.25	0.25
1.0			
2.0			
3.0			

Table 11.1: For Question 4a.

b   When the current is 0.50 A, the voltage across the cell is measured as 1.25 V. The label on the cell is marked as 1.5 V. Explain what has happened to the e.m.f. of the cell.

c   Explain how the external resistance is adjusted to obtain different points on the graph.

5   When a starter motor used to start the engine of a car, the p.d. across the motor is only 2.0 V. However, the battery has e.m.f. 12 V. Explain why the p.d. across the motor is less than the e.m.f. of the battery.

Exercise 11.2 Using the internal resistance equations

This exercise will give you practice using, rearranging and performing calculations involving internal resistance. You will use equations such as $V = IR$ but must choose the right voltage and resistance.

1   The e.m.f. of a battery is 9.0 V. When a resistor is connected to the battery, the voltmeter reading drops to 8.0 V and the current is 0.40 A.

a   Calculate the resistance of the external resistor.

b   Calculate the internal resistance of the battery.

2   A 9.0 Ω resistor is connected to a battery of e.m.f. 4.0 V and internal resistance 1.0 Ω.

a   Calculate the current in the circuit.

b   Calculate the p.d. across the 9.0 Ω resistor.

c   State the p.d. across the battery terminals.

d   State the p.d. across the battery terminals when the resistor is removed. (Without any resistor, the battery is said to be in an open circuit.)

3   A battery of e.m.f. 6.0 V is connected across a 10 Ω resistor. The p.d. across the resistor is 4.0 V.

a   Calculate the current in the circuit.

b   Calculate the internal resistance of the battery.

TIP

Only the e.m.f. is given, so choose as R the total resistance of the circuit.

TIP

In question 3a, you cannot use the e.m.f. as the 'voltage' in $V = IR$ because you do not know the total resistance. Take care to use the right 'voltage'.

4   This graph shows the variation of the potential difference across a cell with the current in it:

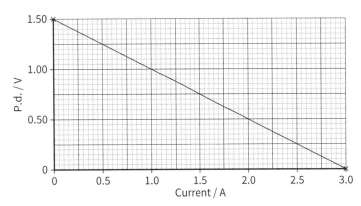

Figure 11.2: For Question 4. Graph showing the variation of the potential difference across a cell with the current in it.

a   Rearrange $E = V + Ir$ to make V the subject of the formula and find expressions for the gradient of the graph and for the y-intercept of the graph in terms of E and r.

b   Use the graph to find the internal resistance of the cell.

c   Draw a circuit diagram of all the apparatus needed to be able to take the measurements shown in the graph. Your apparatus should enable the current to be adjusted.

5   A torch is powered by a 4.5 V battery. The p.d. across the filament lamp in the torch is 3.8 V and the power produced in the lamp is 0.80 W.

a   Calculate the current in the lamp.

b   Calculate the internal resistance of the battery.

c   Calculate the energy lost per second as heat in the internal resistance of the battery.

> **TIP**
>
> Without knowing a resistance you must use an equation for power.

6   A 1.2 Ω resistor is connected across a battery which has an internal resistance of 0.30 Ω. The current is 3.0 A.

a   Calculate the e.m.f. of the battery.

b   Calculate the potential difference across the terminals of the battery.

c   The 1.2 Ω resistor is replaced with another resistor. The current is 1.5 A. Calculate the resistance of the new resistor.

7   A battery of internal resistance 2.0 Ω and e.m.f. 6.0 V is connected to a variable resistor R:

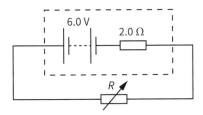

Figure 11.3: For Question 7. Circuit diagram.

a Copy and complete this table, which gives some values of R, the current I and the power P dissipated in R:

R/Ω	I/A	P/W
0	3.0	0
1.0	2.0	
2.0		
3.0		4.3
4.0		

Table 11.2: For Question 7a.

When $R = 1.0\,\Omega$:

b Calculate the power dissipated in the internal resistance.

c Calculate the total power produced by the e.m.f. of the battery.

d Compare P and the values obtained in **b** and **c**.

8 A battery with e.m.f. of 6.0 V and internal resistance of $12\,\Omega$ is connected to two resistors in parallel, as shown:

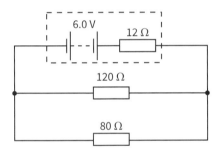

Figure 11.4: For Question 8. Circuit diagram.

a Calculate the total resistance of the circuit.

b Calculate the current in the battery.

c Calculate the potential difference across the terminals of the battery.

Exercise 11.3 The potential divider

Sometimes it is useful to calculate voltage by using the principle of **a potential divider**. You may then not have to calculate a current at all. This exercise gives practice with the equation for a potential divider.

1 Two resistors with resistance R_1 and R_2 are connected in a potential divider arrangement, as shown in the following circuit diagram.

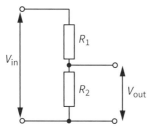

Figure 11.5: For Question 1. Circuit diagram of a potential divider.

The voltage V_{in} is divided between the two resistors R_1 and R_2 in the ratio $R_1 : R_2$. One of the parts is the output voltage V_{out}.

a Divide the number 30 in the ratio 6:4.

b Divide the voltage 80 V in the ratio 6:4.

c Divide the voltage 60 V in the ratio 12:3.

d In terms of V_{in}, R_1 and R_2 find an expression for the current in the potential divider.

e In terms of V_{out} and R_2 find an expression for the current in the potential divider.

f The current in parts **d** and **e** is the same. Use this fact to show that:

$$V_{out} = V_{in} \frac{R_2}{R_1 + R_2}$$

g Copy and complete this table. You may use the formula or basic ideas of splitting a voltage into parts:

V_{out} / V	V_{in} / V	R_1 / Ω	R_2 / Ω
	6.0	50	250
2.0	10.0	100	
4.0	24.0		200
5.1	16.2	400	

Table 11.3: For Question 1g.

2 A variable resistor is connected to a 2000 Ω fixed resistor and a battery of e.m.f. 6.0 V and zero internal resistance, as shown:

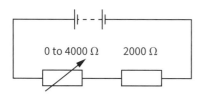

0 to 4000 Ω 2000 Ω

Figure 11.6: For Question 2. Circuit diagram.

The resistance of the variable resistor is varied from 0 to 4000 Ω.

Calculate the maximum voltage and the minimum voltage across the 2000 Ω resistor.

3   This diagram shows a potential divider circuit. The voltmeter has a very high resistance:

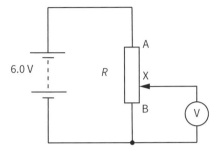

Figure 11.7: For Question 3. Circuit diagram.

The resistor R is divided into two sections, AX and XB, by the slider X.

a   State the reading on the voltmeter when the slider is at A.

b   State the reading on the voltmeter when the slider is at B.

c   Calculate the reading on the voltmeter when the resistance of AX is $4.0\,\Omega$ and the resistance of XB is $8.0\,\Omega$.

4   A potential difference of $6.0\,\text{V}$ is applied to a combination of resistors, as shown:

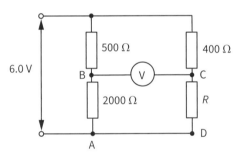

Figure 11.8: For Question 4. Circuit diagram.

a   Calculate the p.d. between points A and B.

b   Calculate the p.d. between C and D when the resistor R has resistance:

   i $200\,\Omega$ **ii** $400\,\Omega$ **iii** $1600\,\Omega$.

c   Calculate the p.d. between B and C when the resistor R has resistance:

   i $200\,\Omega$ **ii** $400\,\Omega$ **iii** $1600\,\Omega$.

5   A light-dependent resistor (LDR) is connected in series to a fixed resistor of $3000\,\Omega$ and a $6.0\,\text{V}$ battery to make a light-sensing circuit.

a   A voltmeter is to be connected to the circuit so that the voltmeter reading increases when light intensity increases. Explain why the voltmeter should be connected across the fixed resistor.

b   Calculate the resistance of the thermistor when the voltage across the fixed resistor is $2.0\,\text{V}$.

> **TIP**
>
> Think of the line AD as being at 0V. Find the voltage at B and at C and subtract them.

Exercise 11.4 The potentiometer

A **potentiometer** can be used to compare voltages quickly and accurately. This exercise gives you practice in using the readings from a potentiometer.

KEY WORD

potentiometer: a device used to compare potential difference or e.m.f.

1 A uniform resistance wire PQ of length 100 cm is connected in parallel with a supply of e.m.f. 10 V and zero internal resistance. A cell of e.m.f. 2.0 V is connected across part of the wire, as shown:

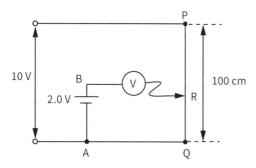

Figure 11.9: For Question 1. Circuit diagram.

a Calculate the potential difference across 1.0 cm of the resistance wire.

b Calculate the p.d. across points R and Q when the distance RQ is:

   i   20 cm   ii   25 cm   iii   40 cm.

c Calculate the reading of the voltmeter when the distance RQ is:

   i   20 cm   ii   25 cm   iii   40 cm.

2 This circuit is a potentiometer used to measure a potential difference V_B:

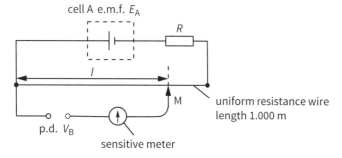

Figure 11.10: For Question 2. Labelled circuit diagram of a potentiometer.

KEY WORDS

galvanometer: an instrument used to measure or detect small electric currents

null method: an experimental technique where a zero reading is sought

The movable contact M is always adjusted until the sensitive meter (**galvanometer**) records zero current (a **null method**). The resistance of the 1.000 m length of resistance wire is 10 Ω.

a Assume $R = 0$. Copy and complete this table:

E_A / V	V_B / V	l / m
2.0	0.60	0.30
2.0	0.44	
	0.60	0.40
6.0		0.80

Table 11.4: For Question 2a.

b Assume $E_A = 2.00\,\text{V}$; $R = 90\,\Omega$.

  i Calculate the p.d. across the resistance wire.

  ii Calculate V_B if $l = 0.245\,\text{m}$.

  iii Having a large resistance R allows small voltages to be measured. Explain why.

c The circuit can be used to measure a small voltage of 2.0 mV. Cell A is a power supply of known voltage 6.00 V. The resistance of the wire is still $10\,\Omega$.

  i Calculate the value of R which produces a p.d. of 3.0 mV across the wire.

  ii Outline the procedure and measurements to be taken that allow the small voltage to be obtained.

  iii Explain how the small voltage is calculated from the measurements.

EXAM-STYLE QUESTIONS

1 A battery has e.m.f. E and internal resistance r. It is connected to six lamps, as shown:

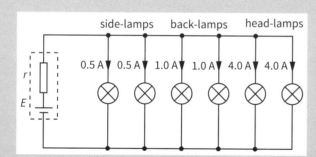

Figure 11.11

The switches to the individual lamps are not shown. The currents in the lamps, when they are all switched on, are shown. The e.m.f. E of the battery is 12.0 V and the internal resistance r is $0.150\,\Omega$.

a Explain what is meant by the *internal resistance* of the battery. [1]

b Use energy considerations to explain why the e.m.f. of the battery is not equal to the p.d. across the battery. [2]

c Calculate the p.d. across the terminals of the battery when all the lamps are switched on. [3]

CONTINUED

    d   Calculate the resistance of a single head-lamp bulb.   **[2]**

    e   Calculate the current in the battery when only the two head-lamp
bulbs are switched on.   **[1]**

    f   The car driver notices that the side-lamps are slightly dimmer when
the head-lamps are on. Explain why.   **[2]**

                                       [Total: 11]

2   A battery of e.m.f. 6.0 V is connected to two resistors in series. One resistor
has resistance 1600 Ω and the other 1200 Ω. The two resistors in series are a
potential divider.

    a   Explain what is meant by a *potential divider*.   **[1]**

    b   Explain why the p.d. across the 1600 Ω resistor is larger than the p.d.
across the 1200 Ω resistor.   **[2]**

    c   The internal resistance of the battery is very small. Calculate the p.d.
across the 1600 Ω resistor.   **[2]**

    d   A resistor of resistance R is connected in parallel across the 1600 Ω
resistor. The p.d. across this resistor falls to 2.0 V. Calculate the
value of R.   **[2]**

    e   A potentiometer is a device for comparing voltages. Draw a circuit
diagram of a potentiometer used to compare the e.m.f. of two cells.
You will need another cell, a resistance wire and a sensitive ammeter.
Explain the procedure used to find the ratio of the e.m.f.s of the
two cells.   **[3]**

                                         [Total: 10]

3   The diagram shows a battery of e.m.f. 4.0 V and negligible internal resistance
connected to a thermistor and a 380 Ω resistor. The voltmeter has a very high
resistance.

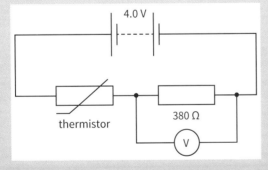

Figure 11.12

The reading on the voltmeter is 2.8 V.

    a   Calculate the current in the circuit and the resistance of the
thermistor.   **[3]**

    b   State and explain how the current in the circuit and the reading of
the voltmeter change as the temperature of the thermistor increases.   **[3]**

                                         [Total: 6]

> Chapter 12
Waves

Exercise 12.1 Basic terms and wave diagrams

KEY WORDS

wave: a periodic disturbance travelling through space, characterised by a vibrating medium

phase difference: a measure of the amount by which one oscillation leads or lags another, expressed as an angle, e.g. 360° if they are one whole oscillation out of step

transverse wave: a wave in which the points of the medium oscillate at right angles to the direction in which the wave travels

amplitude: the maximum displacement from the equilibrium position

wavelength: the distance between two adjacent peaks or troughs in a wave or between adjacent points having the same phase

period: the time taken to complete one cycle of an oscillation

progressive wave: a wave that carries energy from one place to another

In this exercise you use terms related to **waves** and practise with **phase differences** and wave diagrams.

1 These two diagrams represent a **transverse wave**. The one on the left shows how the displacement varies with distance at one instant in time. The one on the right shows how the displacement varies with time at one distance from the source:

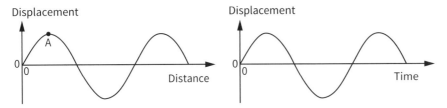

Figure 12.1: For Question 1. Displacement against distance and displacement against time for a transverse wave.

a Copy both diagrams and, on either one or both of them, label the quantities:

amplitude, wavelength, period, $\dfrac{1}{\text{frequency}}$

Use your displacement–distance diagram to answer parts **b–d**:

b On the left diagram mark a point that is in phase with A. Label this B.

c On the left diagram mark a point that has a phase difference of 180° compared with A. Label this C.

d On the left diagram mark a point that has a phase difference of 90° compared with A. Label this D.

Remember: 360° is one whole circle and one whole wavelength further along the wave.

2 a Complete these statements about **progressive waves**:

In longitudinal waves the vibrations are _____ to the direction of the energy transfer.

In transverse waves the vibrations are _____ to the direction of the energy transfer.

b State whether these waves are longitudinal or transverse:

type of wave	longitudinal or transverse
radio waves	
ultrasound waves	
microwaves	
ultra violet waves	
waves on a rope	

Table 12.1: For Question 2b.

c   Describe how to use a long spring to produce a **longitudinal wave** that travels along the spring.

d   Describe how the same spring can be used to produce a transverse wave.

3   A spring is vibrating longitudinally, modelling a sound wave, at a **frequency** of 2.0 Hz. At one instant the distance between a **compression** and the adjacent **rarefaction** is 16 cm. Calculate the speed of the wave.

Remember: a compression is where the coils are close together; it is half a wavelength from the nearest rarefaction, where the coils are far apart.

4   This diagram shows a transverse wave travelling to the right at 6.0 cm s⁻¹:

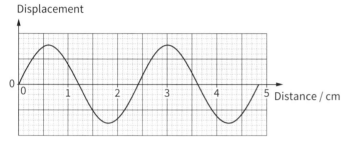

Figure 12.2: For Question 4. Diagram showing a transverse wave travelling to the right.

a   Determine the wavelength of the wave.

b   Use the formula $v = f\lambda$ to calculate the frequency of the wave.

c   Determine the time period of the oscillations of the wave.

d   Copy the diagram and, on the same axes, draw the position of the wave 0.20 s later. You might find how far the wave has moved using speed = distance × time.

5   This diagram shows how the displacement of a particle in a wave varies with time:

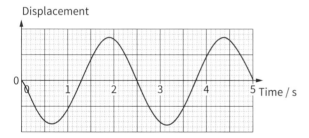

Figure 12.3: For Question 5. Diagram of the displacement of a particle in a wave with time.

a   Determine the time period of the wave.

b   Determine the frequency of the wave.

c   The speed of the wave is 16 cm s⁻¹. Calculate the wavelength of the wave.

d   Copy the diagram and, on the same axes, draw the displacement–time graph for a particle that has a phase difference of 90° to the oscillation shown.

Remember: as 360° is one whole circle, your new graph should be shifted by $\frac{90}{360}$ of a time period.

KEY WORDS

longitudinal wave: a wave in which the points of the medium oscillate along the direction in which the wave travels

frequency: the number of complete oscillations or waves that pass a point in unit time

compression: a region in a sound wave where the air pressure is greater than its mean value

rarefaction: a region in a sound wave where the air pressure is less than its mean value

Exercise 12.2 More about phase difference

This exercise focuses on phase difference and how it can be shown in wave diagrams.

1   This diagram shows five points on a wave:

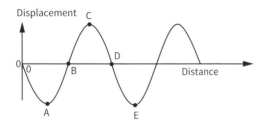

Figure 12.4: For Question 1. Diagram showing five points on a wave.

    a   State which two points have a phase difference of zero.

    b   State which two pairs of points have a phase difference of 270°.

    c   The wave moves to the right. At the instant shown in the diagram:

        i   state the direction in which a particle at A moves.

        ii   state the direction in which a particle at B moves.

2   Two points on a progressive wave are 25 cm apart and differ in phase by 90°.

    a   Explain how this information shows that the wavelength of the wave is 100 cm.

    b   Determine the distance between two points on the wave that have a phase difference of 270°.

    c   Two points on the wave are separated by a distance of 15 cm. Calculate the phase difference between the two points.

3   Explain in your own words what is meant by *a phase difference*.

4   This diagram shows the variation of displacement with time of two points A and B on the same rope:

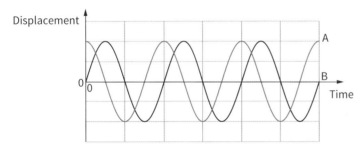

Figure 12.5: For Question 4. Diagram showing the variation of displacement with time of two points A and B on the same rope.

    a   Compare the amplitude of the motions of A and B.

    b   Compare the frequency of the motions of A and B.

    c   Compare the phases of the motions of A and B.

Exercise 12.3 Wave intensity, measuring time and the electromagnetic spectrum

This exercise involves some more complex ideas about waves, such as **intensity**, the **electromagnetic spectrum** and using the time base on an oscilloscope to measure a time.

1 Two waves of the same frequency have amplitudes of 1.5 cm and 3.0 cm.

Calculate the ratio $\dfrac{\text{intensity of wave of amplitude 1.5 cm}}{\text{intensity of wave of amplitude 3.0 cm}}$.

Remember: intensity $\propto$ (amplitude)^2.

2 A wave has amplitude A_0 and intensity I_0. The other waves in this table have the same frequency but different intensities and amplitudes:

	Amplitude	Intensity
initial wave	A_0	I_0
wave A	$\frac{1}{2} A_0$	
wave B		$\frac{1}{2} I_0$
wave C	$3A_0$	
wave D		$16I_0$

Table 12.2: For Question 2.

Copy and complete the table, determining the missing amplitudes and intensities, in terms of A_0 and I_0.

3 A wave of light has intensity $2000\,\mathrm{W\,m^{-2}}$.

a Calculate the energy incident per second on a square of side 0.50 m placed at right angles to the wave.

b Explain why your answer to **a** is reduced when the area is not at right angles to the wave.

c Calculate the area of surface that receives 6000 J in 30 s from the light.

4   Copy and complete this table. It shows the wavelengths and frequencies of some electromagnetic waves. The speed of all the waves is $3.0 \times 10^8 \, \mathrm{m \, s^{-1}}$:

Frequency / Hz	Wavelength / m	Region of the spectrum
	3.0×10^{-2}	
	5.0×10^{-7}	visible
	6.0×10^{-10}	
5.0×10^{7}		
6.0×10^{22}		
3.0×10^{13}		

Table 12.3: For Question 4.

5   A sound is investigated by connecting a microphone to a cathode-ray oscilloscope (c.r.o.).

This diagram shows the trace of the sound wave on the c.r.o. One division on the x-axis of the c.r.o. represents 0.5 ms:

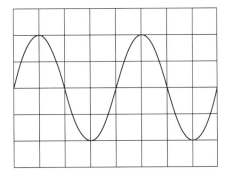

Figure 12.6: For Question 5. Diagram showing the trace of a sound wave on a cathode-ray oscilloscope.

a   Determine the time period of the sound.

b   Use the equation period $= \frac{1}{\text{frequency}}$ to determine the frequency of the sound.

c   Another sound is connected to a different c.r.o. and the same trace is produced. Determine the frequency of the sound if one division on the x-axis of the new c.r.o. represents 2.0 ms.

TIP

The x-axis measures time so find the number of divisions or squares for one cycle and then use the 'time base' of 0.5 ms per division.

Exercise 12.4 The Doppler effect

This exercise tests your understanding of what causes the **Doppler effect**, particularly with sound. You will also practise using the equation for the Doppler effect when a source is moving.

KEY WORDS

Doppler effect: (also called Doppler shift) the change in frequency or wavelength of a wave when the source of the wave is moving towards or away from the observer (or when the observer is moving relative to the source)

1 A stationary observer notices an increase in frequency when a source of sound moves towards him.

   Three students suggest that the increase in frequency is caused because:

   - the velocity of the sound in the air is larger because the source is moving
   - the waves are squashed together because the source is moving towards him
   - the sound is louder as the source comes nearer.

   a State which of the suggestions is the best description.

   b Explain why the sound has a higher frequency as the source approaches.

2 A train sounding a whistle of frequency 400 Hz travels at 40 m s⁻¹. The sound heard by an observer standing very close to the track has a frequency greater than 400 Hz as the train approaches. The speed of sound in air is 340 m s⁻¹.

   a Calculate the frequency heard by the observer as the train approaches.

   b Calculate the frequency heard by the observer as the train travels away from her.

3 A police car drives at 30 m s⁻¹ with its siren blaring at a frequency of 2500 Hz. Calculate the frequency heard as the car approaches directly towards some observers. The speed of sound in air is 340 m s⁻¹.

4 A loudspeaker which emits a note of frequency 300 Hz is whirled in a horizontal circle at a speed of 20 m s⁻¹. Calculate the maximum and minimum frequencies heard by a stationary observer. The speed of sound in air is 340 m s⁻¹.

5 An aircraft flies directly over, and just above the head of, a stationary observer. The engine note heard on the ground before take-off is 250 Hz. As the plane approaches the observer, the frequency heard by the observer is 300 Hz. The speed of sound in air is 340 m s⁻¹.

   a Calculate the speed of the aircraft.

   b Calculate the frequency heard by the observer as the aircraft moves away from him at the same speed.

6 A train travels along a straight track with a constant velocity. The train driver sounds a horn with a frequency of 600 Hz. A stationary observer next to the track hears the sound from the horn at a frequency of 660 Hz. The speed of sound in air is 340 m s⁻¹.

   a Determine the magnitude and the direction of the velocity of the train relative to the observer.

   b State and explain what maximum frequency is heard by another observer further away from the track.

Exercise 12.5 Polarisation

This exercise tests your understanding of **polarisation** and gives you practice in using **Malus's law**.

1   Electromagnetic waves consist of oscillating **electric** and **magnetic fields**. In this diagram of a **plane polarised** electromagnetic wave, E indicates the oscillation of the electric field and B the magnetic field. The plane of polarisation is that of the electric field.

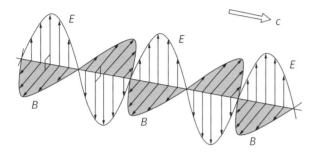

Figure 12.7: For Question 1. Diagram of an electromagnetic wave consisting of oscillating electric (E) and magnetic (B) fields.

   a   Explain why this wave is called a transverse wave.

   b   Describe the difference between a polarised and an unpolarised wave. Draw a diagram to illustrate your answer.

2   Vertically plane polarised light with an incident intensity I_0 and amplitude A_0 passes through a perfect polarising filter. When the angle θ between the plane of polarisation of the light and the transmission axis in the filter is 0° all the light is transmitted.

   a   Calculate the intensity I and the amplitude A on the other side of the filter when

   i $\theta = 30°$

   ii $\theta = 45°$.

   b   Calculate the angle θ when the intensity of light on the other side of the filter is $0.25I_0$.

EXAM-STYLE QUESTIONS

1 These diagrams show the same progressive wave on a string. Diagram 1 shows the wave at time $t_1 = 0$, and diagram 2 shows the wave at $t_2 = 0.10\,\text{s}$. The wave is moving from left to right.

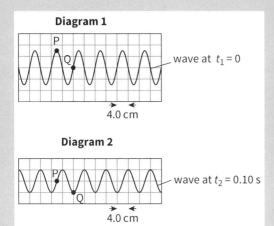

Figure 12.8

Two points P and Q are marked on the string and appear in both diagrams.

a Determine the wavelength of the wave. [1]

b Calculate the speed of the wave, stating any assumption that you make. [3]

c Calculate the frequency of the wave. [2]

d Compare the amplitude of the wave at P and Q. [1]

e Calculate the phase difference between the oscillations of P and Q. [2]

f At time t_1, the amplitude of the oscillation of P is 6.0 cm and at time t_2 the amplitude is 4.0 cm. Calculate this ratio:

intensity of the wave at t_1 : intensity of the wave at t_2 [2]

[Total: 11]

2 a Waves can be longitudinal or transverse.

    i State one difference and one similarity between longitudinal and transverse waves. [2]

    ii Give one example of each type of wave. [2]

b This diagram shows a longitudinal wave of frequency 3.0 Hz:

Figure 12.9

A, B, C, D and E are points through which the wave travels.

CONTINUED

    i   Explain what is meant by *frequency*.   [1]

    ii   State which two points are one wavelength apart.   [1]

    iii The distance between points A and B is 14.0 cm. Calculate the speed of the wave.   [2]

    iv Determine the phase difference between the oscillation of the wave at point A and B. (First work out the fraction of one wavelength that exists between A and B.)   [2]

                             [Total: 10]

3 **a** Explain why only transverse waves can be polarised and non-polarised. **[2]**

    b Describe in outline how you would show that light from a laser is completely plane polarised.   **[3]**

                             [Total: 5]

4 **a** State what is meant by Doppler effect in sound.   **[2]**

    b The diagram shows wavefronts spreading out from a fixed source of sound at the centre of the circles. In the diagram on the right the same wavefronts are shown from a source of sound that moves to the right with a speed of $20\,\text{m s}^{-1}$. The diagrams are not to scale.

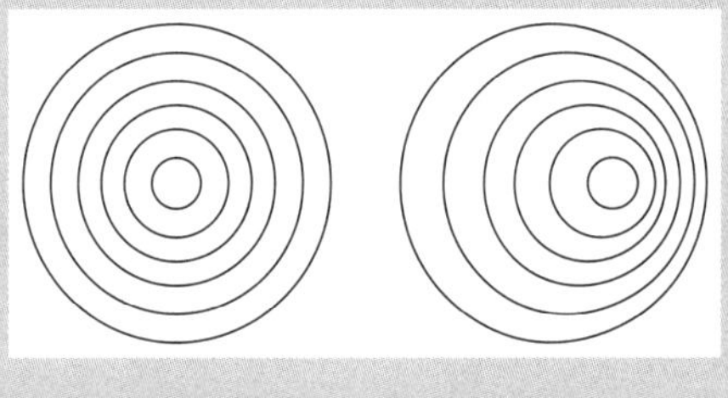

Figure 12.10

The distance between the wavefronts in the diagram on the left is equal to the wavelength of the sound. The frequency of the sound emitted by the source is 200 Hz. The speed of sound in air is $340\,\text{m s}^{-1}$.

Calculate:

    i   the wavelength of the sound   **[2]**

    ii   the time t for one complete oscillation of the sound   **[1]**

    iii the distance moved by the source of sound, travelling at a speed of $20\,\text{m s}^{-1}$, in time t **[1]**

    iv the maximum and minimum distances between the wavefronts in the diagram on the right   **[2]**

    v   the frequency heard by two people, one standing to the right and one to the left of the moving source.   **[2]**

                             [Total: 10]

> Chapter 13

Superposition of waves

CHAPTER OUTLINE

- explain the meaning of the term diffraction

- show an understanding of experiments that demonstrate diffraction

- understand the terms interference and coherence

- understand the conditions required if two-source interference fringes are to be observed and understand experiments that demonstrate two-source interference using water ripples, light and microwaves

- recall and solve problems using the equation $\lambda = \frac{ax}{D}$ or double-slit interference using light

- recall and solve problems using the formula $d \sin \theta = n\lambda$

- describe the use of a diffraction grating to determine the wavelength of light

KEY EQUATIONS

$\lambda = \dfrac{ax}{D}$ for double-slit interference

$d \sin \theta = n\lambda$ for the diffraction grating

Exercise 13.1 Superposition and interference

This exercise helps you to think about **interference** and **path difference**. Remember that path difference is an actual distance and it is not the same as phase difference, although the two are related.

KEY WORDS

interference: the cancellation and reinforcement when two waves pass through each other

path difference: the extra distance travelled by one wave compared with another; often given in terms of the wavelength λ of the waves

1   This diagram shows how the displacement of a particle at a point on the surface of water varies with time:

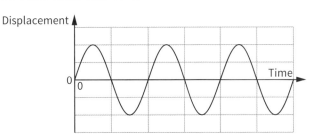

Figure 13.1: For Question 1. Diagram of the displacement of a particle at a point on the surface of water with time.

Copy the diagram and, using the same axes:

a   sketch the variation with time of a wave with twice the amplitude; your wave should be in phase with the wave in the diagram.

b   show the resultant displacement if both waves pass through the same point.

c   draw a wave that has the same amplitude as the original wave but is out of phase with it.

d   show the resultant displacement if the original and the wave in part **c** pass through the same point.

2   Circular waves are produced at points P and Q. This diagram shows the wavefronts produced that are one wavelength apart:

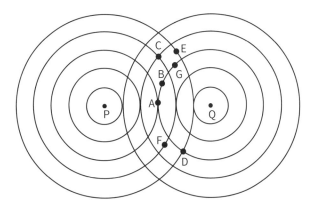

Figure 13.2: For Question 2. Diagram showing wavefront produced at points P and Q.

Look at point A. Two sets of waves arrive at A, one from source P and the other from source Q. There are three whole wavelengths between A and P (i.e. AP = 3λ). There are also three whole wavelengths between A and Q, so AQ = 3λ. The path difference between the two sets of waves AP − AQ = 0.

Look at point B. There are $3\frac{1}{2}$ whole wavelengths between B and P (i.e. BP = $3\frac{1}{2}\lambda$). There are three whole wavelengths between B and Q, so BQ = 3λ. The path difference between the two sets of waves BP − BQ = $\frac{1}{2}\lambda$.

a   Explain why there is **constructive interference** at point A.

b   Explain why there is **destructive interference** at point B.

c   Copy and complete this table to find the path difference for each of the points C to G. For each, decide whether the interference is constructive or destructive.

Point X	Distance from X to P	Distance from X to Q	Path difference	Interference at the point
A	3λ	3λ	0	constructive
B	$3\frac{1}{2}\lambda$	3λ	$\frac{1}{2}\lambda$	destructive
C				
D				
E				
F				
G				

Table 13.1: For Question 2c.

d   Copy and complete these sentences:

   i   At points A, C and D, the path difference from the point to the two sources is _____.

   ii   The two waves arrive _____ phase and they _____ interfere.

   iii   At points B, E, F and G, the path difference from the point to the two sources is _____.

   iv   The two waves arrive _____ phase and they _____ interfere.

e   Copy or trace the two sets of wavefronts in Figure 13.2. On your diagram, join up all the points where the path difference from the point to P and Q is 0. You will find these points where a circle from P crosses the 'same' circle from Q.

f   Using your diagram, join up all the points on one side of the point A where the path difference is λ. To do this: Starting at source Q, count three circles outwards from Q and four circles outwards from P. Where these two circles cross there are two points where the path difference is λ. Now repeat with four circles out from Q and five from P and also $3\frac{1}{2}$ circles out from Q and $4\frac{1}{2}$ circles out from P, and so on. You can also find points on the left-hand side where the path difference is such that Q is further than P from the point chosen.

Exercise 13.2 Two-source interference experiments

This exercise helps you to think about the apparatus used and results found in two-source interference experiments.

1   This diagram shows light from a laser that passes through two slits:

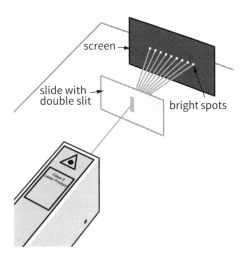

Figure 13.3: For Question 1. Diagram showing light from a laser that passes through two slits.

The equation $\lambda = \frac{ax}{D}$ is used to determine the wavelength λ of the laser light.

a   State what is meant by the other quantities in the formula and, on a sketch of the diagram, mark the distances a, x and D.

b   State how you would measure each distance used in finding the wavelength. Indicate the instrument used in each case and include one precaution that you would take to ensure an accurate result.

c   The wavelength of red light is about 7×10^{-7} m. Use this value to suggest suitable values for all of the other distances in the formula.

d   The bright spots are found to be too close together on the screen for accurate measurement. Suggest two changes that can be made to the experiment to increase the separation of the spots.

e   A laser is used in the experiment. Give two reasons why a laser is preferred to an ordinary white lamp.

> **TIP**
>
> Think about brightness and the effect of the different colours in white light.

2   Two-source interference can be shown with water waves and microwaves as well as light.

a   Draw the apparatus that is used to show two-source interference of water waves.

b   Draw the apparatus that is used to show two-source interference of microwaves.

c   The wavelengths of light and microwaves are different. For a double-slit experiment, suggest how the wavelength of the microwaves leads to differences in the quantities a, x and D as compared with those used in light experiments.

Exercise 13.3 Calculations and descriptions with the double-slit experiment

This exercise helps you practise using the double-slit interference formula and applying it to experiments. For fringes to be observed in two-source interference the waves must have the same wavelength (frequency and speed) and be **coherent**.

1   This diagram shows a double-slit experiment using coherent light:

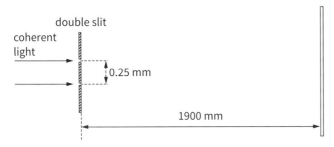

Figure 13.4: For Question 1. Diagram showing a double-slit experiment using coherent light.

The wavelength of the light is 5.0×10^{-7} m.

a   Calculate the spacing of the fringes on the screen.

b   The pattern on the screen of intensity against distance can be drawn graphically. Copy and complete this graph to show other fringes:

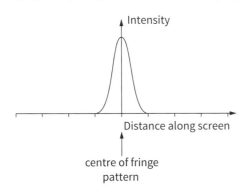

Figure 13.5: For Question 1b. Graph of intensity against distance.

In the following situations, **c** to **g**, state what happens, if anything, to the dark and bright fringes.

c   The slits are moved closer together.

d   The wavelength of the light is increased.

e   The intensity of the light passing through both slits is reduced.

f The intensity of the light passing through only one of the slits is reduced.

g The coherent light is replaced by light of the same wavelength, but from two different sources that are not coherent.

2 A double-slit interference experiment uses a source of wavelength 5.86×10^{-7} m. The separation of the two vertical slits is 0.30 mm and the distance from the slits to the screen is 1.7 m.

a Describe the appearance of the fringes.

b Calculate the fringe separation.

c Calculate the distance on the screen between the middle of the central fringe and the middle of the first dark fringe.

3 This diagram shows the central section of the double-slit interference pattern on a screen:

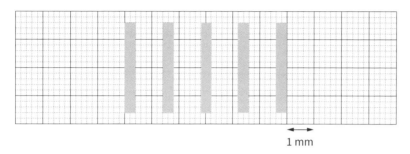

1 mm

Figure 13.6: For Question 3. Diagram showing the central section of the double-slit interference pattern on a screen.

a Determine a value for the separation of the fringes on the screen.

b The screen is 2.0 m from the slits and the separation of the slits is 1.0 mm. Calculate the wavelength of the light.

c Draw the pattern obtained when the separation of the slits is halved. Make sure you include the scale.

d Describe the pattern obtained when a white light source is used. The light from the two slits is still coherent, even though it is now white and contains a mixture of wavelengths.

4 Two coherent light sources are 0.30 mm apart. They each emit light of wavelength 4.95×10^{-7} m. An interference pattern is produced on a screen placed 2.00 m from the sources. Calculate the distance between two neighbouring bright fringes on the screen.

5 In a two-source interference experiment, the distance from the two sources to the screen is 1.6 m. A pattern of dots is seen on the screen with one central dot and three dots on either side of the central dot.

The distance between the central dot and the third dot on one side is 10.0 mm.

The wavelength of the light from the laser used is 6.0×10^{-7} m.

The third dot away from the central dot is three fringe spacings away.

a Calculate the fringe separation, x.

b Calculate the separation of the sources, a.

TIP

In **f**, think about what happens in destructive and constructive interference when waves have different amplitude.

TIP

Consider what happens if the phase of one source suddenly changes.

6   Two slits in a metal barrier are placed in front of a source of microwave radiation, as shown:

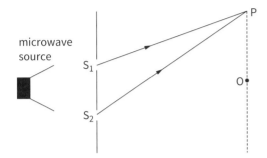

Figure 13.7: For Question 6. Diagram showing microwave radiation passing through two slits in a metal barrier.

The wavelength of the microwaves is 3.0 cm.

The distance S_1P is 90.0 cm and the distance S_2P is 99.0 cm.

a   Calculate the path difference between the two waves, one travelling from S_1 to P and the other travelling from S_2 to P. Give your answer in cm.

b   State the phase difference between the two waves arriving at P.

c   State the type of interference occurring at P.

d   A detector of microwaves is placed at O and moved slowly towards P. Describe what is observed. Use your answer to **b** to see how many maxima and minima there are between O and P.

Exercise 13.4 Diffraction and the diffraction grating

This exercise helps you understand the role of **diffraction** and gives you practice in using the diffraction grating formula. You will also consider the **dispersion** produced by a grating and the different orders of the spectrum it produces.

1   Match the four wave terms with the correct statement:

Term	Statement
diffraction	needs a constant phase difference between two waves
interference	occurs when waves meet and the resultant displacement is the sum of the displacements of each wave
coherence	causes a pattern due to cancellation and reinforcement of the waves
superposition	causes waves to spread out as they pass through narrow gaps

Table 13.2: For Question 1.

2   This diagram shows a student's drawing of the diffraction pattern of a water wave as it passes from left to right through a gap which is larger than the wavelength:

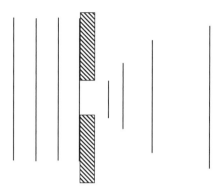

Figure 13.8: For Question 2. A student's drawing of the diffraction pattern of a water wave as it passes from left to right through a gap which is larger than the wavelength.

a   State two things that are incorrect about the diagram.

b   Draw a diagram of the diffraction pattern if the gap is much smaller than the wavelength.

3   The speed of sound is $320\,\mathrm{m\,s^{-1}}$.

a   Calculate a value for the wavelength of the sound of frequency 2.0 kHz.

b   Draw a diagram of apparatus you could use to show the diffraction of sound. Suggest the size of the gap used.

TIP

Take care to use the equation $v = f\lambda$ with the frequency in Hz.

4   A diffraction grating has 500 lines per millimetre. Light is incident normally on the grating.

a   Calculate the distance, in metres, between one line and the next on the diffraction grating.

b   Calculate the wavelength of light that gives a first-order maximum at an angle of 22.0°.

c   Calculate the angle of the second-order maximum when light of this wavelength is used.

d   State what happens when you try to use the diffraction grating formula for the third-order. This limits the number of orders to only two in this case.

e   State the total number of lines seen in the diffraction pattern if only two orders are present in the spectrum of a monochromatic source of light.

5   Light of wavelength 590 nm is incident normally on a diffraction grating of width 30.0 mm which contains 10 000 lines.

a   Calculate the spacing of the lines in the grating.

b   Calculate the angular positions of the various orders.

6   When red light of wavelength 700 nm is passed normally through a diffraction grating, the first-order maximum is found at an angle of 25° to the zero-order beam.

a   Calculate the grating spacing and the number of lines per millimetre in the grating.

b Calculate the angle for the first-order maximum using blue light of wavelength 400 nm.

c Calculate the difference in angle between the blue light and the red light in the first-order spectrum.

7 Light of wavelength 600 nm is incident normally on a diffraction grating, as shown:

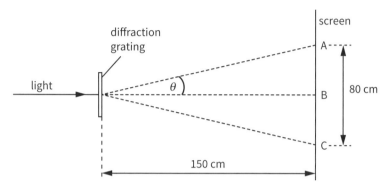

Figure 13.9: For Question 7. Light of wavelength 600 nm incident normally on a diffraction grating.

First-order maxima are seen at positions A and C on the screen.

a Calculate the angle θ.

b Calculate the grating spacing.

c Calculate the distance on the screen between B and the position of a second-order maximum.

EXAM-STYLE QUESTIONS

1 A vertical screen is placed some metres from a vertical double slit. A single beam of red light from a laser shines on the double slit and a pattern of red dots is seen on the screen.

   a Explain how the pattern of red dots is formed on the screen. Use ideas about path difference, phase difference and interference in your answer. [3]

   b Explain, using ideas about diffraction, why this pattern becomes less bright towards the edge of the screen. [2]

   [Total: 5]

2 Diffraction gratings can be used to find the wavelength of light.

   a Describe how you would use a diffraction grating to find the wavelength of light from a laser. [4]

   b State an advantage of using a diffraction grating rather than double slits in your experiment. Explain your reasoning. [2]

   [Total: 6]

CONTINUED

3 In an experiment using double slits, eight fringe spacings on the screen are found to occupy a distance of 0.40 cm. The screen is 50 cm from the slits. The wavelength of the light is 700 nm.

    a Calculate the fringe spacing. [1]

    b Calculate the separation of the slits. [2]

    c The double slits are replaced with a diffraction grating. The slits in this grating are separated by the same distance as the double slits. Light of the same wavelength (700 nm) is shone through the grating. Calculate the angle of the first-order maximum. [2]

    d State two differences between the patterns seen when the double slits and the diffraction grating are used. [2]

    e **Suggest** why having lines as far apart as this for a diffraction grating experiment is not suitable. [2]

[Total: 9]

COMMAND WORD

Suggest: apply knowledge and understanding to situations where there are a range of valid responses in order to make proposals

Chapter 14

Stationary waves

CHAPTER OUTLINE

- explain and use the principle of superposition in simple applications of stationary waves
- show an understanding of experiments that demonstrate stationary waves using microwaves, stretched strings and air columns
- explain the formation of a stationary wave using a graphical method, and identify nodes and antinodes
- determine the wavelength of sound using stationary waves

KEY EQUATIONS

distance from one node to the next (or one antinode to the next) $= \dfrac{\lambda}{2}$

distance from one node to the nearest antinode $= \dfrac{\lambda}{4}$

Exercise 14.1 How superposition leads to stationary waves

This exercise gives you practice using graphs of **stationary waves** and in applying the principle of **superposition**.

1   This diagram shows a string fixed at both ends vibrating with a stationary wave pattern:

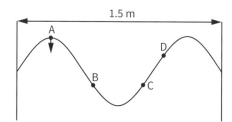

Figure 14.1: For Question 1. Diagram showing the wave pattern of a vibrating string (fixed at both ends).

At the time shown, the displacement is a maximum.

a   Draw the string vibrating between the same ends a quarter of cycle later than in the diagram.

b   Draw the string vibrating between the same ends a half-cycle later than in the diagram. Remember the stationary wave is not moving along – some of the points on it are just moving up and down and some points do not move up and down at all, they stay as zero all the time.

c Calculate the wavelength of the wave. Use the idea that the distance between successive **nodes** is $\frac{\lambda}{2}$.

d In Figure 14.1, the arrow on point A shows the direction in which the string at A is about to move. State the directions in which points B, C and D are about to move.

2 This diagram shows the displacement of two progressive waves P and Q at one instant in time:

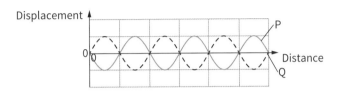

Figure 14.2: For Question 2. Displacement of two waves P and Q.

The two waves travel in opposite directions. Wave P moves to the right and wave Q moves to the left. These two waves combine by the principle of superposition to form a stationary wave.

a Copy the diagram onto a piece of graph paper, leaving enough space below for three similar diagrams. Draw and label the resultant of P and Q on your diagram.

A short time t later, the waves have moved a quarter of a wavelength in opposite directions, as shown:

Figure 14.3: For Questions 2b–e.

b Copy this diagram underneath your part **a**, on the same sheet of paper. Draw the resultant of P and Q.

c Draw the diagram and resultant again, with each wave having moved a further quarter of a wavelength in opposite directions.

A progressive wave moves along. Half the distance between the vertical lines is $\frac{\lambda}{4}$.

d Draw the diagram and resultant again, with each wave having moved a further quarter of a wavelength in opposite directions.

e Mark on your diagram the letter A at all the places where the resultant wave always has a maximum amplitude. Add the letter N at all places where the resultant is always zero.

3 A stationary wave is formed by the superposition of two progressive waves.

This diagram shows a stationary wave and *one* of the two progressive waves at one instant of time. The distance along the *x*-axis is the horizontal distance along the wave:

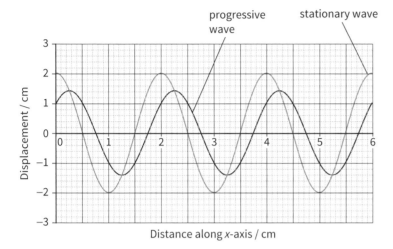

Figure 14.4: For Question 3. A stationary wave and one of the two progressive waves at one instant of time.

a Complete this table. Show the values of:
- the displacement of the stationary wave
- the displacement of the progressive wave at the distances along the *x*-axis shown in the table
- the displacement of the other progressive wave (the one not shown on the diagram).

One row has been done for you.

> **TIP**
>
> Remember that the two progressive wave displacements add together to make the displacement of the stationary wave.

Distance along *x*-axis / cm	Displacement of stationary wave / cm	Displacement of progressive wave shown / cm	Displacement of other progressive wave / cm
0	+2.0	+1.0	+1.0
0.50			
1.00			
1.50			
2.00			

Table 14.1: For Question 3a.

b State the values of the distances along the *x*-axis on the diagram where nodes are formed.

c State the values of the distances along the *x*-axis on the diagram where **antinodes** are formed.

d State the distance in centimetres between a node and the nearest antinode and compare this distance with the wavelength λ of the progressive wave.

> **KEY WORD**
>
> **antinode:** a point on a stationary wave where the amplitude is a maximum

Exercise 14.2 Using stationary wave patterns

This exercise helps you to use stationary wave patterns to find wavelengths, frequencies and speed.

1   This diagram shows three stationary wave patterns on the same wire PQ:

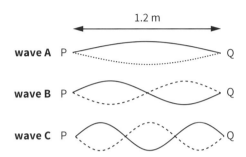

Figure 14.5: For Question 1. Three stationary wave patterns on the same wire PQ.

The distance between points P and Q is 1.2 m.

a   State the wavelengths of waves A, B and C.

b   The frequency of the **fundamental** wave A is 240 Hz. State the frequencies of the **harmonic** waves B and C.

c   State the number of antinodes shown on each of the waves A, B and C.

d   Describe the motion of wave A, starting with the wave position shown by the solid line.

2   The length of a string fixed at both ends is 60 cm.

a   Calculate the longest wavelength (the fundamental) of a stationary wave that can be set up on the string.

b   The sound heard from the wave in **a** has a frequency of 100 Hz. Calculate the speed of the wave on the string.

3   A wire of length 0.24 m is fixed at both ends. An oscillator makes the wire move up and down as a stationary wave. At certain values of the oscillator frequency, stationary waves are formed; the different stationary waves have different wavelengths.

a   State the three largest wavelengths of stationary waves that can form on the wire.

b   The speed of the wave along the wire is 100 m s^{-1}. Calculate the three smallest frequencies that produce stationary waves.

KEY WORDS

fundamental frequency: the lowest-frequency stationary wave

harmonic: a mode of vibration with a frequency that is a multiple of the fundamental frequency

TIP

Remember, node to node is $\lambda/2$.

4   A loudspeaker creates a stationary wave in a tube. The dust in the tube collects in piles at the nodes. There is also a node at the closed end:

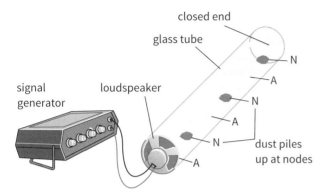

Figure 14.6: For Question 4. Creation of a stationary wave in a closed glass tube.

a   Explain why the dust collects at the nodes.

b   The distance between successive nodes in the pattern is 5.0 cm. The speed of sound in the tube is 320 m s⁻¹. Calculate the wavelength and frequency of the sound from the loudspeaker.

c   In the diagram, starting from the open end, there is a sequence ANANAN of antinodes and nodes, where A is an antinode and N is a node. Suggest two other possible sequences within the tube where the distance between successive nodes is larger than 5.0 cm.

Exercise 14.3 Using the correct terms to explain stationary waves

It is important to be able to use terms such as *amplitude* and *phase* correctly and to make comparisons. This exercise provides practice in using these terms and making comparisons.

1   This diagram shows a string carrying a stationary wave at the instant when the displacement is a maximum:

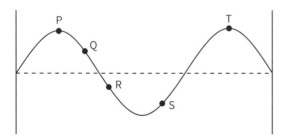

Figure 14.7: For Question 1. A stationary wave at one instant.

P, Q, R, S and T are points marked on the string.

a The point P is at an antinode. Explain what is meant by an *antinode*.

b Explain what is meant by a *node*.

c State how many nodes there are on the diagram.

d Complete this table to give the phase difference between different points on the stationary wave. Two values have been done for you.

Remember that points between nodes on a stationary wave move up and down in phase.

Points	Phase difference between the points
P and Q	0
P and R	180°
P and S	
P and T	
Q and R	
Q and S	
R and S	

Table 14.2: For Question 1d.

e Describe where points with no phase difference will be found on a stationary wave.

f Compare the phase difference between points at different distances along a *stationary wave* with the phase difference between points along a *progressive wave*.

g Point Q vibrates up and down in phase with point P but with a lower amplitude. Place the amplitudes of the oscillations at P, Q, R, S and T in order, from largest to smallest.

h Describe how the amplitude of oscillation of a point on a stationary wave varies along the wave. Compare this with the amplitude of oscillation of different points along a progressive wave.

i Compare the transmission of energy along a stationary wave and along a progressive wave. Explain why there is a difference.

2 This diagram shows the shape of one stationary wave formed on a guitar string when a note is played:

Figure 14.8: For Question 2. The shape of one stationary wave formed on a guitar string when a note is played.

Points P, Q and R are three marks on the string, placed at the antinodes.

a   Explain how a stationary wave is formed on the guitar string from a progressive wave travelling along the string.

b   Describe the motion of point P.

c   Compare the oscillation at the three points. You should describe any similarities and differences in the *amplitude* and in the *phase difference* between the points.

d   Draw the shape of another stationary wave that forms on the same length of string but which has a larger wavelength than shown in the diagram. Mark the nodes on your diagram.

3   This diagram shows a mode of vibration of a stationary sound wave set up in a closed tube:

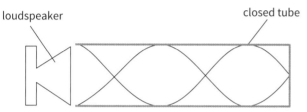

Figure 14.9: For Question 3. Diagram showing a mode of vibration of a stationary wave in a closed tube.

a   Describe the motion of a molecule of air at an antinode.

b   Explain how waves from the loudspeaker produce stationary waves in the tube.

c   The wavelength of sound from the loudspeaker is 8.0 cm. Determine the length of the tube. (Ignore end corrections.)

The frequency of sound from the loudspeaker is gradually increased and the next mode of vibration is found.

d   Sketch this mode.

e   Determine the wavelength of the wave formed in this mode.

> **TIP**
>
> The antinode is an antinode in the displacement of a molecule of air. Your answer should bring in the fact that sound is a longitudinal wave.

Exercise 14.4 Planning experiments on stationary waves

Being able to describe and plan experiments needs practice and thought. This exercise includes a number of structured approaches to experiments involving stationary waves.

1 This diagram shows apparatus that can be used to show a stationary wave on a string and to measure the wavelength of the wave:

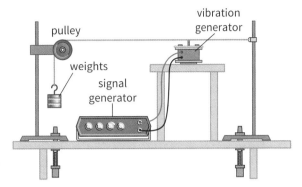

Figure 14.10: For Question 1. Diagram of apparatus that can be used to show a stationary wave on a string and to measure the wavelength of the wave.

a State how you can obtain a stationary wave on the string and how you would recognise the positions of nodes and antinodes.

b Suggest how you can measure the wavelength of the wave. Include one precaution that enables an accurate value to be found.

c The frequency of the wave is the frequency of the signal from the signal generator. Explain how this frequency can be measured using an oscilloscope.

d Suggest how the experiment can be used to determine how the speed of the wave on the string depends on the tension in the string.

2 This diagram shows apparatus that can be used to produce a stationary microwave:

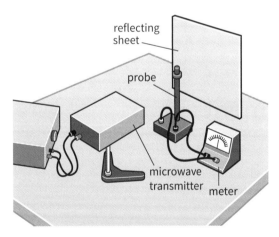

Figure 14.11: For Question 2. Diagram of apparatus that can be used to produce a stationary microwave.

a Describe how you would use the apparatus to demonstrate a stationary wave.

b Explain why a stationary wave is set up.

c Explain how to use the stationary wave to measure the frequency of the microwave from the transmitter.

3   This diagram shows a column of water and a tuning fork:

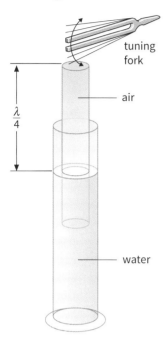

tuning fork

air

$\frac{\lambda}{4}$

water

Figure 14.12: For Question 3. Producing a stationary wave with a column of water and a tuning fork.

When the length of the air column is $\frac{\lambda}{4}$, a stationary sound wave is produced with one node and one antinode.

a   State whether a node or an antinode is found at the top of the air column.

b   State whether a node or an antinode is found at the surface between the water and the air.

c   State, in terms of λ, what length of air column produces a stationary wave with two nodes and two antinodes.

d   Describe how you would use the apparatus to demonstrate that stationary waves can be set up.

e   Describe and explain how you would use the apparatus to measure the wavelength of sound. Since the antinode at the open end of the tube is slightly outside the tube, your method should involve the difference in the lengths of two air columns where there is a stationary wave.

f   The frequency of a tuning fork is marked on the tuning fork. The experiment is repeated with different tuning forks. Describe the graph obtained when the wavelength λ of the sound wave is plotted against the frequency f of the tuning fork.

g   Suggest a graph that may be plotted involving f and λ to give a straight line with a gradient equal to the speed of the sound in the air column.

EXAM-STYLE QUESTIONS

1   A string is fixed at one end and made to vibrate by a vibrator close to that end. The frequency of the vibrator is altered until a stationary wave forms, as shown:

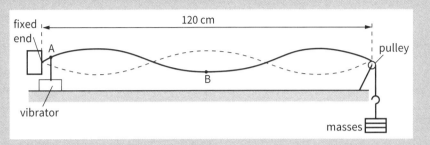

Figure 14.13

a   Explain how a progressive wave produced by the vibrator causes the stationary wave to form. **[2]**

b   Copy the wave pattern and mark on your diagram where nodes are found. **[1]**

c   State the number of antinodes shown on the diagram. **[1]**

d   Compare:

   i   the phase **[1]**

   ii   the amplitude **[1]**

   of the oscillations of points A and B on the string.

e   The frequency of the vibrator is 150 Hz and the length of the string between the pulley and the fixed end is 120 cm.

   i   Calculate the wavelength of the progressive wave on the string. **[2]**

   ii   Calculate the speed of the progressive wave along the string. **[2]**

f   Adding more masses to the hook hanging from the string increases the speed of the progressive wave along the string.

   A small mass is added and the stationary wave shown disappears.

   i   Explain why the stationary wave pattern shown disappears. **[2]**

   ii   State whether the frequency of the vibrator must be increased or decreased to form the same stationary wave pattern on the string as shown in the diagram. Explain your thinking. **[2]**

   [Total: 14]

2   This diagram shows a demonstration of a stationary wave on a string:

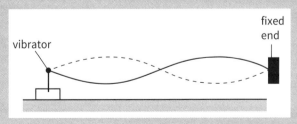

Figure 14.14

CONTINUED

A vibrator is attached near one end of the string and the other end of the string is fixed. The vibrator causes a progressive wave to travel along the string.

a Use the principle of superposition to explain the formation of the stationary wave. **[2]**

b The speed of the progressive wave is $24\,\text{m s}^{-1}$ and the vibrator has a frequency of $50\,\text{Hz}$.

   i Calculate the wavelength of the progressive wave on the string. **[1]**

   ii Calculate the distance between the nodes on the string. **[1]**

c When the frequency of the vibrator is *doubled*, the number of loops on the stationary wave changes from two to four. **Predict** whether this change affects the speed of the progressive wave along the string. Explain your thinking. **[2]**

[Total: 6]

> **COMMAND WORD**
>
> **Predict:** suggest what may happen based on available information

3 **a** Describe how progressive waves and stationary waves on a string differ in regard to the:

   i transfer of energy along the string **[1]**

   ii variation of amplitude with distance along the string. **[1]**

b When used to describe a stationary wave, explain what is meant by:

   i a displacement node **[1]**

   ii a displacement antinode. **[1]**

c A loudspeaker is placed close to the open end of a long tube which is closed at the other end, as shown. The length of the tube is $30\,\text{cm}$:

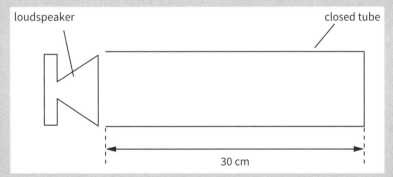

Figure 14.15

The frequency of the loudspeaker is altered slowly. A loud sound is heard at several frequencies.

   i Explain what causes these loud sounds to occur. **[2]**

   ii Sound of wavelength $24\,\text{cm}$ from the loudspeaker causes a loud sound. Describe the position of the nodes and antinodes within the tube at this wavelength. **[2]**

   iii The speed of sound in the tube is $320\,\text{m s}^{-1}$. Determine the lowest frequency at which a loud sound is produced in the tube. **[3]**

[Total: 11]

Atomic structure and particle physics

CHAPTER OUTLINE

- describe a simple model for the nuclear atom and infer from the results of the α-particle scattering experiment the existence and small size of the nucleus

- distinguish between nucleon number and proton number

- understand that an element can exist in various isotopic forms, each with a different number of neutrons

- represent nuclides with notation, and appreciate that nucleon number, proton number and mass–energy are all conserved in nuclear processes

- show an understanding of the nature and properties of α-, β^+-, β^-- and γ-radiations

- understand that an antiparticle has the same mass but opposite charge to the corresponding particle, and that a positron is the antiparticle of an electron

- describe leptons including electrons and neutrinos, including how (electron) antineutrinos and (electron) neutrinos are produced during β^- and β^+ decay

- understand that α-particles have discrete energies but that β-particles have a continuous range of energies because (anti)neutrinos are emitted in β decay

- describe a simple quark model of hadrons, including protons and neutrons, which are not fundamental particles

- describe β^- and β^+ decay in terms of a simple quark model and also with decay equations involving nuclide notation

- understand that quarks are fundamental particles and that there are six flavours (or types) – up, down, strange, charm, top and bottom – and know the charge of each type and their antiquarks

- recall that electrons and neutrinos are fundamental particles and that hadrons are classified as baryons (three quarks or antiquarks) or mesons (one quark and antiquark)

KEY EQUATIONS

nucleon number = proton number + neutron number

In β^- decay $d \rightarrow u + {}^{0}_{-1}e + \bar{\nu}$

In β^+ decay $u \rightarrow d + {}^{0}_{+1}e + \nu$

Exercise 15.1 Discovering the nuclear model of the atom

In this exercise you will discover how we know that an atom has a small central, positive **nucleus**. Remember the **alpha-particle** (α-particle) and the nucleus are both positive.

KEY WORDS

nucleus (of an atom): the very small, but very dense, positively charged centre of an atom

alpha-particle: two protons and two neutrons ($_2^4\alpha$, the nucleus of a helium atom $_2^4$He) emitted from a nucleus during radioactive decay

1   This diagram shows three α-particles approaching a gold nucleus in a scattering experiment:

α-particle 1 ⟶
α-particle 2 ⟶
α-particle 3 ⟶

gold nucleus

Figure 15.1: For Question 1. Diagram showing three alpha-particles approaching a gold nucleus in a scattering experiment.

All three α-particles have the same initial energy.

a   State which α-particle is deviated through the *smallest* angle. Explain why.

b   Copy the diagram and draw the paths of the three α-particles as they approach and leave the nucleus.

c   A force acts on each α-particle as it approaches the gold nucleus. On your diagram add an arrow to show the direction of this force at the point where α-particle 3 is closest to the nucleus. Explain why it acts in the direction that you have shown.

2   In an experiment, a large number of α-particles are fired at random towards a thin gold foil. The particles pass through the foil. Some are deviated only a little and some are deviated through large angles.

Compare the number of particles that deviate through small and large angles if:

a   the gold nuclei are far apart from each other

b   the gold nuclei are very close together.

Experiments show that most α-particles pass straight through the foil with only a small deviation.

c   Explain what this shows about the amount of empty space in the atom.

3   Link the observation in the α-particle scattering experiment with the best explanation.

Observation	Explanation
most α-particles pass straight through the gold foil	there are electrons outside the nucleus
	electrons have a negative charge
some α-particles are deflected	most of an atom is empty space
	the mass of an atom is concentrated in a small space
a few α-particles are deflected by more than 90°	the nucleus is positively charged
	the nucleus contains neutrons

Table 15.1: For Question 3.

4 In a scattering experiment, α-particles are fired at a thin gold foil.

  a State the direction in which the maximum number of α-particles will be detected after hitting the foil.

  b State what this observation suggests about the structure of an atom.

  c Some α-particles are scattered through more than 90°. State and explain what this suggests about the structure of a gold atom.

Exercise 15.2 Particles in the atom and some decay equations

This exercise give you practice completing decay equations, making the total **proton number** (or charge) and total **nucleon number** match on either side of the equation.

1 a Copy and complete this table to show the number of protons, the number of neutrons, the number of electrons in a neutral atom, and the full **nuclide** notations:

Nuclide notation	Number of protons	Number of neutrons	Number of electrons in a neutral atom
$^{238}_{92}U$			
He	2	2	
^{63}Cu	29		
^{58}Ni		30	
^{14}N	7		
^{15}O		7	

Table 15.2: For Question 1a.

b State the differences in structure between a neutral *atom* of ^4_2He, a singly charged **ion** of ^4_2He and an α-particle.

c This diagram represents three different nuclei:

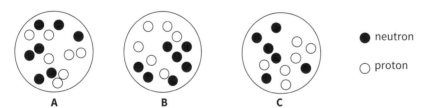

Figure 15.2: For Question 1c. Diagram representing three different nuclei.

State and explain which of the nuclei are **isotopes** of the same element.

2 State three quantities that are conserved in a nuclear process. There are several quantities to choose from – do not just say *mass* or *energy*.

3   An isotope of phosphorus $^{30}_{15}P$ decays by emitting a **beta-minus**-particle (β^- or $^{0}_{-1}e$) and an **electron antineutrino** ($\bar{v}$) to form a Si nucleus.

    a   Copy and complete this equation:

        $^{30}_{15}P \rightarrow Si + {}^{0}_{-1}e + \bar{v}$

        Note: $\bar{v}$ is an electron antineutrino; neutrinos have no proton number nor nucleon number.

    b   In the reaction, the total **rest mass** of the products is smaller than the mass of the $^{30}_{15}P$ nucleus. Explain why rest mass does not appear to be conserved.

    c   Give the nuclide notation of another isotope of phosphorus.

4   Calculate the values of p, q, r and s in each of these nuclear reactions:

    a $^{241}_{95}Am \rightarrow {}^{p}_{q}Np + {}^{r}_{s}He$

    b $^{14}_{6}C \rightarrow {}^{p}_{q}N + {}^{0}_{-1}e + \bar{v}$

    c $^{23}_{12}Mg \rightarrow {}^{p}_{q}Na + {}^{0}_{+1}e + v$

Notes:

$^{r}_{s}He$ is an α-particle, which you should know about.

$^{0}_{-1}e$ is a β^--particle and $\bar{v}$ is an electron antineutrino.

$^{0}_{+1}e$ is a β^+-particle and v is an **electron neutrino**.

5   A nucleus of uranium $^{238}_{92}U$ undergoes a series of nuclear decays, as shown by the arrows in this diagram. Each circle represents a nucleus present during the decay series:

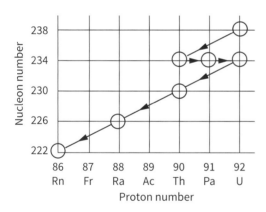

Figure 15.3: For Question 5. Diagram showing a nucleus of uranium undergoing a series of nuclear decays.

    a   State the nuclide notation of the final nucleus in the series.

    b   Write out the decay equation for one example of α decay in this series.

    c   Write out the decay equation for one example of β^- decay in this series.

    d   State how many β^--particles and α-particles are emitted during the series.

    e   State the nuclide notation of two pairs of isotopes in this series.

    f   Imagine a nucleus emits a **beta-plus**-particle (β^+). Describe the arrow that needs to be added to the diagram for this decay.

KEY WORDS

beta-minus (β^-) decay: the emission of an electron (β^--particle, $^{0}_{-1}e$) from a nucleus as a neutron decays into a proton (proton number increases by 1 and an antineutrino is also emitted)

electron antineutrino: an antiparticle that is emitted in β^- decay, with virtually no mass (at rest) and no charge

rest mass: the mass of a particle when at rest

electron neutrino: a particle that is emitted during β^+-decay with virtually no mass (at rest) and no charge

KEY WORDS

beta-plus (β^+) decay: the emission of a positron (β^+-particle, $^{0}_{+1}e$) from a nucleus as a proton decays into a neutron (proton number decreases by 1 and a neutrino is also emitted)

6 An atom of $^{238}_{92}U$ decays progressively into $^{206}_{82}Pb$ by emitting eight α-particles and a number of β⁻-particles. How many β⁻-particles are emitted?

7 This question is about the **unified atomic mass unit**: $1\,u = 1.66 \times 10^{-27}\,kg$.

- The mass of a carbon-12 atom is exactly 12 u.
- The mass of a hydrogen-1 atom is close to 1.0 u.
- The mass of a helium-4 atom is close to 4.0 u.

  a Calculate the mass of a carbon-12 atom in kg.

  b Calculate the number of atoms in 1.0 kg of carbon-12.

  c Calculate the mass of a helium-4 atom in kg.

  d Calculate the mass of an electron ($9.11 \times 10^{-31}\,kg$) in unified atomic mass units.

Exercise 15.3 The nature and properties of nuclear radiation

This exercise helps you understand that the *nature* of radiation is what it is made of; its *properties* are what it can do. The properties involved in radioactivity are a result of the nature of the particles.

1 A student lists some of the properties of α-particles, β⁻-particles, β⁺-particles and γ-radiation. Link the property to the correct radiation. One of the particles is linked to two properties.

Property
has the most positive charge
passes through paper but not 2 cm lead
is not affected by an electric field
travels at the speed of light
is an antiparticle of a common particle

Radiation
α-particle
β⁻-particle
β⁺-particle
γ-radiation

Table 15.3: For Question 1.

2 **a** Copy and complete this table to show the mass and charge of the four types of radiation. Give values of charge in terms of e where e is $1.60 \times 10^{-19}\,C$.

The rest mass of a proton and a neutron are each $1.7 \times 10^{-27}\,kg$ to two significant figures.

The rest mass of an electron is $9.1 \times 10^{-31}\,kg$.

	α-particle	β⁻-particle	β⁺-particle	Photon of γ-radiation
Mass / kg				
Charge		−1e		

Table 15.4: For Question 2a.

b The speed of a typical β^--particle leaving a nucleus is $0.9c$, where c is the speed of light.

  i State the speed of a β^+-particle and the speed of a photon of γ-radiation, each of which has approximately the same energy as the β^--particle.

  ii Calculate the speed of an α-particle which has approximately the same energy as the β^--particle. Give your answer as a fraction of c.

3 Describe and explain what happens to a neutral atom as an α-particle passes near and causes ionisation.

4 State which of the four types of radiation (α, β^-, β^+ or γ):

 a produces the most ionisation per mm along its path through air atoms

 b has the shortest range in air

 c is not affected by a magnetic field

 d is attracted by a negatively charged object

 e is deflected the opposite way to α-radiation by an electric field

 f has the highest speed

 g is emitted with a range of speeds (consider those emissions that are emitted with a neutrino or antineutrino from a nucleus)

 h is the same as a **fundamental particle** found in the atom

 i is an electromagnetic wave

 j is made up of protons and neutrons.

5 Explain why each type of radiation that you chose in question **4**, parts **a–g**, has the property described.

6 A **positron** (β^+-particle) is an **antiparticle**.

 a State the name of the corresponding *particle*.

 b State one property of an antiparticle that is the same for its corresponding particle.

 c State one property of an antiparticle that is different for its corresponding particle.

7 Outline how you could use the absorption properties of nuclear radiation to show that a radioactive source emits only γ-radiation. Include one precaution you would take to reduce the effect of random errors.

Exercise 15.4 Fundamental particles including quarks

This exercise helps you to learn about some types of **quark** and where they are found in the nucleus, and which particles are **leptons** and which particles are **hadrons**.

1 Copy the following table and add ticks to show if a particle is fundamental, whether it is a lepton or a hadron, and if it contains quarks. There may be one or more ticks for each particle.

> **TIP**
>
> Think about why ionisation happens in question 4, parts **a** and **b**.

> **KEY WORDS**
>
> **fundamental particle:** an elementary particle not made from other particles, for example leptons and quarks
>
> **positron:** the antiparticle of the electron; has the same mass as the electron but charge $+e$
>
> **antiparticle:** a particle with the same mass and opposite charge as another particle
>
> **quark:** the fundamental particle of which hadrons are made; there are six types or flavours: up, down, strange, charge, top and bottom
>
> **lepton:** a fundamental particle not affected by the strong nuclear force, for example electron, positron and neutrino
>
> **hadron:** any particle made from quarks

Particle	Fundamental	Lepton	Hadron	Contains quarks
neutron				
proton				
electron				
neutrino				

Table 15.5: For Question 1.

2   Leptons include electrons and neutrinos. State two differences between electrons and neutrinos.

3   An up quark is written as u, a down quark as d and a strange quark as s. The charge on an electron is e.

    a   State the quark structure of a neutron.

    b   An up quark has a charge $+\frac{2}{3}e$. Use your answer to **a** to show that the charge on a down quark is $-\frac{1}{3}e$.

    c   State the quark structure of a proton.

    d   Show that your choice of quarks in **c** have a total charge of $+e$.

4   When a neutron decays it produces a β^--particle (an electron $_{-1}^{0}e$) and two other particles.

    a   State the name of the two other particles and complete this decay equation:

$$_{0}^{1}n \rightarrow {_{-1}^{0}e} + \underline{\hspace{1cm}} + \underline{\hspace{1cm}}$$

    b   State what happens to the quarks inside the neutron during the decay.

    c   State which of the particles in the decay equation in **a** are leptons and which are antiparticles.

5   One step in the fusion process that takes place in the Sun involves the β^+ decay of a proton (p) into a neutron (n) and a neutrino (ν).

    The equation for the step is: $p \rightarrow n + \beta^+ + \nu$

    a   Show that charge is conserved in the equation shown.

    b   Show that nucleon number is conserved in the equation shown.

    c   State what happens to the quarks inside the proton during β^+ decay.

6   A neutral carbon atom $_{6}^{12}C$ contains quarks, leptons and hadrons.

    a   State which particles in the carbon atom are leptons and how many leptons in total are found in one neutral atom of carbon.

    b   State which particles in the carbon atom are hadrons and how many hadrons in total are found in one neutral atom of carbon.

    c   State how many quarks there are in one neutral atom of carbon.

7   **a**   A nuclear decay is written in terms of the quarks in the nucleus as:

$$d \rightarrow u + \underline{\hspace{1cm}} + \underline{\hspace{1cm}}$$

    State the two particles that are not shown on the right-hand side.

b A nuclear decay is written in terms of the quarks in the nucleus as:

u ⟶ d + _____ + _____

State the two particles that are not shown on the right-hand side.

8 A nuclear process that does *not* occur is $v + p \rightarrow n + \beta^-$.

a Show that this process does not conserve charge.

b Show that the nuclear process $\bar{v} + p \rightarrow n + \beta^+$ conserves charge, proton number and nucleon number.

9 Hadrons such as the neutron and proton contain either three quarks or three antiquarks. They do *not* contain a mixture of quarks and antiquarks.

a Using only up (u) and down (d) quarks and their antiparticles ($\bar{u}$ and $\bar{d}$), write all the quark combinations of three quarks or three antiquarks.

b Write all the combinations of quarks that contain one strange quark (s) with up and down quarks to make a combination of three quarks.

c Write all the combinations of three antiquarks that contain two strange antiquarks ($\bar{s}$) with an up or down antiquark.

d Suggest a name for the hadron which contains two $\bar{u}$ quarks and one $\bar{d}$ quark.

10 Copy and complete the table to show the charges of all six types of quark.

Charge / e	Quark type (flavour)		
$+\dfrac{2}{3}$	up		
$-\dfrac{1}{3}$	down		bottom

Table 15.6: For Question 10.

11 A **baryon** contains three quarks made from any of the six types (flavours). Calculate all possible values of the charge on a baryon. Show your working.

12 A pion (π) is a **meson** that is composed of only up and down quarks and their antiquarks.

State the possible combinations of quark that make:

a a π^- meson which has a charge of -1 (i.e. the same charge as on an electron)

b a π^+ meson which has a charge of $+1$ (i.e. the same charge as on a proton)

c a π^0 meson which has no charge.

13 A sigma-plus-particle contains two up quarks and a strange quark (uus).

a Show that the charge on the sigma-plus-particle is $+1$.

b State the quark structure of an antisigma-plus-particle.

KEY WORDS

baryon: a hadron made from three quarks or three antiquarks (an antibaryon)

meson: a hadron made from a quark and an antiquark

EXAM-STYLE QUESTIONS

1 This table shows some of the isotopes of aluminium and their type of nuclear decay:

Isotope	$^{25}_{13}Al$	$^{26}_{13}Al$	$^{27}_{13}Al$	$^{28}_{13}Al$	$^{29}_{13}Al$
Type of decay	β^+	β^+	stable	β^-	β^-

Table 15.7

a Describe the similarities and the differences in the structure of neutral atoms of the isotopes. [3]

b Describe the structure of a nucleus of $^{27}_{13}Al$ in terms of:

   i the number of protons and neutrons it contains [2]

   ii the number of up (u) and down (d) quarks it contains. [2]

c Describe what happens during beta-minus (β^-) decay using a quark model. [2]

d State two quantities conserved in beta decay. [2]

e By considering the difference between the isotopes in the table, suggest why some isotopes emit β^--radiation and some emit β^+-radiation. [2]

[Total: 13]

2 a Complete this table for the three types of radiation: [8]

Radiation	Nature	Charge	Penetrating ability in air	Affected by magnetic fields
α			6 cm	a little
β^-		$-1e$		
β^+	positron		2.0 m	
γ				

Table 15.8

b i A radioactive nucleus decays with the emission of an α-particle and a photon of γ-radiation. Describe the changes that occur in the proton number and the nucleon number of the nucleus. [2]

   ii Describe briefly, with the aid of a sketch diagram, an experiment to distinguish between the α-, β- and γ-radiation emitted from a radioactive source using a magnetic field. Explain why the experiment is difficult to perform with α-radiation and how the experiment shows that β^--particles are emitted with a range of speeds. [4]

c About 100 years ago, experiments were performed by firing α-particles at gold foil. A detector was used to see how many particles were scattered at different angles. Summarise the results of these experiments and explain the conclusions that were drawn. [3]

[Total: 17]

CONTINUED

3   Leptons and hadrons are two classes of particles.

a   Some classes of particles are fundamental; others are not. State and explain whether leptons and hadrons are fundamental or not fundamental.   [3]

b   Name the class of particles of which the neutron is a member.   [1]

c   Give two examples of a lepton.   [2]

d   In beta-minus (β^-) decay, a nucleus of calcium (Ca) emits a β^--particle as shown in the reaction:

$$^{45}_{20}\text{Ca} \rightarrow\ ^{45}_{21}\text{Sc} + \beta^- + \bar{\nu}_e$$

   i   State the name of the particle $\bar{\nu}_e$.   [1]

   ii   Explain, in terms of the neutrons and protons involved, how this change occurs.   [2]

   iii   Explain, in terms of the quarks involved, how this change occurs.   [2]

e   State the quark change that happens during beta-plus (β^+) decay.   [1]

[Total: 12]

4   Hadrons are a group of particles that contain quarks. Hadrons can be either mesons or baryons.

a   i   State the quark structure of a baryon.   [1]

   ii   State the quark structure of a meson.   [1]

b   i   State one similarity and one difference between a particle and an antiparticle.   [2]

   ii   Complete the table with properties of the antiproton.   [2]

	Charge / C	Quark structure
antiproton		

Table 15.9

c K^- particles are mesons made from strange, up and down quarks. The K^--particle contains one strange particle (s) and one antiquark. The K^--particle has a charge of −1, equal to the charge on an electron.

   i   Determine the charge on the antiquark.   [1]

   ii   Determine which antiquark is present in the K^--particle.   [1]

[Total: 8]

5   a   The quark composition of a neutron is written as udd. Explain why this is the only combination of u and d quarks that is possible for a neutron.   [1]

b   The quark composition of a π^- particle is written as d$\bar{\text{u}}$.

There is a particle called Δ^- whose quark composition is ddd.

   i   Show that the magnitudes of the charges on the π^- and the Δ^- are equal.   [1]

   ii   Explain, in terms of quarks, why the π^- is a meson but the Δ^- is a baryon.   [2]

[Total: 4]

Practical skills at AS Level

CHAPTER OUTLINE

- use appropriate techniques for the measurement of length, volume, angle, mass, time, temperature and electrical quantities

- understand and explain the effects of systematic errors and random errors

- understand the distinction between precision and accuracy

- assess the uncertainty in a calculated quantity by addition of absolute, fractional or percentage uncertainties

---

KEY EQUATIONS

$$\text{gradient} = \frac{\text{change in } y}{\text{change in } x} = \frac{\Delta y}{\Delta x}$$

$$\text{uncertainty} = \frac{1}{2}(\text{maximum reading} - \text{minimum reading})$$

$$\text{percentage uncertainty} = \frac{\text{uncertainty}}{\text{mean value}} \times 100\%$$

When $A = B \pm C$; absolute uncertainty in A = sum of absolute uncertainties in B and C

When $A = \dfrac{B}{C}$ or BC; percentage uncertainty in A = sum of percentage uncertainties in B and C

Exercise P1.1 Scales and uncertainties

This exercise gives you practice reading the scales of a number of different instruments and estimating the **uncertainties** in measurements.

The number of significant figures given in a reading should be decided by looking at the measuring instrument used. For example, it is not sensible to record a distance measured on a ruler with a millimetre scale as 3 cm or 3.00 cm; it should be recorded as 3.0 cm.

KEY WORD

uncertainty: an estimate of the spread of values around a measured quantity within which the true value will be found

1 a Record the position of the left-hand and right-hand edge of the coin placed
on this metre rule:

Figure P1.1: For Question 1a.

b Read the temperature shown on this thermometer:

Figure P1.2: For Question 1b.

c Read the current shown on this **analogue** meter:

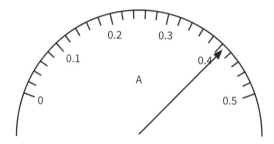

Figure P1.3: For Question 1c.

> **KEY WORDS**
>
> **analogue display:** a continuous display which represents the quantity being measured on a dial or scale

d Read the volume shown on measuring cylinder A:

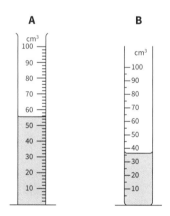

Figure P1.4: For Question 1d.

> **KEY WORDS**
>
> **precision:** the smallest change in value that can be measured by an instrument or an operator or that is shown in a measurement
>
> **zero error:** the measurement of a quantity when the true value is zero

e State whether cylinder A or B has the lower **precision**. Explain why.

f A small volume, $6 \, \text{cm}^3$, of glue has become solid at the bottom of cylinder
A. Unless taken into account, this causes a **zero error** when the cylinder is
used to measure the volume of a liquid, and makes cylinder A less accurate.
Explain what is meant by a *zero error* and how cylinder B is likely to be more
accurate.

2 Copy and complete the following table, giving units for any values. Include columns for any instruments that you have available or for which there is a diagram in your textbook.

	Metre rule	30 cm ruler	Callipers	Micrometer	Analogue thermometer	Analogue voltmeter	Measuring cylinder A	Protractor	Top pan balance	Stopwatch
Is there a possibility of a zero error?										
What is the smallest scale division?										
What is the uncertainty (assume no zero error)?										
What is the largest possible reading?										
What is the percentage uncertainty in the largest possible reading?										

Table P1.1: For Question 2.

TIP

To decide the uncertainty, you will have to think about whether it is possible to read the scale within the divisions on the instrument. Some of the instruments were shown in question 1. If you cannot read within a division then the smallest division is the uncertainty.

Exercise P1.2 Finding the uncertainty in a reading

This exercise considers different uncertainties in measurements and how they arise.

Calculated quantities should be given to the same number of significant figures as (or one more than) the measured quantity with the least **accuracy**, except when produced by addition or subtraction.

1 When a student hears the starting pistol at the start of the race, he starts his stopwatch and stops it as he sees a runner crossing the finishing line.

The reading on the **digital** stopwatch is 26.02 s.

a Suggest the value that the student should write down as his best estimate for the time and for the uncertainty in the time, based on only one reading.

b Three other students also record the same time and the readings on their stopwatches are:

25.90 s   26.34 s   26.14 s

Calculate the mean value of all four readings and an estimate of the uncertainty of the time.

KEY WORDS

accuracy: how close the value of a measured quantity is to the true value of the quantity

digital display: a display that gives the information in the form of characters (numbers or letters)

c   The true value of the time is 26.40 s. Explain how this value shows that the students' readings have a **systematic error**.

d   Suggest one cause of a systematic error and one cause of a **random error** in the readings.

2   A student times a number of oscillations of a ball along a curved track.

Figure P1.5: For Question 2.

Timing one complete oscillation, her readings were:

    2.12 s

    2.32 s

Timing ten complete oscillations, her readings were:

    21.20 s

    21.32 s

The time for one complete oscillation is T.

a   Use the first set of readings to determine the value and uncertainty for T.

b   Use the second set of readings to determine the value and uncertainty for T.

c   Calculate the percentage uncertainty in the two values of T that you have determined.

d   Suggest one reason why timing a large number of oscillations – 200, for example – is not possible.

Exercise P1.3 Combining uncertainties

This exercise helps you understand percentage uncertainties and absolute uncertainties.

There are two simple rules:

- When quantities are added or subtracted, you add *absolute uncertainties* to find the total absolute uncertainty.

- When quantities are multiplied or divided, you add *percentage uncertainties* to find the total percentage uncertainty.

1   a   State the number of significant digits in 0.0254.

b   Write $T = 1.25578 \pm 0.1247$ s, keeping two significant digits in the uncertainty.

c   Calculate the percentage error for $v = 12.25\,\mathrm{m\,s^{-1}} \pm 0.25\,\mathrm{m\,s^{-1}}$.

d   Calculate the absolute error if the accepted value is 120 s and the percentage error is 5%.

KEY WORDS

systematic error: an error of measurement that differs from the true value by the same amount in each measurement

random error: an error in a measurement that is unpredictable and which may vary from one measurement to the next

---

TIP

You should find that the percentage uncertainty in T found using ten complete oscillations is the smaller. Using more oscillations gives a smaller percentage uncertainty.

2 a Each of these measurements was taken several times.

The uncertainty is half the **range** of the readings:

$T = 7.5\,\text{s} \pm 0.2\,\text{s}$

$L = 10.0\,\text{m} \pm 0.2\,\text{m}$

$D = 5.6\,\text{cm} \pm 4\%$

Determine which measurement has the smallest percentage uncertainty.

b Two sides of a piece of paper are measured as $A = 29.5 \pm 0.1\,\text{cm}$ and $B = 21.0 \pm 0.1\,\text{cm}$. The circumference C of the paper is $2A + 2B$. Calculate the absolute error in C.

c A pressure P is calculated using the formula $P = \dfrac{F}{\pi R^2}$. The percentage uncertainties are $\pm 2\%$ in F and $\pm 1\%$ in R. Calculate the percentage uncertainty in P.

3 The area A of a circle of radius r is given by $A = \pi r^2$.

If r measures $10.0 \pm 0.2\,\text{cm}$, calculate:

a the percentage uncertainty in r

b the percentage uncertainty in A (r is squared and so is multiplied by itself; there is no error in π)

c the absolute uncertainty in A (changing from percentage to absolute uncertainty, you will need the value of $A = 314\,\text{cm}^2$).

4 These readings were obtained in an experiment to measure the density of a ball-bearing:

- mass $= 7.0 \pm 0.1\,\text{g}$
- volume $= 1.20 \pm 0.05\,\text{cm}^3$

A student obtains the density as $5.8333\,\text{g cm}^{-3}$.

a Calculate the percentage uncertainty of each reading.

b Calculate the percentage uncertainty in the density value.

c Calculate the absolute uncertainty in the density.

d Write down the density and uncertainty to a reasonable number of significant figures.

5 Measurements taken as a ball falls a distance D in a time T are:

- $D = 1.215 \pm 0.004\,\text{m}$
- $T = 0.495, 0.498, 0.503, 0.496, 0.501\,\text{s}$

The mean average value of T is $0.499\,\text{s}$ and the acceleration due to gravity g is $9.77\,\text{m s}^{-2}$ (calculated using the formula $g = \dfrac{2D}{T^2}$).

Calculate the:

a percentage uncertainty in D

b range in the measurements of T

c absolute uncertainty in the average value of T

d percentage uncertainty in the average value of T

e percentage uncertainty in g

f absolute uncertainty in g.

Exercise P1.4 Tables, graphs and gradients

This exercise gives you practice tabulating results, drawing graphs and finding gradients.

1   A student investigates the speed of water waves in a shallow tray:

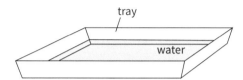

Figure P1.6: For Question 1.

One end of the tray is lifted and then lowered quickly. A wave moves backwards and forwards across the tray several times before it dies away.

The student measures the depth d of the water and the time T taken by the wave to travel from one end of the tray to the other and back again. She repeats the reading of T. The distance travelled by the wave in time T is 5.00 m.

The student's measurements for different values of d are shown in this table:

d / m	T / s first value	T / s second value
0.005	22.2	22.3
0.010	15.9	16.0
0.015	12.9	13.1
0.020	11.3	11.4
0.025	10.1	10.1
0.030	9.2	9.3
0.035	8.5	8.4

Table P1.2: Data for Question 1.

The speed v of the water wave is found using the formula:

$$v = \frac{5.00}{t}$$

where t is the average value of the two values of T.

When T is measured in s, the formula gives a value for v in m s^{-1}.

a   Produce a table for the readings showing the depth d in m, the average time t and the speed v. Also include values of v^2 in your table. Give appropriate units for all quantities.

b   Plot a graph of v^2 on the y-axis against d on the x-axis.

c   Draw a straight line of best fit.

d Determine the gradient and *y*-intercept of this line.

e The quantities *v* and *d* are related by the formula:

$v^2 = Ad + B$

where *A* and *B* are constants.

Use your answer to part **d** to determine the values of *A* and *B*. Give appropriate units.

2 During half of an oscillation of a simple pendulum, the string holding the pendulum bob hits against a stationary horizontal rod:

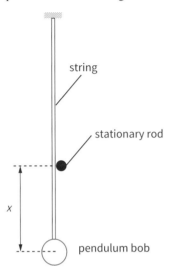

Figure P1.7: For Question 2.

The distance between the pendulum bob and the rod is the distance *x*. The total length of the string is kept constant.

The distance *x* and the time T_{10} for ten complete oscillations are measured by a student.

This is part of the student's notebook showing the readings:

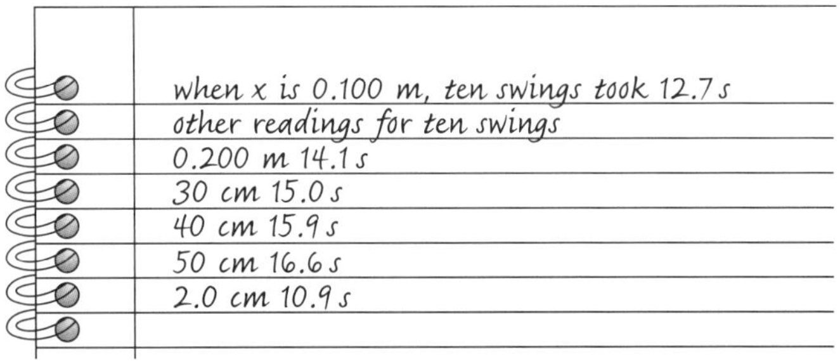

> when *x* is 0.100 m, ten swings took 12.7 s
> other readings for ten swings
> 0.200 m 14.1 s
> 30 cm 15.0 s
> 40 cm 15.9 s
> 50 cm 16.6 s
> 2.0 cm 10.9 s

Figure P1.8: Data for Question 2.

a Produce a table for the readings showing the distance *x* in metres, T_{10} and the time *t* for one oscillation. Include $\sqrt{x}$ in your table. Give units for all quantities.

b Plot a graph of *t* on the *y*-axis against $\sqrt{x}$ on the *x*-axis.

c Draw the straight line of best fit.

d   Determine the gradient and y-intercept of this line.

e   The quantities t and $\sqrt{x}$ are related by the formula:

$t = A\sqrt{x} + B$

where A and B are constants.

Use your answer to part **d** to determine the values of A and B. Give appropriate units.

Exercise P1.5 Mathematical relationships and sources of uncertainty

This exercise allows you to test mathematical relationships, suggest sources of uncertainty and improvements to reduce uncertainty.

1   It is suggested that two quantities F and x are related by the formula:

$F = kx$

where k is a constant.

This table shows values of F and x:

F / N	x / cm
20	18.0
4.2	2.0

Table P1.3: Data for Question 1.

a   Use data from the table to calculate two values for k.

b   The uncertainty in each value of x is ± 0.1 cm. The uncertainty in F is very small. Calculate the percentage uncertainty in each reading of x.

c   State a criterion you can use to determine whether the data supports the relationship.

d   Explain whether the data supports the suggested relationship.

2   It is suggested that two quantities y and x are related by the formula:

$y = kx^2$

where k is a constant.

This table shows values of y and x:

y / cm	x / cm
18	6.00
32	7.83

Table P1.4: Data for Question 2.

a   Use data from the table to calculate two values for k.

b   The uncertainty in each value of y is ± 1 cm. The uncertainty in x is very small. Calculate the percentage uncertainty in the smallest value of y.

c State a criterion you can use to determine whether the data supports the relationship.

d Explain whether the data supports the suggested relationship.

3 It is suggested that two quantities T and x are related by the formula:

$T^2 = kx$

where k is a constant.

This table shows values of T and x:

T / s	x / cm
2.0	4.00
6.3	41.3

Table P1.5: Data for Question 3.

a Use data from the table to calculate two values for k.

b The uncertainty in each value of T is ±0.1 s. The uncertainty in x is very small. Calculate the percentage uncertainty in the smallest value of T.

c State a criterion you can use to determine whether the data supports the relationship.

d Explain whether the data supports the suggested relationship.

4 In this question you will need to describe sources of uncertainty and improvements in a basic experiment. Many such sources of uncertainty or limitations in the procedure will depend on the actual apparatus used. You may have to look up the apparatus in your textbook.

For each situation described:

- imagine that you have taken two sets of readings of two quantities that are related; you have used your readings to see whether a suggested relationship is supported by these readings (remember that in any formula, k represents a constant)

- suggest sources of error or limitations and then suggest improvements to reduce the errors or limitations.

a A metre rule is balanced on a pivot and two masses are placed on it, one either side of the pivot. You check the relationship clockwise moment = anticlockwise moment.

b You check that the resistance R of a wire of constant length is related to the area of cross-section A by the relationship $R = \frac{k}{A}$.

c A hacksaw blade is clamped at one end. You check that the period of oscillation t is related to the length l of the hacksaw blade that is free to vibrate by the relationship $t^2 = kl^3$.

d You check that the width w of a piece of paper tape is related to the maximum force F needed to break the tape when it is pulled by a newtonmeter by the relationship $F = kw$.

EXAM-STYLE QUESTIONS

1   A student connects a resistor of resistance R to a cell, as shown in this circuit diagram:

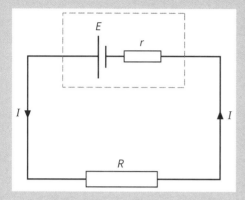

Figure P1.9

The e.m.f. of the cell is E and its internal resistance is r. The current I is measured by an ammeter, which is not shown.

The student uses a number of different resistances, R. She records the current and the value of R each time. The cell is only switched on for a short time to take the readings.

The readings the student obtains are shown in the table:

R / Ω	10	20	5	2	15	25	30
I / A	0.118	0.068	0.186	0.286	0.086	0.056	0.048

Table P1.6

a   Copy the table, placing the readings in order of increasing resistance. Include values of $\frac{1}{I}$ in your table.   [1]

b   Plot a graph of $\frac{1}{I}$ on the y-axis against R on the x-axis.   [3]

c   Draw the straight line of best fit.   [1]

d   Determine the gradient and y-intercept of this line.   [2]

e   The quantities I and R are related by the formula:

$$\frac{1}{I} = \frac{1}{E}(R+r)$$

where E is the e.m.f. of the cell and r is the internal resistance of the cell.

Use your answers to part **d** to determine the values of E and r. Give appropriate units.   [2]

[Total: 9]

CONTINUED

2 A mass M hanging on the end of a spring was twisted slightly. The time T for one complete oscillation was measured accurately by recording the time T_5 for five complete oscillations.

The results obtained for T_5 were 2.46 s and 2.64 s when $M = 100$ g.

a Determine the value of T when $M = 100$ g. [1]

b Estimate the percentage uncertainty in the average value of T_5. [1]

The measurement of T_5 was repeated using a mass of 300 g.

The results obtained for T_5 were 4.26 and 4.32 s.

c Determine the new value of T when $M = 300$ g. [1]

It is suggested that the quantities T and M are related by the equation:

$T^2 = kM$

where k is a constant.

d Use your answers to parts **a** and **c** to calculate two values of k. [2]

e Explain whether the results support the suggested relationship. [1]

f Describe four sources of uncertainty or limitations of the procedure for this experiment. [4]

g Describe four improvements that could be made to this experiment. You may suggest the use of other apparatus or different procedures. [4]

[Total: 14]

> # Chapter 16
Circular motion

CHAPTER OUTLINE

- use degrees and radians as measures of angle, including the expression of angular displacement in radians

- explain uniform circular motion in terms of a resultant force causing a centripetal acceleration

- solve problems involving angular displacement and velocity, including use of the equations $v = r\omega$ and $\omega = \frac{2\pi}{T}$

- solve problems involving centripetal acceleration, including use of the equations $a = r\omega^2 = \frac{v^2}{r}$ and $F = mr\omega^2 = \frac{mv^2}{r}$

KEY EQUATIONS

angular velocity $= \dfrac{\text{angular displacement}}{\text{time}}$; $\omega = \dfrac{\Delta\theta}{\Delta t}$

speed $=$ radius $\times$ angular velocity; $v = r\omega$

centripetal acceleration $=$ radius $\times$ (angular velocity)^2; $a = r\omega^2 = \dfrac{v^2}{r}$

centripetal force $=$ mass $\times$ centripetal acceleration; $F = mr\omega^2 = \dfrac{mv^2}{r}$

Exercise 16.1 Angular measure

The **radian** is a more 'natural' unit of measurement of angles than the degree. Angles in radians can be calculated knowing the length s of the arc subtended by the angle and the radius r of the circle: $\theta = \frac{s}{r}$. This exercise provides practice in calculating angles in radians and converting between degrees and radians.

KEY WORD

radian: a unit of angle such that 2π radians $= 360°$

1   For each diagram **a–f**, calculate the unknown quantity θ in radians, s or r, from the other two:

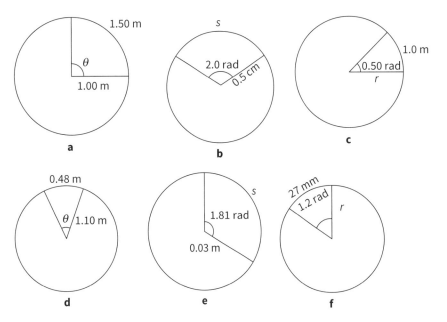

Figure 16.1: For Question 1. Circles with angle, radius and arc labelled.

2   When an object moves around a complete circle, its **angular displacement** is 2π radians or 360°.

a   Show that one radian is approximately equal to 57°.

b   Convert each of these angles in degrees to radians:

   i   20°

   ii   75°

   iii   175°.

c   Convert each of the following angles in radians to degrees:

   i   0.40 rad

   ii   1.35 rad

   iii   2.0 rad.

d   Express each of these angles as multiples of π radians:

   i   180°

   ii   90°

   iii   45°.

KEY WORDS

angular displacement: the angle through which an object moves in a circle

3 This diagram shows how an angle of one radian is defined – *the arc subtended by the angle is equal in length to the radius of the circle*:

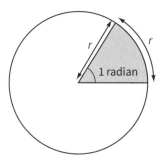

Figure 16.2: For Question 3. Diagram showing how an angle of one radian is defined.

> **TIP**
>
> If a question about circular motion seems unclear, draw a diagram of the circle and angles involved to help your understanding.

a Draw a similar diagram to show the dimensions of an angle of 2.0 radians.

b Draw a similar diagram to show the dimensions of an angle of $\frac{\pi}{3}$ radians.

4 You may need to find the value of a trigonometric function (such as sine or cosine) of an angle whose value is given in radians. Make sure that you know how to set your calculator to work with angles in radians.

Check that your calculator shows that sin (1.0 rad) = 0.841.

a Calculate the values of the following, where all angles are given in radians; give your answers to three significant figures:

   i cos 1.0

   ii tan 1.0

   iii sin 0.10

   iv $\sin\left(\dfrac{\pi}{4}\right)$

   v $\cos\left(\dfrac{\pi}{3}\right)$

   Your calculator is likely to have a π key.

b Determine the following angles; give your answers in radians to three significant figures:

   i $\sin^{-1} 0.50$

   ii $\cos^{-1} (-0.65)$

Exercise 16.2 Uniform circular motion

An object that moves around a circular path at a steady speed is described as having uniform circular motion. This is an exercise to develop understanding of the relationships between velocity, **angular velocity**, period, angle and radius.

1 A fairground ride consists of several cars travelling around on a vertical wheel of radius $r = 20.0$ m. Each car makes one complete circuit in a time $T = 35$ s.

> **KEY WORDS**
>
> **angular velocity:** the rate at which the angular displacement changes

a   During each circuit, a car travels around 360°. This is its angular displacement θ. Give the value of θ in radians.

b   Calculate the car's angular velocity ω.

c   Calculate the distance travelled by the car during one circuit ($= 2\pi r$).

d   Calculate the car's speed v using speed $= \dfrac{\text{distance}}{\text{time}}$.

e   Calculate the car's speed using $v = r\omega$. Check that your answers to **d** and **e** are the same.

2   Two runners, A and B, are jogging side by side around a circular running track.

a   The radius of runner A's circular path is 100.0 m. Calculate the distance travelled in one complete circuit. (Give your answer to one decimal place.)

b   Runner B jogs beside runner A, at a distance of 0.80 m further from the centre of the track. How much further does runner B travel than runner A when completing a circuit?

c   Runner A runs at a steady speed of 5.0 m s^{-1}. Determine the speed at which runner B must run in order to stay beside runner A.

3   A train moves along a curved section of track at a steady speed of 18.0 m s^{-1}.

a   The curved section of track has a length of 900 m. Deduce how long it will take the train to travel this distance.

b   The radius of curvature of the track is 3.60 km. Calculate the angle through which the train has moved (its angular displacement). Remember:

angle in radians $= \dfrac{\text{length of arc}}{\text{radius}}$

c   Calculate the angular velocity of the train.

d   Draw a diagram to show the curved section of the track. Add arrows to show the velocity of the train at the start of the section and at the end.

Exercise 16.3 Centripetal acceleration

An object moving in a circle must be acted on by a resultant force which is not zero. In this exercise, you need to decide whether an object is acted on by a non-zero resultant force. If there is a non-zero resultant force towards the centre, you can then calculate quantities such as angular velocity and acceleration.

1   a   Describe the motion of an object which is acted on by balanced forces (resultant force = 0).

b   The resultant force acting on an object as it travels around in a circle is a cause of **centripetal acceleration**. State the direction of the force.

KEY WORDS
centripetal acceleration: the acceleration of an object towards the centre of its circular motion

2   This diagram shows an object at several points around its path. It is moving with uniform circular motion in a clockwise direction:

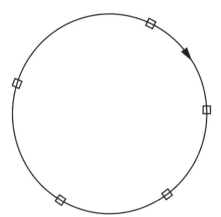

Figure 16.3: For Question 2. Diagram showing an object at several points around its path, moving with uniform circular motion in a clockwise direction.

a   Explain what the word *uniform* tells you about the object's speed.

b   State whether the object's velocity is constant. Explain your answer.

c   Copy the diagram and add an arrow (labelled *v*) to each image of the object to represent its velocity. Add a second arrow (labelled *F*) to represent the resultant force acting on it.

3   This diagram shows a rubber bung being moved around in a circle on the end of a length of string:

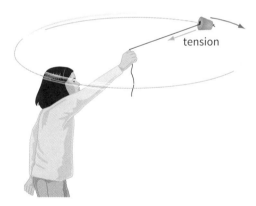

tension

Figure 16.4: For Question 3. A rubber bung being moved around in a circle on the end of a length of string.

The bung travels with constant speed around eight complete circuits in 10 s. The radius *r* of its path is 40.0 cm.

a   State the name of the force that provides the centripetal force which causes the bung to travel in a circle.

b   Calculate the speed *v* of the bung.

c   Use the equation $a = \frac{v^2}{r}$ to calculate the bung's centripetal acceleration.

d Draw a diagram of the bung, as viewed from above, and add arrows to show the directions of its velocity and its acceleration.

e State the other quantity you would need to know in order to determine the centripetal force acting on the bung.

f Describe how the bung will move if the girl releases the string.

4 The Earth is kept in its orbit by the gravitational pull of the Sun:

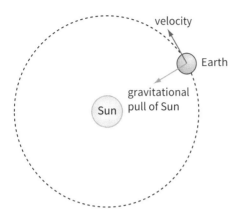

Figure 16.5: For Question 4. The Earth is kept in its orbit by the gravitational pull of the Sun.

a State how long it takes the Earth to orbit the Sun. Give your answer in seconds.

b Calculate the Earth's angular velocity ω around the Sun.

c The radius of the Earth's orbit is 150×10^6 km. Use the equation $a = r\omega^2$ to calculate the Earth's centripetal acceleration around the Sun.

d The gravitational acceleration of an object near the Earth's surface is $9.8\,\mathrm{m\,s^{-2}}$. How many times greater is this than your answer to part **c**?

5 A car is travelling at $28\,\mathrm{m\,s^{-1}}$ along a curved section of road. The radius of curvature of the road is $300\,\mathrm{m}$.

a Calculate the car's centripetal acceleration.

b The car has a mass of $1200\,\mathrm{kg}$. Calculate the centripetal force acting on the car.

The road surface is banked at an angle θ (that is, it slopes across the direction of travel) so that the car can travel around the bend without slipping. This diagram shows the forces acting on the car: its weight mg and the contact force of the road N. There is no frictional force acting up or down the slope.

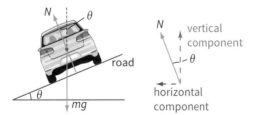

Figure 16.6: For Question 5b. Diagram showing the forces acting on a car on a banked road.

> **TIP**
>
> Any force that has a component at right angles to an object's velocity will provide a centripetal acceleration.

c   What force provides the car's centripetal acceleration? State its direction.

d   The best angle of banking is given by this equation:

$$\tan\theta = \frac{v^2}{rg}$$

Find the value of θ for vehicles travelling at $28\,\text{m s}^{-1}$.

6   This diagram shows a rubber bung on the end of a length of string:

Figure 16.7: For Question 6. Diagram showing a rubber bung on the end of a length of string moving in a horizontal circle.

The bung is being swung around in a horizontal circle at constant speed. The string makes an angle of 60° with the vertical.

a   Two forces act on the bung. Name these forces and draw a free body diagram to show their directions.

b   The mass of the bung is 150 g. Calculate its weight.

c   The weight of the bung is balanced by the vertical component of the tension in the string. Use this fact to calculate the tension in the string.

d   The centripetal force acting on the bung is provided by the horizontal component of the tension. Calculate the value of this horizontal component.

e   Calculate the bung's acceleration.

f   The radius of the bung's path is 60 cm. Calculate its speed.

g   Calculate the time taken for one complete revolution of the bung.

EXAM-STYLE QUESTIONS

1   a   **Explain** what is meant by the term *angular velocity*.   [2]

     b   A merry-go-round in a children's park completes 10 revolutions in one minute. Calculate its angular velocity.   [2]

     c   A child sitting on the edge of the merry-go-round is at a distance of 1.20 m from the entre. Calculate the child's centripetal acceleration.   [2]

     d   The child moves closer to the centre of the ride. State whether each of these quantities increases, decreases or stays the same:
          i   angular velocity
          ii   centripetal acceleration
          iii   resultant force that causes centripetal acceleration.   [3]

[Total: 9]

COMMAND WORD

Explain: set out purposes or reasons / make the relationships between things evident / provide why and/or how and support with relevant evidence

CONTINUED

2   A racing cyclist is practising by cycling around a flat, circular track. The track has a radius of 50.0 m.

   a   The cyclist travels half-way around the track. Show that his angular displacement is π radians. **[2]**

   b   The electronic timing system indicates that the cyclist took 11.51 s to complete this ride. Calculate his angular velocity and his speed. **[3]**

   c   The cyclist, together with his bicycle, has a mass of 94.2 kg. Calculate the centripetal force acting on the cyclist. **[2]**

   d   The centripetal force is provided by the frictional force of the track on the bicycle's tyres. Describe how the cyclist will move if there is insufficient friction to keep him on course as he travels around the track. **[2]**

[Total: 9]

3   The diagram shows an aircraft flying in a horizontal circle at a constant speed. The weight of the aircraft is shown by the force W and the lift by the force L.

Figure 16.8

   a   Explain how the lift force keeps the aircraft flying in a horizontal circle at a constant speed. **[3]**

   b   The aircraft has a mass of 1.5×10^5 kg and flies in a horizontal circle of radius 2.5 km. The centripetal force acting on the aircraft is 1.9×10^6 N and the lift force $L = 2.4 \times 10^6$ N. Calculate:

     i   the speed of the aircraft **[2]**

     ii   the angle between the lift force L and the horizontal. **[2]**

[Total: 7]

Chapter 17

Gravitational fields

CHAPTER OUTLINE

- understand the concept of a gravitational field, represent a gravitational field using field lines and define gravitational field strength and gravitational potential

- recall how, in gravitational problems, the mass of a uniform sphere may be considered to be a point mass at its centre

- derive a formula for the gravitational field strength of a point mass

- solve problems involving gravitational field strength and potential, including the potential due to two point masses

- recall and use Newton's law of gravitation to solve problems

- analyse circular orbits in an inverse- square- law field, including geostationary orbits

- appreciate that on the surface of the Earth, g is approximately constant

KEY EQUATIONS

$$\text{gravitational field strength} = \frac{\text{gravitational force}}{\text{mass}}; g = \frac{F}{m}$$

$$\text{gravitational potential} = \frac{\text{work done}}{\text{mass}}; \phi = \frac{W}{m}$$

$$\text{Newton's law of gravitation} = F = \frac{Gm_1m_2}{r^2}$$

$$\text{gravitational field strength } g = \frac{GM}{r^2}$$

$$\text{potential energy of two masses } E_p = \frac{-Gm_1m_2}{r}$$

$$\text{centripetal force} = \text{mass} \times \text{centripetal acceleration}; F = mr\omega^2 = \frac{mv^2}{r}$$

Exercise 17.1 Newton's law of gravitation

Isaac Newton discovered the law that describes the gravitational pull of one object on another. This exercise provides practice in drawing and interpreting field diagrams, and using the equation for gravitational force.

1 This diagram shows how we can represent the **gravitational field** of the Earth:

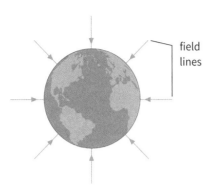
field lines

> **KEY WORDS**
>
> **gravitational field:** a region where an object feels a force because of its mass

Figure 17.1: For Question 1. Diagram showing a representation of the gravitational field of the Earth.

a Explain why the arrows on the field lines are all directed into the Earth.

b At what point do all the field lines appear to meet?

The building you are sitting in is on the surface of the Earth. Here, the Earth's gravitational field is described as *uniform*.

c Draw a diagram to show gravitational field lines in the area around you.

d State how the field lines you have drawn show that the field is uniform.

e Look back at Figure 17.1. Explain how this shows that the Earth's gravitational field is not uniform on this scale.

2 This diagram shows two objects, A and B. The mass of A is greater than the mass of B. A and B attract each other with a gravitational force. These forces are shown as F_1 and F_2:

> **TIP**
>
> In question **2c**, you will need to think about the masses of the objects.

Figure 17.2: For Question 2. Diagram showing two objects, A and B, and gravitational forces F_1 and F_2.

a What can you say about the *directions* of forces F_1 and F_2?

b What can you say about the *magnitudes* of forces F_1 and F_2?

c A and B are initially stationary. The gravitational forces cause them to accelerate towards each other. Which object will have the greater acceleration? Explain your answer.

3 **Newton's law of gravitation** is represented by the equation $F = \frac{Gm_1m_2}{r^2}$, where G is the gravitational constant.

a Rearrange the equation to make G its subject.

b Show that the units of G are $N\,m^2\,kg^{-2}$ and in SI base units $m^3\,s^{-2}\,kg^{-1}$.

> **KEY WORDS**
>
> **Newton's law of gravitation:** any two point masses attract each other with a force that is directly proportional to the product of their mass and inversely proportional to the square of their separation

4   This diagram shows an object of mass M on the surface of the Earth:

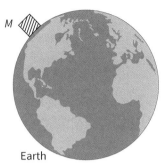

Earth

Figure 17.3: For Question 4. An object of mass M on the surface of the Earth.

a   Copy the diagram and add an arrow to show the direction of the Earth's gravitational force F on the object.

b   The object is attracted to all points within the Earth. Which region of the Earth causes the *strongest* gravitational pull on the object? Label this region A. Explain your answer.

c   Which region of the Earth causes the *weakest* gravitational pull on the object? Label this region B. Explain your answer.

d   We can consider the Earth's gravitational pull as if all of its mass were concentrated at one point, its centre of gravity. Label this point C. Explain your answer.

5   The value of the gravitational constant is $G = 6.67 \times 10^{-11}\,\mathrm{N\,m^2\,kg^{-2}}$.

a   Use Newton's law to calculate the gravitational force of the Earth on a mass of $6.0\,\mathrm{kg}$ placed on its surface (mass of Earth $= 6.0 \times 10^{24}\,\mathrm{kg}$; radius of Earth $= 6400\,\mathrm{km}$).

b   Calculate the gravitational force of the Sun on the Earth (mass of Sun $= 2.0 10^{30}\,\mathrm{kg}$; radius of Earth's orbit around Sun $= 150 \times 10^{6}$ km).

Exercise 17.2 Gravitational field strength

The idea of **gravitational field strength** g is familiar because we use the quantity g to calculate the weight W of an object of mass m, using $W = mg$. On the Earth's surface, $g = 9.8\,\mathrm{N\,kg^{-1}}$ approximately. This is an exercise in calculating and using gravitational field strength for different objects in the Solar System.

1   Partly because the Earth is not a perfect sphere, the value of g varies from $9.78\,\mathrm{N\,kg^{-1}}$ at the equator to $9.83\,\mathrm{N\,kg^{-1}}$ at the poles.

An object of mass $20.0\,\mathrm{kg}$ is transported from the equator to the North Pole.

a   Calculate the weight of an object of mass $20.0\,\mathrm{kg}$ at a point where the Earth's gravitational field strength $g = 9.80\,\mathrm{N\,kg^{-1}}$.

KEY WORDS

gravitational field strength: the gravitational force exerted per unit mass on a small object placed at a point

b Calculate the amount by which the object's weight increases in moving from the equator to the North Pole.

c Explain how g will change if you climb to the top of a high mountain.

2 The gravitational force of one mass on another is given by Newton's law, $F = \frac{Gm_1m_2}{r^2}$. The definition of gravitational field strength g says that its value is the gravitational force acting *per unit mass* on a body.

a Show that this leads to the equation for the gravitational field strength at a distance r from a point mass M: $g = \frac{GM}{r^2}$.

b Calculate the gravitational field strength at the Earth's surface. Give your answer to two significant figures. (mass of Earth = 6.0×10^{24} kg; radius of Earth = 6400 km; gravitational constant $G = 6.67 \times 10^{-11}$ N m^2 kg^{-2})

3 The Moon has a mass of 7.4×10^{22} kg and its mean radius is 1.74×10^6 m.

a Calculate the gravitational force on a mass of exactly 1 kg on the surface of the Moon. (gravitational constant $G = 6.67 \times 10^{-11}$ N m^2 kg^{-2})

b State the value of the gravitational field strength on the surface of the Moon.

c Calculate the weight of an object of mass 20.0 kg on the surface of the Moon.

d Imagine that you dropped an object close to the surface of the Moon. Determine the object's acceleration.

4 The dwarf planet Pluto is orbited by its moon Charon, as shown:

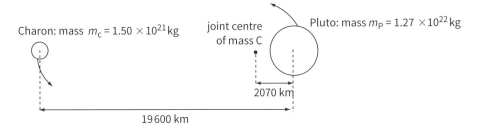

Figure 17.4: For Question 4. Diagram showing the dwarf planet Pluto orbited by its moon Charon.

In fact they orbit one another around their joint **centre of mass** C.

a Calculate the gravitational field strength at C due to Pluto. Give its direction (gravitational constant $G = 6.67 \times 10^{-11}$ N m^2 kg^{-2}).

b Calculate the gravitational field strength at C due to Charon. Give its direction.

c What is the gravitational force on an object of mass 1.0 kg placed at C? Explain your answer.

TIP

In question **1c**, remember that the gravitational force of one object on another depends on the distance between their centres of mass.

KEY WORDS

centre of mass: the point at which we can consider the total mass of the object to be concentrated

---

TIP

Think about the definition of field strength and remember that it is a vector quantity.

Exercise 17.3 Gravitational potential

The **gravitational potential** at a point is defined in terms of the work done in bringing unit mass from infinity to the point. You can think of it as the gravitational potential energy per unit mass, but remember that its value is zero at infinity and less than zero everywhere else. This is an exercise in understanding and using the equation for calculating gravitational potential.

KEY WORDS

gravitational potential: the work done per unit mass in bringing a mass from infinity to a point in a gravitational field

1   At point P, the gravitational potential $\phi = -60$ J kg^{-1}.

Thinking about the definition of ϕ:

a   state the gravitational potential energy of a mass of 1.0 kg at point P

b   calculate the gravitational potential energy of a mass of 50.0 kg at point P

c   state the work done in moving a mass of 50.0 kg from infinity to point P

d   state the work done in moving a mass of 50.0 kg from point P to infinity.

At point Q, the gravitational potential $\phi = -40$ J kg^{-1}.

e   Which point is at a higher potential, P or Q?

f   Calculate the work done in moving a mass of 50.0 kg from point P to point Q.

2   You will need this data for this question:

gravitational constant $G = 6.67 \times 10^{-11}$ N m^2 kg^{-2}

Earth: mass $= 6.0 \times 10^{24}$ kg; radius $= 6.4 \times 10^6$ m

Moon: mass $= 7.4 \times 10^{22}$ kg; mean radius $= 1.74 \times 10^6$ m

The gravitational potential ϕ in the field of a point mass is given by $\phi = -\frac{GM}{r}$.

a   State the meaning of each of the symbols G, M and r.

b   Use the equation for ϕ to calculate the gravitational potential on the surface of the Earth.

c   Calculate the gravitational potential ϕ on the surface of the Moon.

d   An astronaut of mass 120 kg stands on the surface of the Moon. Calculate his gravitational potential energy (taking the zero of potential energy at a point an infinite distance from the Moon).

e   A second astronaut is in a spacecraft orbiting above the Moon's surface. Which astronaut is at the higher gravitational potential?

TIP

Remember that, although the gravitational potential near a mass is always negative, it *increases* with distance from the mass – it becomes *less negative*.

3   When an object of mass m is raised through a height h, its increase in gravitational potential energy $= mgh$.

You should be familiar with this equation, but note that it only applies close to the Earth's surface where g is roughly constant. In this question, you can check that you get the same answer using this equation as using the more general relationship $\phi = -\frac{GM}{r}$

a   An object of mass 1.0 kg is placed on the Earth's surface. It is now at a distance of 6.40×10^6 m from the centre of the Earth. Calculate its gravitational potential energy using the general relationship given. The mass of the earth is given in **Q2**. Give your answer to eight significant figures.

TIP

You will need to use an electronic calculator.

b The object is now lifted a distance of 100 m vertically upwards. Its distance from the Earth's centre of mass is now $6.400\,100 \times 10^6$ m. Using the equation $\phi = -\frac{GM}{r}$, calculate the new value of its gravitational potential energy.

c Calculate the *increase* in its gravitational potential energy.

d Calculate the same quantity using the equation:

change in gravitational potential energy $= mgh$

Do you get the same answer as you did for part **c**?

Exercise 17.4 Orbiting under gravity

Gravity is the most important force for astronomical objects such as the planets and moons of the Solar System. It also holds satellites in their orbits around the Earth. This is an exercise that considers spacecraft and satellites in different types of orbits around the Earth.

1 This diagram shows three similar spacecraft that share a circular orbit around the Earth. Each spacecraft has a mass of 450 kg:

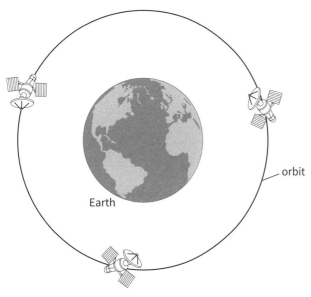

Figure 17.5: For Question 1. Three spacecraft that share a circular orbit around the Earth.

a Copy the diagram and add a force arrow to each spacecraft to show the force of the Earth's gravitational pull on it.

b Each spacecraft orbits at a distance of 2600 km above the Earth's surface. Calculate the distance of each spacecraft from the centre of the Earth and the gravitational force on it (gravitational constant $G = 6.67 \times 10^{-11}\,\mathrm{N\,m^2\,kg^{-2}}$; Earth: mass $= 6.0 \times 10^{24}$ kg; radius $= 6.4 \times 10^6$ m).

TIP

Remember to always calculate a spacecraft's distance from the centre of the Earth, not its distance above the Earth's surface.

c   A spacecraft must travel at the correct speed if it is to stay in its orbit. Calculate this speed for the spacecraft, using the circular motion equation

$$F = \frac{mv^2}{r}$$

d   Calculate the time for one of the spacecraft to complete a single orbit of the Earth. Give your answer in minutes.

2   This diagram shows a spacecraft in an elliptical orbit around the Earth. Its distance from the Earth varies as it travels around its orbit:

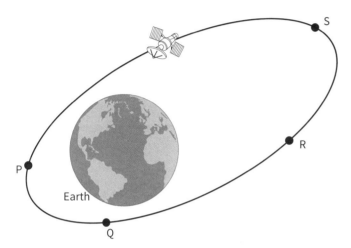

Figure 17.6: For Question 2. Diagram showing a spacecraft in an elliptical orbit around the Earth.

Include reasons with your answers to these questions:

a   Four points P–S are marked on the orbit. State the point at which the spacecraft is furthest from the Earth.

b   State the point at which the Earth's gravitational pull on the spacecraft is weakest.

c   State the point at which the spacecraft's gravitational potential energy is greatest.

d   The spacecraft's total energy (KE + PE) is constant. State the point at which the spacecraft will be moving most slowly.

3   A spacecraft is in a **geostationary orbit** and orbits a planet once each day. It appears to remain at a fixed point in the sky, above the planet's equator.

a   Determine the period of orbit of a geostationary spacecraft around the Earth. Give your answer in seconds.

A geostationary spacecraft could be placed in orbit around the planet Mars in order to maintain communication with a lander on the planet's surface. The period T of such a spacecraft would be given by the equation:

$$T^2 = \left(\frac{4\pi^2}{GM}\right) r^3$$

b   State which quantities are represented by the symbols M and r.

c   Calculate the radius of orbit for a geostationary planet orbiting Mars. Use a reference book or the internet to supply the necessary data.

KEY WORDS

geostationary orbit: an orbit of a satellite such that the satellite remains directly above the same point on the equator at all times

Exercise 17.5 Field and potential with two masses

In this exercise, you will consider that gravitational field strength is a vector and gravitational potential is a scalar.

1   When travelling from the Earth to the Moon, there is one point P where the gravitational pull of the Earth is equal to the gravitational pull of the Moon. This is at a distance of 3.41×10^8 m from the centre of the Earth and 3.8×10^7 m from the centre of the Moon.

Given that Earth's mass = 6.0×10^{24} kg and Moon's mass = 7.4×10^{22} kg, calculate:

a   the gravitational field and potential at P due to the Earth

b   the gravitational field and potential at P due to the Moon

c   the total gravitational field due to the Earth and Moon at P

d   the total potential due to the Earth and Moon at P.

2   The diagram shows a binary star system in which two stars orbit each other. The masses of the stars and distances to a point P are shown:

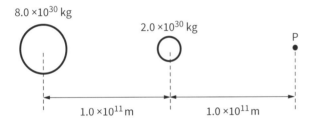

Figure 17.7: For Question 2. Diagram showing a binary star system and a point P.

a   Calculate the total gravitational field strength at point P.

b   Calculate the total gravitational potential at point P.

Gravitational constant $G = 6.67 \times 10^{-11}$ N m^2 kg^{-2}

Earth: mass = 6.0×10^{24} kg; radius = 6.4×10^6 m

1   a   Explain what is meant by the term *gravitational field strength*.   [2]

b   A spacecraft of mass of 220 kg lands on the surface of Mars. An on-board sensor determines its weight to be 836 N. Calculate the gravitational field strength on the surface of Mars.   [2]

c   Measurements from Earth show that the diameter of Mars is 6.75×10^6 m. Determine the planet's mass.   [3]

d   The gravitational field on the surface of Mars is described as *uniform*. Explain what this means.   [2]

[Total: 9]

CONTINUED

2 a Explain what is meant by the term *gravitational potential*. [2]

A spy spacecraft orbits the Earth in a circular orbit, 500 km above the planet's surface.

b **Calculate** the gravitational potential at this height. [3]

c State the amount of energy per kilogram that would be required to move the spacecraft entirely out of the Earth's gravitational field. [1]

d Calculate the speed of the spacecraft in its orbit. [2]

e Calculate the time taken for the spacecraft to complete one orbit around the Earth. [2]

[Total: 10]

COMMAND WORD

Calculate: work out from given facts, figures or information

3 The diagram shows three gravitational equipotential surfaces round the Earth.

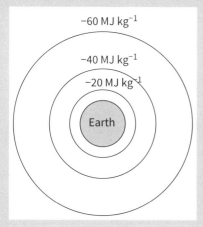

−60 MJ kg⁻¹

−40 MJ kg⁻¹

−20 MJ kg⁻¹

Earth

Figure 17.8

At every point on the outer circle the gravitational potential is −60 MJ kg⁻¹.

a Explain what is meant by the statement that gravitational potential is −60 MJ kg⁻¹. [2]

b Explain why the gravitational potential is negative. [2]

c Explain how the distances between the equipotential surfaces in the diagram show that the gravitational force on a mass decreases with distance above the Earth. [2]

d A spacecraft returns to the Earth under the attraction of gravity alone from a point where the gravitational potential is −20 MJ kg⁻¹. Calculate the speed of the spacecraft when it is at a distance from the Earth where the gravitational potential is −1.0 MJ kg⁻¹. [3]

[Total: 9]

CONTINUED

4 **a** **State** Newton's law for the gravitational force between two masses. [2]

 b Use Newton's law of gravitation to show that the speed v of a satellite in circular orbit around the Earth is given by the expression $v = \sqrt{\frac{GM}{R}}$, where G is the constant of gravitation, M is the mass of the Earth and R is the distance between the satellite and the centre of the Earth. [2]

 c The diagram shows two identical objects each of mass M.

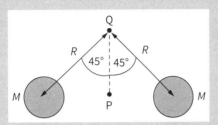

Figure 17.9

 i Explain why the gravitational field strength at point P, equidistant from the two objects, is zero. [2]

 ii In terms of M, R and the gravitational constant G:

   1. derive an expression for the total gravitational field strength at point Q [2]

   2. state the total gravitational potential at point Q. [1]

[Total: 9]

COMMAND WORD

State: express in clear terms

> Chapter 18
Oscillations

CHAPTER OUTLINE

- describe oscillations using appropriate terminology

- express the period of oscillation in terms of both frequency and angular frequency

- analyse graphical representations of simple harmonic motion, including changes in displacement, velocity, acceleration and the interchange between kinetic and potential energy

- recall and use the equations of simple harmonic motion, including those for displacement, velocity, acceleration and total energy

- describe the effects of damping, including the importance of critical damping

- describe forced oscillations and resonance, including examples of resonance that are useful or that should be avoided

KEY EQUATIONS

$\text{frequency} = \dfrac{1}{\text{period}}; f = \dfrac{1}{T}$

Defining s.h.m.: acceleration α, displacement x, angular frequency ω; $a = -\omega^2 x$

sinusoidal displacement in s.h.m.: $x = x_0 \sin 2\pi\, ft$ or $x = x_0 \sin \omega t$

maximum velocity = amplitude $\times$ angular frequency $v_0 = \omega x_0$

velocity $v = v_0 \cos \omega t$

$v = \pm\omega\sqrt{(x_0^2 - x^2)}$

total energy $E = \frac{1}{2} m\omega^2 x_0^2$

Exercise 18.1 Describing oscillations

There are many types of oscillation, but they can all be described in terms of basic quantities: amplitude, frequency and period. This exercise provides practice in using these key terms and calculating these quantities.

1 The *frequency* is the number of oscillations per second; the *period* is the number of seconds per oscillation.

   a State the SI units of frequency and period. Give their names and symbols.

   b State how the units of frequency and period are related.

   c Write down an equation relating frequency f and period T.

   d A mass on the end of a spring oscillates up and down with a period of 0.40 s. Calculate its frequency.

e   A pendulum completes 40 swings in one minute. Calculate its period and frequency.

f   A loudspeaker can oscillate with frequencies between 20 Hz and 20 kHz. Determine the corresponding periods of oscillation.

g   If the frequency of an oscillation increases, state whether its period increases, decreases or stays the same.

2   This graph represents the oscillations of a simple pendulum:

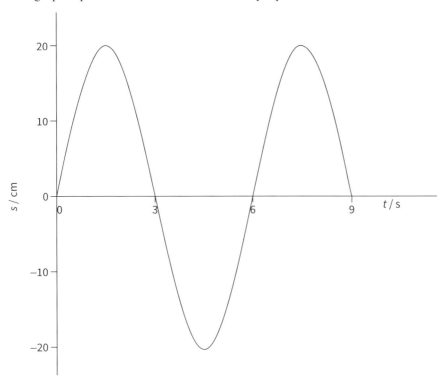

Figure 18.1: For Question 2. Graph representing the oscillations of a simple pendulum.

a   State the quantity shown on the *y*-axis.

b   State the amplitude of the oscillation.

c   State the quantity shown on the *x*-axis.

d   State the period of the oscillation.

e   Determine the frequency of the oscillation.

f   Explain the meaning of the term *simple pendulum*.

3   A mass suspended from a spring oscillates up and down.

•   The highest point in the oscillation is 0.20 m above the lowest point.

•   The mass completes 250 oscillations in 30 s.

a   State the amplitude of the oscillation. Give your answer in cm.

b   Calculate the period of the oscillation. Give your answer in ms.

c   Determine the frequency of the oscillation.

d   Draw a graph to represent the oscillation. Your graph should show 1.5 complete oscillations.

4 Two masses A and B are oscillating with the same frequency, but there is a **phase** difference between them. This graph represents their motion:

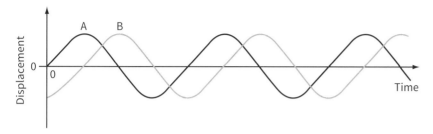

Figure 18.2: For Question 4. Graph representing the displacement of oscillating masses A and B.

a   Determine the displacement of B when A has maximum displacement.

b   Determine the displacement of A when B has maximum displacement.

c   The graphs start at time $t = 0$. State which oscillation is first to reach its maximum after this time.

d   There is a phase difference between A and B. Calculate the fraction of a complete oscillation that this phase difference represents.

e   Express the phase difference in radians (one oscillation $= 2\pi$ rad).

f   Express the phase difference in degrees (one oscillation $= 360°$).

Exercise 18.2 Graphical representations

In exercise 12.1 you drew and interpreted displacement–time graphs for waves. We can draw similar graphs to represent how the velocity and acceleration of an oscillating mass change with time.

1   a   State, in words, the mathematical relationship between velocity and displacement.

b   Describe how you could find velocity from a displacement–time graph.

c   Write the mathematical relationship between acceleration and velocity.

d   Describe how you could find acceleration from a velocity–time graph.

e   In considering the motion of an oscillating mass, we talk about *displacement* and *velocity*. Explain why it would be wrong to consider *distance* and *speed*.

2 This graph is a distance–time graph for an oscillating mass:

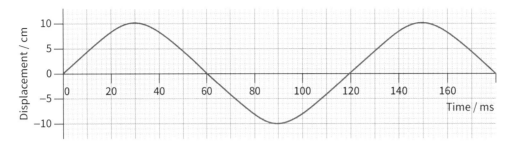

Figure 18.3: For Question 2. Distance–time graph for an oscillating mass.

a State two times at which the mass has maximum positive displacement.

b What is the mass's velocity at these times? Explain how you can deduce this from the graph.

c State one time at which the mass has maximum negative displacement. State the velocity at this time.

d State two times at which the mass has maximum positive velocity. Explain how you can deduce this from the graph.

e State two times at which the mass has maximum negative velocity.

f Draw two sets of graph axes, one above the other. On the upper set of axes, sketch the displacement–time graph shown in Figure 18.3. On the lower set of axes, sketch the corresponding velocity–time graph using the information you have deduced in **b**–**e**. (There is no need to include numbers on either set of axes.)

3 This velocity–time graph represents the motion of an oscillating mass:

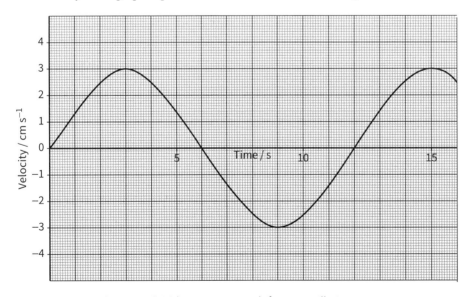

Figure 18.4: For Question 3. Velocity–time graph for an oscillating mass.

a From the graph, deduce the period and frequency of the oscillations.

b State three times at which the acceleration of the mass is zero. Explain how you can deduce this from the graph.

c The acceleration of the mass has its greatest positive values when time $t = 12\,\text{s}$. At what time does the acceleration have its maximum negative value?

d You can estimate the maximum acceleration as follows: lay a ruler on the graph so that it lies along the steepest slope of the graph (e.g. at $t = 12\,\text{s}$). Note the points where it crosses the top and bottom of the grid. Use these values to deduce the maximum acceleration.

e You can also estimate the amplitude of the oscillation. This is equal to half of the area under the first 'bump' of the graph (between $t = 0\,\text{s}$ and $t = 6\,\text{s}$). Each large square on the graph represents $1\,\text{cm}$. Use this idea to estimate the amplitude.

f Draw two sets of graph axes, one above the other. On the upper set of axes, sketch the velocity–time graph shown in Figure 18.4. On the lower set of axes, sketch the corresponding acceleration–time graph using the information you have deduced in **b**–**d**. Your sketch graphs should indicate maximum and minimum values of the quantities on the y-axes.

Exercise 18.3 Equations of s.h.m.

Simple harmonic motion (s.h.m.) is the term used to describe a very specific type of oscillation. The graphs of displacement, velocity and acceleration against time are all sinusoidal. This is an exercise about representing s.h.m. using diagrams, graphs and equations.

1 This diagram shows a mass fixed between two springs:

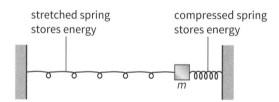

stretched spring
stores energy

compressed spring
stores energy

m

Figure 18.5: For Question 1. Diagram showing a mass fixed between two springs.

When released, it will oscillate back and forth. Its equilibrium position is half-way between the two fixed ends.

a Copy the diagram and mark the equilibrium position of the mass.

b Add an arrow labelled x to show the displacement of the mass.

c Add an arrow labelled F to show the restoring force acting on the mass.

2 Simple harmonic motion is defined as 'the motion of an oscillator in which its acceleration is directly proportional to its displacement from its equilibrium position and is directed towards that position'. It can also be defined simply by the equation $a = -\omega^2 x$.

a In this equation, ω is the angular frequency of the oscillation. State the quantities represented by a and x. Give their names and standard SI units.

b The angular frequency ω is related to the frequency f. Write down the equation that relates them.

KEY WORDS

simple harmonic motion (s.h.m.): motion of an oscillator in which its acceleration is directly proportional to its displacement from its equilibrium position and is directed towards that position

c The definition of s.h.m. states that acceleration is directly proportional to displacement. What is the constant of proportionality in the equation?

d Explain why there is a minus sign in the equation.

e For a mass undergoing s.h.m. the acceleration–displacement graph is a straight line. Sketch such a graph. Indicate the maximum positive and negative displacements of the mass ($\pm x_0$).

3 The displacement of an oscillating mass can be represented by an equation of the form $x = x_0 \sin \omega t$, where x_0 is the amplitude of the motion. This can also be written as $x = x_0 \sin 2\pi ft$.

By comparing a specific equation to this 'standard equation', you can deduce a great deal of information about the motion of an oscillating mass.

The displacement (in mm) of an oscillating mass is given by $x = 25 \sin 40\pi t$.

It may help you to write down this equation with the 'standard equation' below it, for ease of comparison.

a State the amplitude of the oscillation.

b Show that the frequency $f = 20\,\text{Hz}$.

c Calculate the period of the oscillation.

d The maximum velocity of the moving mass is given by $v_0 = \omega x_0$. Calculate this quantity. State its units.

e Calculate the maximum acceleration of the mass.

> **TIP**
>
> You can find the maximum acceleration using the equation that defines s.h.m.

4 This graph shows how the velocity of a mass varies as it executes s.h.m:

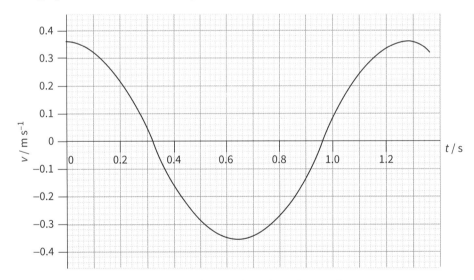

Figure 18.6: For Question 4. Graph showing how the velocity of a mass varies as it executes s.h.m.

a From the graph, deduce information so that you can write an equation for this motion in the form $v = v_0 \cos \omega t$.

b State the units of v and t in this equation.

c Calculate the displacement x (in metres) of the mass when $t = 0$.

d Deduce an equation for the displacement x of the mass as a function of time.

e Using the formula $v = \pm\,\omega\sqrt{(x_0^2 - x^2)}$, calculate the velocity v when $x = \pm\,0.060\,\text{m}$.

f The mass has value $0.20\,\text{kg}$. Calculate the total energy of the oscillating mass.

g State the times shown on the graph when the mass has maximum kinetic energy and the times when the oscillation has maximum potential energy.

Exercise 18.4 Energy and damping in s.h.m.

As a mass oscillates, there is a constant interchange of energy between kinetic and potential (stored) forms. **Damping** the oscillation introduces an extra force that removes energy from the system. This exercise explores damping and **resonance**.

1 The diagram shows how a simple pendulum can be set in motion:

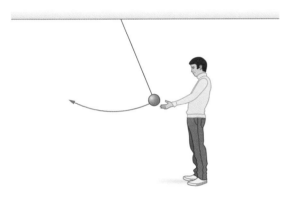

Figure 18.7: For Question 1. A simple pendulum set in motion.

a The student does work against gravity in pulling the mass to one side. State the form of energy that the mass now has.

b Describe how you could calculate the energy stored by the mass in this position. Include a diagram in your answer.

c The student releases the mass. State the point at which the mass is moving fastest.

d Describe how you could calculate the speed of the mass from your answer to part **b**.

A student suggests that an object with a greater mass will swing faster because it has more energy.

e Is the student correct that a greater mass will have greater energy? Explain your answer.

f Is the student correct that a greater mass will move faster? Explain your answer.

TIP

For part **d**, think carefully: will the displacement vary as a sine or cosine function?

KEY WORDS

damped oscillation: an oscillation in which resistive forces cause the energy of the system to be transferred to the surroundings

resonance: when the frequency of a driving force is equal to the natural frequency of the oscillating system, the system absorbs the maximum energy from the driver and has maximum amplitude

2 A mass is fixed between two springs so that it can oscillate horizontally:

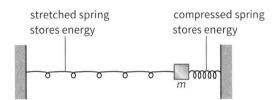

Figure 18.8: For Question 2.

a Name the form of energy stored by a stretched or compressed spring.

b State the equation you would use to calculate the energy stored in a stretched spring. Explain any symbols used in the equation.

c Explain how you would use this equation to calculate the maximum velocity of a mass executing s.h.m. between two springs.

d The period T of a simple pendulum does not depend on the mass that is oscillating. How will the period of oscillation of this mass–spring system change if the mass is increased? Explain your answer.

3 A simple pendulum can be made by attaching a polystyrene (Styrofoam) ball to a length of thread. As the pendulum swings, air resistance causes the amplitude of the oscillations to decrease. This is an example of damping.

This diagram shows how the pendulum swings:

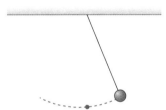

Figure 18.9: For Question 3. Diagram showing a swinging pendulum.

a Copy the diagram and mark the point where the ball will be moving most quickly. Label this point X.

b At point X, add an arrow to show the direction of the ball's velocity. Label this arrow v.

c At point X, add a second arrow to show the direction of the force of air resistance on the ball. Label this arrow F.

d Sketch a displacement–time graph to show the pattern of the ball's oscillations. Your graph should show the amplitude of oscillation decreasing significantly in the time of about five oscillations.

e Sketch an amplitude–time graph to show how the amplitude decreases towards zero over a longer period of time.

f Imagine that you could gradually increase the density of the air in which the pendulum is swinging. This will increase the damping of the oscillations. How would this affect the rate at which the amplitude of the oscillations would decrease to zero?

g   Eventually, the pendulum would be **critically damped**. Explain how you would recognise this condition.

4   This diagram shows two identical masses hanging from strings of equal lengths. The upper ends of the strings are tied to a horizontal string:

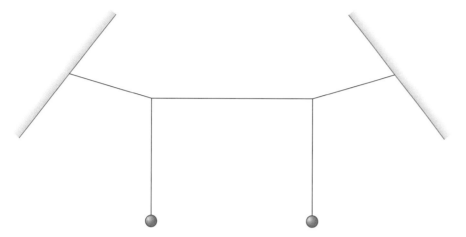

Figure 18.10: For Question 4. Diagram showing two identical masses hanging from strings of equal lengths. The upper ends of the strings are tied to a horizontal string.

At the start of the experiment, one mass is pulled forwards and released so that it swings back and forth. As time passes, its oscillations become smaller but the second mass starts to swing. After a while, the first mass stops swinging while the second mass has its maximum amplitude. Then the process goes into reverse and the second mass gradually slows down while the first mass starts to swing again.

a   What can you say about the **natural frequencies** of oscillation of the two pendulums?

b   The second mass is forced to oscillate at its natural frequency by the motion of the first one. State the name of the phenomenon that occurs when a mass is driven at its natural frequency.

c   It is surprising to see one pendulum come to a halt while the other starts moving. Explain whether energy is conserved in this experiment.

d   If the second pendulum were 20% longer it would not swing with such great amplitude. Explain why.

EXAM-STYLE QUESTIONS

1 This graph represents the displacement of an oscillating mass:

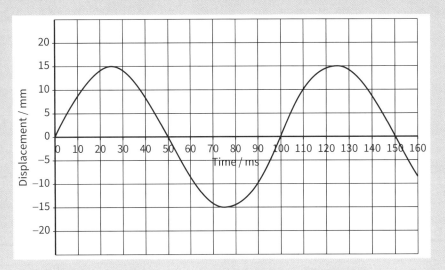

Figure 18.11

a   Deduce the period and frequency of the oscillations. **[3]**

b   Write an equation to represent the oscillations of the form
$x = x_0 \sin \omega t$. **[2]**

c   Deduce the maximum velocity of the mass. **[2]**

d   The oscillating object has a mass of 17 kg. Calculate the maximum restoring force acting on the mass as it oscillates. **[3]**

[Total: 10]

2 One end of a long ruler is clamped to a bench. A large mass is attached to the other end. The mass is pushed downwards and released. It oscillates up and down, executing simple harmonic motion about its equilibrium position.

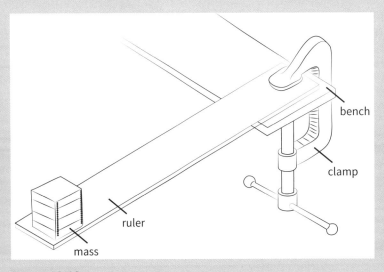

Figure 18.12

CONTINUED

a   Explain what is meant by *simple harmonic motion*.   [2]

b   Describe how you would find the equilibrium position of the mass.   [2]

An accelerometer is attached to the mass. This measures and records its acceleration.

c   **Sketch** a graph to show how you would expect the mass's acceleration to vary with time, starting with the mass in its position of maximum negative displacement.   [3]

This graph shows how the acceleration of the mass depends on its displacement:

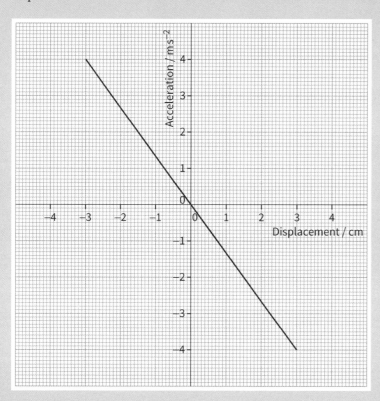

Figure 18.13

d   Explain why the graph has a negative gradient.   [1]

e   From the graph, determine the value of the amplitude of the oscillations.   [1]

f   Deduce the angular frequency of the oscillations.   [2]

g   Calculate the period of the oscillations.   [2]

h   The mass of the object attached to the ruler is 0.40 kg. Calculate the total energy of the mass when it is oscillating with the amplitude in **e** and the frequency in **f**.   [2]

[Total: 15]

> **COMMAND WORD**
>
> **Sketch:** make a simple freehand drawing showing the key features

CONTINUED

3 **a** An object undergoes simple harmonic motion. State the difference between its

   i amplitude and displacement [2]

   ii frequency and angular frequency. [2]

b Tides cause the surface of the water in a harbour to vary. The motion of the surface of the water is modelled as being simple harmonic motion with a period of 12.4 hours and an amplitude of 4.0 m. The depth d of the water at any time t is the height of the water above its mean position.

   i Calculate the maximum difference in d during one complete period. [1]

   ii Calculate the frequency of the oscillation of the water surface. [2]

   iii Calculate the maximum vertical speed of the water surface. [2]

   iv Calculate the vertical speed of the water surface when $d = 2.0$ m. [2]

   v Write down an expression for d in metres in terms of t in seconds. [2]

   [Total: 13]

> Chapter 19
Thermal physics

CHAPTER OUTLINE

- understand and explain the transfer of thermal energy and the concept of thermal equilibrium
- understand how certain physical properties can be used to measure temperature
- understand the **thermodynamic temperature scale** and convert between temperatures measured in kelvin and in degrees Celsius
- use a simple kinetic model of matter to explain the different states of matter, temperature and energy changes
- understand that the internal energy of a system is determined by the state of the system
- recall and use the first law of thermodynamics
- define and use specific heat capacity and specific latent heat

KEY EQUATIONS

First law of thermodynamics:

increase internal energy = energy supplied by heating + energy supplied by doing work; $\Delta U = q + W$

$$\text{specific heat capacity} = \frac{\text{energy supplied}}{\text{mass} \times \text{temperature change}}; \; c = \frac{E}{m\Delta\theta}$$

$$\text{specific latent heat} = \frac{\text{energy supplied}}{\text{mass}}; \; L = \frac{E}{m}$$

Converting between Celsius and Kelvin scales of temperature: $T(\text{K}) = \theta\,(°\text{C}) + 273.15$

Exercise 19.1 Kinetic model and internal energy

In the kinetic model of matter, we picture matter as being made of many particles (atoms, ions or molecules). The model can be used to explain many phenomena, and this exercise develops an understanding of the model at its simplest.

1   The following diagrams show how we can picture the arrangement of particles in a solid, a liquid and a gas.

KEY WORDS

thermodynamic temperature scale: a temperature scale that does not depend on the properties of any particular substance

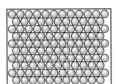 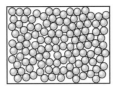 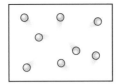

Figure 19.1: For Question 1. Three diagrams showing the arrangement of particles in a solid, a liquid and a gas.

a   In which state (or phase) of matter are the particles packed most closely together? In which state are they farthest apart?

b   If a solid is heated, its particles gain energy. Describe how the motion of the particles changes.

c   In a solid, the particles are closely packed together. State whether the force between neighbouring particles is attractive or repulsive.

d   To change a solid to a gas, its particles must be separated. State how the potential energy of the particles changes as they are pulled apart. Is energy being added to the material, or being removed?

e   By comparing the diagrams for a solid and a gas, you can see two ways in which the particles of a gas have more energy than the particles of a solid. State the two differences and name the corresponding forms of energy.

2   In which of the following changes does the **internal energy** of the body increase?

   water freezing at constant temperature; a stone falling in a vacuum; water evaporating at constant temperature; a wire being stretched at constant temperature

3   Two identical beakers, A and B, contain equal amounts of water. The water in A is at a temperature of 20 °C while the water in B is at 50 °C. The water in each beaker gradually evaporates.

   a   In which beaker do the water molecules have the greater average energy?

   b   Explain why the initial rate of evaporation of the water in beaker B is greater than that of the water in beaker A. Refer to your answer to part **a**.

   c   Explain why the temperature of the water in each beaker decreases as the water evaporates.

   d   Explain why the temperature of the water in beaker B falls more quickly than that of the water in beaker A.

4   This diagram shows particles of gas in a cylinder:

   A piston is being pushed downwards to compress the gas.

   a   In a collision, momentum is transferred from one object to another. The piston and the particles collide with one another. Momentum is transferred from the piston to the particles. Describe the effect this has on the average speed of the particles.

   b   Describe any changes in the total kinetic energy of the particles.

   c   Describe any changes in the temperature of the gas.

   d   State the phrase that describes this way of transferring energy to a gas.

KEY WORDS

internal energy: the sum of the random distribution of kinetic and potential energies of the atoms or molecules of a system

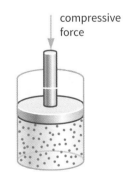

compressive force

Figure 19.2: For Question 4. Piston compressing a gas.

The average force pushing the piston is 20 N and it moves through a distance of 12 cm.

e Calculate the amount of energy transferred to the gas.

In practice, the force needed to compress the gas would increase as the piston is pushed downwards (because the pressure of the gas would increase). This graph shows how the force might increase:

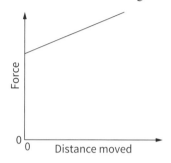

Figure 19.3: For Question 4f. Graph showing increase of force.

f Describe how you could determine the energy transferred to the gas from such a graph. Include a sketch graph in your answer.

5 The internal energy of a material can be increased in two ways: by heating it and by doing work on it. The first law of thermodynamics tells us how the internal energy changes, and can be represented by this equation:

$\Delta U = q + W$

a State the meaning of each of the symbols in this equation, and their units.

b A gas is heated by transferring 400 kJ to it. At the same time, it is compressed so that 300 kJ of work is done on it. Calculate the increase in its internal energy.

c A cylinder of air is compressed by an average force of 240 N moving through a distance of 0.05 m. Because the temperature of the air increases, it loses 4.0 J of energy through the walls of the cylinder to its surroundings. Calculate the increase in the internal energy of the air.

> **TIP**
>
> Think carefully about whether W is positive or negative.

6 If two objects are in contact with each other, energy will transfer from the hotter object to the colder object. A temperature difference leads to the transfer of energy.

This diagram shows three objects in contact with each other. Their temperatures are: A 20 °C; B 30 °C; C 20 °C.

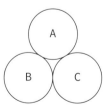

Figure 19.4: For Question 6. Three objects in contact with each other.

a   There will be a net transfer of **thermal energy** between A and B. State the direction of this transfer.

b   Explain why we describe this as a *net* transfer of energy.

c   Between which two objects will there be no net transfer of energy? Explain your answer.

d   Which two objects are in **thermal equilibrium**? Explain your answer.

e   Eventually all three objects are in thermal equilibrium. What can you say about their temperatures at this time?

7   Copy and complete the table to show whether in the equation $\Delta U = q + W$

- the internal energy U increases, decreases or stays the same
- thermal energy supplied to the object q is positive or negative
- work W on the object is positive, negative or zero.

	U	q	W
the heating of a solid of constant volume			
a lump of ice melts at 0 °C to give water at 0 °C (note ice is less dense than water)			
a gas expands at constant temperature			

Table 19.1: For Question 7.

8   This diagram shows a mass of gas trapped in a cylinder by a piston:

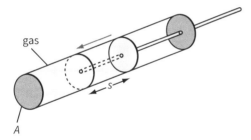

Figure 19.5: For Question 8. Diagram showing a mass of gas trapped in a cylinder by a piston.

The gas exerts pressure on the circular end of the piston. The gas is cooled and it contracts. Work is done on the gas (*w* is positive) *by* the outside atmosphere as the piston moves inwards.

In parts **a** and **b** of this question you will calculate, from first principles, the work done on the gas.

a   The pressure of the gas is 100 kPa. It presses on the piston whose area A is 50 cm². Calculate the force on the piston.

Remember:

$$p = \frac{F}{A}$$

where p = pressure; F = force; A = area.

b As the gas contracts, the piston moves through a distance $s = 80\,cm$. Calculate the work done on the gas.

An alternative way to calculate the work done on the gas is to use the equation:

$W = p\Delta V$

where W is work done, p is pressure and ΔV *is* change in volume of the gas.

Look at the diagram again. The change in volume ΔV is the cylindrical section of length s and area A.

c Calculate ΔV using the values of s and A given. Give your answer in m³.

d Calculate W using $W = p\Delta V$. Do you get the same answer as in part **b**?

e You can only use the equation $W = p\Delta V$ in situations where the pressure p is constant. Explain why this is so. Think about the force exerted by the gas on the piston.

Exercise 19.2 Thermometers and temperature scales

There are many different types of thermometer: liquid-in-glass, thermocouple, electrical resistance, etc. Each is based on a different physical property which varies with temperature. In this exercise, you will answer questions about thermometers and the Celsius and thermodynamic (Kelvin) scales of temperature.

1 In this question, use the approximate relation $T(K) = \theta(°C) + 273.15$.

    a Convert each of the following temperatures from °C to K:

        i   0

        ii   100

        iii   523

        iv   −196.

    b Convert each of the following temperatures from K to °C:

        i   0

        ii   200

        iii   350

        iv   1000.

    c State which temperature is greater, 400 K or 125 °C.

    d A block of ice is allowed to warm from −20 °C until it melts at 0 °C. Calculate the increase in its temperature. Give your answer in K.

2   This graph shows how the resistance of a thermistor changes with temperature:

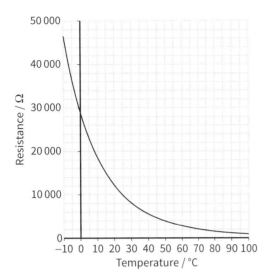

Figure 19.6: For Question 2. Graph showing how the resistance of a thermistor changes with temperature.

   a   State the temperature at which the thermistor has a resistance of 10 kΩ.

   b   State the resistance of the thermistor at 60 °C.

   c   Explain why the thermistor would be more useful for measuring temperatures close to 0 °C than to 100 °C. Use the word *sensitivity* in your answer.

3   Two important types of electrical thermometer are the *resistance thermometer* and the *thermocouple thermometer*.

   a   Which of these two thermometers is constructed from wires of two different metals?

   b   Which of these two thermometers generates a voltage that depends on the temperature difference between two points?

   c   A resistance thermometer may be based on a resistance wire or a thermistor. State which of these two types of thermometer shows a big change in resistance over a small change in temperature.

   d   A resistance thermometer is likely to have a greater mass than a thermocouple. Explain why this means that a thermocouple thermometer is likely to respond more quickly to a change in temperature.

   e   A thermocouple has a non-linear response to temperature and hence will require calibration if it is to be used as a thermometer. Explain the meanings of the terms *non-linear* and *calibration*.

4   The thermodynamic (Kelvin) scale of temperature has two fixed points. The upper one is 273.16 K.

   a   State the lower fixed point and give its value in K and in °C.

   b   Give the value of the upper fixed point in °C.

> **TIP**
>
> Remember, a sensitive thermometer produces a large change in reading for a small change in temperature.

Exercise 19.3 Energy change calculations: s.h.c. and s.l.h.

Knowing the values of a material's **specific heat capacity (s.h.c.)** and its **specific latent heat** (s.l.h.) allows us to calculate energy changes. This is an exercise in calculating and using both of these quantities.

1 The equation $c = \frac{E}{m\Delta\theta}$ defines specific heat capacity.

   a State what each symbol represents, and give its SI unit. (Note: $\Delta\theta$ is a single quantity.)

   The specific heat capacity of lead is $126\,\mathrm{J\,kg^{-1}\,K^{-1}}$.

   b Calculate the amount of energy required to raise the temperature of $1\,\mathrm{kg}$ of lead by $10\,°\mathrm{C}$.

   c $1\,\mathrm{kJ}$ of energy is supplied to $1\,\mathrm{kg}$ of lead. Determine the amount by which the temperature of the lead will rise, to the nearest $1\,°\mathrm{C}$.

2 To cool a $5\,\mathrm{kg}$ block of steel at a temperature of $200\,°\mathrm{C}$, it is plunged into a tank containing $50\,\mathrm{kg}$ of water at $20\,°\mathrm{C}$. You can calculate the final temperature of the water.

   The steel and the water will reach the same final temperature. We can write this as final temperature $= X\,°\mathrm{C}$.

   specific heat capacity of steel $= 450\,\mathrm{J\,kg^{-1}\,K^{-1}}$

   specific heat capacity of water $= 4200\,\mathrm{J\,kg^{-1}\,K^{-1}}$

   a Write down an expression in terms of X for the energy *lost* by the steel in cooling from $200\,°\mathrm{C}$ to $X\,°\mathrm{C}$.

   b Write down a similar expression for the energy *gained* by the water in being heated from $20\,°\mathrm{C}$ to $X\,°\mathrm{C}$.

   c These two quantities are equal (assuming no energy is lost to the surroundings). Write an equation in which these quantities are shown to be equal.

   d Solve the equation for X.

   e You could use a method like this to determine the specific heat capacity of a material. Outline how you would do this. List the quantities you would measure. State one other quantity whose value you would need to know.

3 A block of copper was heated with a 60 W electrical heater. This graph shows how the temperature of the block increased:

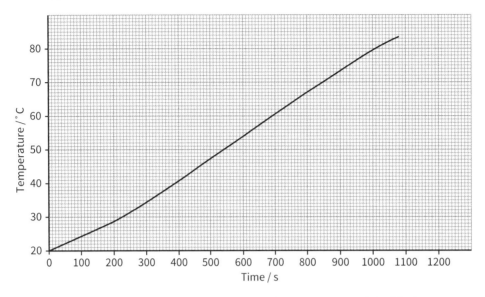

Figure 19.7: For Question 3. Graph showing how the temperature of the block increased.

a Choose the straight-line section of the graph and deduce by how much the block's temperature increased in 200 s.

b Calculate the energy supplied to the block in this time.

c The mass of the block was 2.00 kg. Calculate the specific heat capacity of copper.

d In this experiment, it is likely that some of the heat supplied to the block was lost to the surroundings. What feature of the graph suggests that this was the case? Explain your answer.

e Is the true value for the specific heat capacity of copper likely to be higher or lower than that calculated in part **c**? Explain your answer.

4 The equation $L = \frac{E}{m}$ defines specific latent heat.

a State what each symbol represents, and give its SI unit.

The **specific latent heat of fusion** of water $L = 330\,000\,\mathrm{J\,kg^{-1}}$.

b Explain the meanings of the words *specific* and *fusion* in this sentence.

c A freezer converts 10 g of water at 0 °C to ice at the same temperature in five minutes. Determine the amount of energy that must be removed from the water to achieve this.

5   These diagrams show the typical arrangements of atoms in a solid, a liquid and a gas:

solid 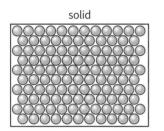   liquid 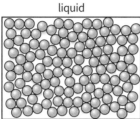   gas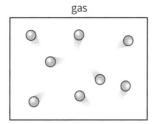

Figure 19.8: For Question 5. The arrangement of particles in a solid, a liquid and a gas.

a   As represented in the diagram of a solid, each atom is in contact with a number of neighbouring atoms. How many?

b   Describe how this number changes when the material is heated so that it changes from a solid to a liquid and then to a gas.

c   Use this idea to explain why the **specific latent heat of vaporisation** is greater than the specific latent heat of fusion for a given substance.

> **KEY WORDS**
>
> **specific latent heat of vaporisation:** the amount of heat energy needed to convert unit mass of liquid to gas without change in temperature

EXAM-STYLE QUESTIONS

1   Solder is an alloy of two metals which is used to join wires together. It has a relatively low melting point.

A block of solid solder was heated at a steady rate until it melted. The graph shows how its temperature increased:

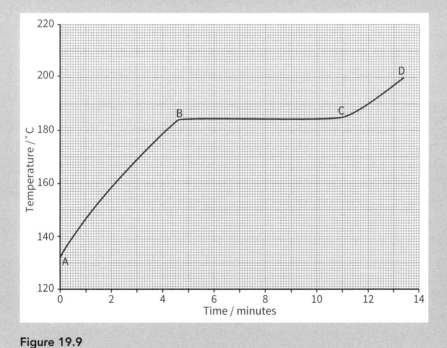

Figure 19.9

CONTINUED

a Deduce the melting point of the solder. [1]

Consider the region BC of the graph. Describe how the following quantities were changing in this part of the heating process:

b the total kinetic energy of the atoms of the solder [1]

c their potential energy [1]

d the internal energy of the solder. [1]

The block had a mass of 25.0 g.

e State the other information you would need in order to deduce the specific heat capacity of the solder. [2]

[Total: 6]

2 This diagram shows a simple method to estimate the specific latent heat of vaporisation of water, L:

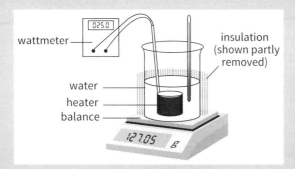

Figure 19.10

A beaker is filled with hot water and placed on a balance. It is then heated with an electrical heater. The thermometer indicates the temperature of the water.

a Explain what is meant by the *specific latent heat of vaporisation* of a liquid. [2]

b The heater has a power rating of 25 W. Calculate the energy it supplies to the water in 500 s. [1]

The water boils and the mass recorded on the balance gradually decreases. This table shows two measurements of the mass separated by a time interval of 500 s:

Time / s	Mass / g
0	131.36
500	127.05

Table 19.2

c Use this data to estimate a value for the specific latent heat of vaporisation of water L. [2]

d Most of the energy supplied by the heater results in vaporisation of the water. However, some energy is lost to the surroundings and does not contribute to the vaporisation of the water. **Suggest** one way in which energy is lost to the surroundings. [1]

e Explain whether energy losses to the surroundings mean that your estimated value for L in part **c** is an under-estimate or an over-estimate. [2]

[Total: 8]

3 a State what is meant by the *internal energy* of a system. [2]

b Explain using the first law of thermodynamics why there is an increase in internal energy when a mass of water at 100 °C becomes an equal mass of steam at 100 °C. [2]

c i A small heater in a greenhouse transfers thermal energy at an average rate of 110 W to the air in a greenhouse. The air in the greenhouse has a volume of 25 m³, a density of 1.2 kg m⁻³ and a specific heat capacity of 980 J kg⁻¹ K⁻¹. Calculate the increase in temperature of the air inside the greenhouse in one hour as a result of this energy transfer. [2]

ii Suggest a reason why the actual increase in temperature may be different from this value. [1]

[Total: 7]

4 The volume of 1.00 kg of water increases from $1.00 \times 10^{-3}\,\text{m}^3$ to $1.70\,\text{m}^3$ when it changes from water at 100 °C to steam at 100 °C.

a Calculate the work done against the atmosphere when 1.00 kg of water turns to steam. Atmospheric pressure is 1.02×10^5 Pa. [2]

b The specific latent heat of vaporisation of water is 2.26×10^6 J kg⁻¹. Use the first law of thermodynamics and your answer to **a** to calculate the increase in internal energy of a mass of 1.00 kg as it turns to steam at 100 °C. [2]

[Total: 4]

COMMAND WORD

Suggest: apply knowledge and understanding to situations where there are a range of valid responses in order to make proposals

TIP

Think carefully about whether the work done is positive or negative.

Ideal gases

- recall the equation of state for an ideal gas and use it to solve problems

- state the assumptions of the kinetic theory and use it to relate the macroscopic properties of a gas to the microscopic properties of its particles

- deduce the relationship between the pressure and volume of a gas and the number and mean-square speed of its particles

- recall and use the definition of the Boltzmann constant

- deduce that the average translational kinetic energy of a molecule is proportional to the thermodynamic temperature

- understand that the root-mean-square speed $c_{r.m.s.}$ is given by $\sqrt{<c^2>}$

KEY EQUATIONS

the ideal gas equation: $pV = nRT$

number of moles $= \dfrac{\text{mass (g)}}{\text{molar mass } (\text{g mol}^{-1})}$

pressure and volume of a gas: $pV = \dfrac{1}{3}Nm<c^2>$; $p = \dfrac{1}{3}\rho<c^2>$

average molecular $\text{KE} = \dfrac{3}{2} \times$ Boltzmann constant $\times$ thermodynamic temperature; $\dfrac{1}{2}m<c^2> = \dfrac{3}{2}kT$

Boltzmann constant $k = \dfrac{R}{N_A}$

root-mean-square speed $c_{r.m.s.} = \sqrt{<c^2>}$

Exercise 20.1 Ideal gases

An 'ideal' gas does not exist! But the idea of an **ideal gas** is very useful. Gases at low pressures behave very much like ideal gases. This is an exercise in using the ideal gas equation and **Boyle's law**.

1   This is the ideal gas equation: $pV = nRT$

    a   State the quantity represented by each symbol, giving the unit of each.

    b   Which two quantities are related by Boyle's law?

    State the two quantities that are constant in Boyle's law.

KEY WORDS

ideal gas: a gas that behaves according to the equation $pV = nRT$

Boyle's law: the pressure exerted by a fixed mass of gas is inversely proportional to its volume, provided the temperature of the gas remains constant c   Which quantity in the ideal gas equation can be used to calculate the mass of gas? Explain how you would carry out such a calculation.

2   To use the ideal gas equation, $pV = nRT$, you need to be able to calculate the number of **moles** n in a sample of gas.

   a   Calculate the number of moles in 0.48 g of oxygen (molar mass of oxygen = $32\,\text{g mol}^{-1}$). It may help to recall that *molar mass* means the mass of one mole.

   b   26 g of helium contains 6.5 mol of particles. Calculate the molar mass of helium.

   c   A classroom has dimensions $2.2\,\text{m} \times 6.0\,\text{m} \times 4.8\,\text{m}$. It contains air of density $1.29\,\text{kg m}^{-3}$. Calculate the number of moles of air this classroom contains. (molar mass of air = $29\,\text{g mol}^{-1}$)

3   A cylinder of volume 40.0 litres is filled with air to a pressure of $200 \times 10^3\,\text{Pa}$. A piston then compresses the air to a volume of 2.5 litres.

   a   Calculate the pressure of the compressed air, assuming that its temperature remains constant. You can think in proportions or use $p_1 V_1 = p_2 V_2$.

   b   Sketch a graph of pressure against volume to show how these quantities will change as the air is compressed.

   c   The experiment is performed at a temperature of 27 °C. Calculate the number of moles of gas contained in the cylinder. (universal molar gas constant $R = 8.31\,\text{J mol}^{-1}\,\text{K}^{-1}$)

4   If a gas is heated at constant pressure, its volume will change.

   The relationship between volume and thermodynamic temperature at constant pressure is known as Charles's law.

   a   State whether the volume of the gas will increase or decrease as the temperature increases at constant pressure.

   b   Sketch a graph to show how the volume of an ideal gas depends on its thermodynamic temperature.

   c   An ideal gas will have zero volume at absolute zero. Describe how you would expect a real gas to behave as its temperature is reduced towards absolute zero.

   d   10 mol of nitrogen is heated from 23 °C to 100 °C at a constant pressure of $100 \times 10^3\,\text{Pa}$. Calculate the change in volume of the gas.

5   Usually, when a gas expands or contracts, both its pressure and temperature change. We can solve problems like this using the relationship:

$$\frac{pV}{T} = \text{constant}$$

   a   What is the constant in this equation? Give its unit.

   A balloon contains $0.040\,\text{m}^3$ of helium at a pressure of $3.5 \times 10^5\,\text{Pa}$ and a temperature of 27 °C. It is heated until it bursts. At this point its volume has expanded to $0.044\,\text{m}^3$ and its temperature has reached 190 °C.

   b   Calculate the value of the quantity $\frac{pV}{T}$ before the balloon is heated.

   c   Using your answer to part **b**, calculate the pressure at which the balloon bursts.

   d   Calculate the temperature at which the balloon bursts if it does not expand as it is heated.

Exercise 20.2 The kinetic model of a gas

We can think of a gas as being made of particles moving about in a box. This is the kinetic model of a gas. Because the particles obey the usual laws of physics, we can use the model to deduce equations linking microscopic behaviour of particles to the macroscopic properties of a gas – pressure, temperature, and so on. This exercise tests your understanding of these relationships.

1   Kinetic theory produces the equation $pV = \frac{1}{3}Nm<c^2>$

   The equation of state for a gas is $pV = nRT$

   a   State what is meant by the symbols n and N.

   b   Explain how these equations lead to the idea that the average translational kinetic energy of a molecule is $\frac{3}{2}kT$.

   c   Show that the average kinetic energy of 1 mole of gas is $\frac{3}{2}RT$.

   d   Three molecules of gas have speeds 200, 300 and 400 m s⁻¹. Calculate:

      i   their mean speed

      ii   their mean-square speed

      iii   their root-mean-square speed.

2   This question relates to the assumptions of the kinetic model of a gas.

   This diagram represents the particles of a gas which is contained in a rectangular box:

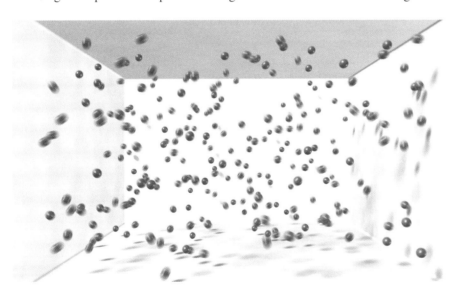

Figure 20.1: For Question 2. Diagram representing the particles of a gas contained in a rectangular box.

   a   What can you say about the total volume of the particles compared with the total volume of the box?

   b   We know that particles attract each other; it is why solids form when matter is cooled. State whether the particles of a gas attract one another.

c Describe the path of an individual particle in between collisions with other particles and with the walls of the box.

d State whether the collisions between particles are elastic or inelastic. Explain what effect this has on the total kinetic energy of the particles.

3 This question relates to the derivation of the relationship between the pressure p of a gas and the motion of its particles. It follows the same steps as the derivation of the relationship:

$$pV = \frac{1}{3}Nm <c^2>$$

Look at this diagram:

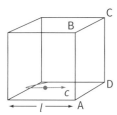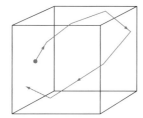

Figure 20.2: For Question 3. The left-hand side of the diagram shows a single particle in a cube-shaped box. A typical particle will be moving around so that it bounces off all six faces of the cube, rather than just two, as shown in the right-hand part of the diagram.

The left-hand side of the diagram shows a single particle in a cube-shaped box. For simplicity, we will suppose its mass is 1 kg and its speed is $c = 500\,\text{m s}^{-1}$. It travels horizontally to the left and right.

a Calculate the particle's momentum.

b The particle strikes the cube face ABCD and bounces off it so that its velocity is reversed. Calculate the change in the particle's momentum. Remember that momentum is a vector quantity.

c The particle now bounces off the opposite face and returns to strike face ABCD again. Suppose that the length of each side of the cube is $l = 1.0\,\text{m}$. Calculate the time interval between collisions on face ABCD. How many times will the particle strike ABCD each second?

d Calculate the force on ABCD due to this one particle. Use the relationship:

$$\text{force} = \frac{\text{change in momentum}}{\text{time}}$$

e Calculate the pressure on ABCD.

f What will be the pressure on the face opposite ABCD?

g In practice, a typical particle will be moving around so that it bounces off all six faces of the cube, rather than just two, as shown in the right-hand part of Figure 20.2. By what fraction will this reduce the pressure on cube face ABCD? Calculate the new value of the pressure.

> **TIP**
>
> Remember that momentum is a vector quantity. So, a change from a positive to a negative momentum can never be a zero change.

h The volume of the cube is $1\,m^3$.

The density of the 'gas' it contains is $1.0\,kg\,m^{-3}$.

The density of air is about $1.29\,kg\,m^{-3}$ at $0\,°C$.

State whether the pressure of the air would be greater or less than the value you have calculated in part **g**.

i State whether the collisions between the particle and the walls of the cube are elastic or inelastic. Justify your answer.

4 We can write the following equation for the average kinetic energy of a particle (atom or molecule) of a gas:

$$\text{average kinetic energy} = \frac{1}{2}m<c^2>$$

a State what the symbols m and $<c^2>$ represent.

We can relate this quantity to the temperature of the gas:

$$\frac{1}{2}m<c^2> = \frac{3}{2}kT$$

b State what the symbols k and T represent.

c If the thermodynamic temperature of a gas is doubled, by what factor does the average kinetic energy of its particles increase?

d Sketch a graph to show how the mean kinetic energy of the particles of a gas changes as its temperature increases.

EXAM-STYLE QUESTIONS

1 a State what is meant by an *ideal gas*. [2]

A container holds $120\,g$ of hydrogen gas at a temperature of $27\,°C$ and a pressure of $100\,kPa$.

b **Determine** the volume of the container. (molar mass of hydrogen = $2.0\,g$; universal molar gas constant $R = 8.31\,J\,mol^{-1}\,K^{-1}$) [2]

c The container is heated to $100\,°C$ at fixed volume. Determine the pressure of the gas at this temperature. [2]

d Determine the density of the hydrogen. [1]

e Determine the root-mean-square (r.m.s.) speed of the hydrogen molecules at $100\,°C$. [2]

[Total: 9]

2 A rigid container holds a mass of gas.

a Use the kinetic model of matter to explain why the gas exerts a pressure on the walls of the container. [2]

b The mass of gas in the container is doubled. Explain why the pressure of the gas doubles. [2]

c Explain why the pressure of the gas increases when the temperature of the gas increases. [2]

> COMMAND WORD
>
> **Determine:** establish an answer using the information available

CONTINUED

  d Calculate the mean kinetic energy of the molecules of a gas
     at 27 °C. (Boltzmann constant $k = 1.38 \times 10^{-23}$ J K^{-1}) [2]

  e The principal constituents of air are nitrogen (molar mass 28 g) and
     oxygen (molar mass 32 g). The root-mean-square speed of the nitrogen
     molecules is greater than that of the oxygen molecules. Explain this. [2]

     [Total: 10]

3 a State what is meant by a *mole* of substance. [2]

   b The volume of 1.5 moles of an ideal gas at −50 °C is 2.5×10^{-2} m^3. The gas
      is heated at constant pressure p.

      Calculate:

      i   the volume of the gas at 250 °C [1]

      ii the value of the pressure p. [1]

      [Total: 4]

Uniform electric fields

KEY EQUATIONS

electric field strength $= \dfrac{\text{force}}{\text{charge}}$; $E = \dfrac{F}{q}$

acceleration of a charged particle $a = \dfrac{qE}{m}$

electric field strength in a uniform field $E = \dfrac{V}{d}$

Exercise 21.1 Representing an electric field

Electric charges are surrounded by electric fields. We draw field lines to represent an electric field. This exercise provides practice drawing electric fields and understanding the rules that should be followed.

1   Each of these statements is *incorrect*. Rewrite them so that they are correct:

   a   Two positive electric charges attract each other.

   b   There is a repulsive force between two opposite electric charges.

   c   Electric field lines are directed from negative to positive.

   d   An electric field line shows the direction of the force on a negative charge placed at a point in a field.

2   Draw diagrams to represent these electric fields:

   a   the uniform field between two parallel plates with opposite charges

   b   the field around a positively charged sphere

   c   the field around a pair of charges, one positive and one negative.

> **TIP**
>
> Remember that field lines always enter a charged surface at right angles; also remember the direction of the arrows on field lines.

3   Each of these diagrams, **a**, **b** and **c**, shows a positive charge Q placed in an electric field produced by other charges:

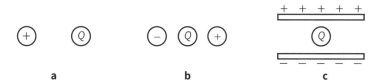

Figure 21.1: For Question 3. Each diagram shows a positive charge Q placed in an electric field produced by other charges.

Copy each diagram and add an arrow to show the direction of the force on Q.

Exercise 21.2 Calculating force and field strength

We define **electric field strength** at a point in a field in terms of the force on a positive charge placed at that point. This exercise tests your understanding of the equations that define electric field strength and how to apply them.

Note: electron charge, $e = 1.6 \times 10^{-19}$ C.

KEY WORDS

electric field strength: the force per unit positive charge at a point

1   Electric field strength is defined by the equation:

$$E = \frac{F}{q}$$

a   State the quantities represented by E, F and q, and give the units of each.

b   Rearrange the equation to make F its subject.

c   Deduce an equation for the acceleration a of a charged particle of mass m in an electric field. Use the equation that relates F, m and a.

2   **a**   Calculate the electric field strength when a force of 2.0×10^{-9} N acts on a charge of 4.5×10^{-6} C.

b   Calculate the force on an electron placed in a field of strength 2.0×10^{4} N C^{-1}.

3   The field strength is the same at all points in a uniform electric field.

A uniform electric field can be produced by applying a potential difference between two parallel plates. The field strength is given by $E = \frac{V}{d}$.

a   State the quantity represented by each of the symbols E, V and d, and give the units of each.

b   Calculate the field strength between two parallel metal plates separated by a distance of 20.0 cm when there is a p.d. of 5.0 kV between them. Your answer can be in V m^{-1} or N C^{-1} as they are the same.

c   What p.d. is needed to produce a field strength of 500 V m^{-1} between two parallel metal plates separated by 1.0 cm?

d   What force will be exerted on a particle of charge $+2e$ placed between two parallel plates separated by a distance of 140 mm when there is a p.d. of 400 V between them?

TIP

You can do this in two steps: first calculate the field strength.

e Calculate the force on the charge shown in this diagram and state its direction.

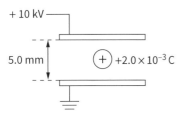

Figure 21.2: For Question 3e. A positive charge between two parallel plates.

Exercise 21.3 Moving in an electric field

This exercise considers charges moving in an electric field. A charged particle moving in a uniform electric field is like a mass moving in a uniform gravitational field (in other words, like a projectile). Remember that the usual laws of motion apply to a charged particle moving in an electric field.

1 Figure 21.3 shows a proton placed in a uniform electric field between two metal plates. The reading on the voltmeter is 240 V.

proton mass $= 1.67 \times 10^{-27}$ kg; proton charge $= +1.60 \times 10^{-19}$ C

a Calculate the electric field strength.

b Calculate the force on the proton.

c Calculate the acceleration of the proton.

d The proton is initially stationary. Describe how it will move in the electric field.

2 This diagram shows the path of a beam of electrons which is moving horizontally as it enters a uniform electric field:

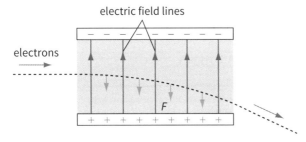

Figure 21.4: For Question 2. Diagram showing the path of a beam of electrons which is moving horizontally as it enters a uniform electric field.

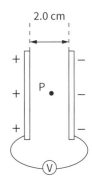

Figure 21.3: For Question 1. Diagram showing a proton in a uniform electric field between two plates.

a   Explain how you can tell from the pattern of the field lines that this is a uniform electric field.

b   Explain why the arrows on the field lines are directed upwards.

c   Explain why the force arrows on the electrons are directed downwards. Think about the electron charge.

d   The horizontal component of the electrons' velocity is constant. Explain why this is so.

e   As the electrons enter the electric field, the vertical component of their velocity is zero. Describe how this vertical component of velocity changes in the field.

f   The electrons follow a curved path. Describe the shape of this path.

> **TIP**
>
> In parts **d–f**, you should recall the equivalent ideas for a projectile moving in a uniform gravitational field (Chapter 2).

EXAM-STYLE QUESTIONS

Gravitational field strength $g = 9.81\,\text{N}\,\text{kg}^{-1}$; elementary charge $e = 1.60 \times 10^{-19}\,\text{C}$

1   a   Explain what is meant by an *electric field*.   **[2]**

> **COMMAND WORD**
>
> **Define:** give precise meaning

   b   **Define** *electric field strength*.   **[2]**

   This diagram shows a charged particle of mass $1.0 \times 10^{-6}\,\text{kg}$ placed in an electric field directed from left to right:

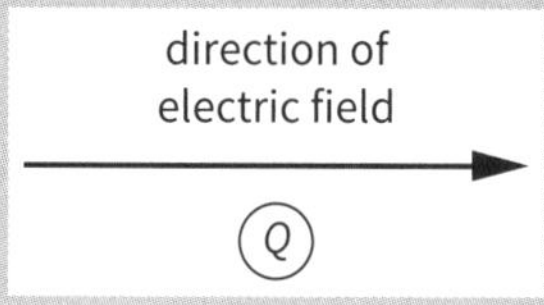

direction of electric field

$\longrightarrow$

(Q)

Figure 21.5

The field has a strength of $2500\,\text{N}\,\text{C}^{-1}$ and the particle has a charge of $-4.5 \times 10^{-9}\,\text{C}$.

   c   Calculate the electric force on the particle.   **[2]**

   d   Calculate the gravitational force on the particle.   **[2]**

   e   Draw a diagram to represent the forces on the particle.
       Add an arrow to your diagram to show the approximate direction of the resultant force on the particle.   **[3]**

   [Total: 11]

2 This diagram shows two metal plates, arranged vertically. There is a potential difference between them, as shown:

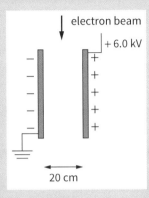

Figure 21.6

A beam of electrons, directed downwards, is about to enter the space between the plates.

a Calculate the electric field strength between the plates. [2]

b Calculate the electric force on an electron in the field, and state its direction. [2]

c Copy the diagram and add electric field lines to represent the field between the plates. [1]

d Show the path of the electron beam as it passes between the plates and into the space beyond. [2]

[Total: 7]

3 An electron moves towards the right in a straight line at a constant speed of $2.0 \times 10^7 \, \text{m s}^{-1}$ within a vacuum. The electron enters a uniform electric field at point P and stops at point Q. The distance PQ is 5.0 cm. The mass of an electron is $9.11 \times 10^{-31} \, \text{kg}$.

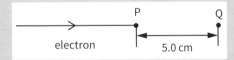

Figure 21.7

a i State the direction of the electric field. [1]

   ii Describe how a uniform electric field can be achieved. [1]

b Calculate the deceleration of the electron. [2]

c Calculate the electric field strength. [2]

d Describe the motion of the electron after it leaves point Q. [2]

[Total: 8]

Chapter 22

Coulomb's law

CHAPTER OUTLINE

- understand that the charge on a spherical conductor may be considered to act as a point charge at its centre

- recall and use Coulomb's law to solve problems

- recall and use the formula for the field strength of a point charge

- define the electric potential at a point and use the equation for the potential of a point charge

- relate field strength and potential due to a point charge

- compare electric fields and gravitational fields

KEY EQUATIONS

Coulomb's law: $F = \dfrac{Q_1 Q_2}{4\pi\varepsilon_0 r^2}$

$E = \dfrac{Q}{4\pi\varepsilon_0 r^2}$

electric potential $= \dfrac{\text{work done}}{\text{charge}}$; $V = \dfrac{W}{Q}$

electric potential due to a point charge $V = \dfrac{Q}{4\pi\varepsilon_0 r}$

field strength $= -(\text{potential gradient})$; $E = -\dfrac{\Delta V}{\Delta d}$

Exercise 22.1 Electric field around a point charge

You have already studied general ideas about electric fields (Chapter 21). You have also studied gravitational fields (Chapter 17). This exercise extends these ideas to consider electric fields around point electric charges.

Note: permittivity of free space, $\varepsilon_0 = 8.85 \times 10^{-12}\,\mathrm{F\,m^{-1}}$.

1   This question revises the idea of an electric field.

a   State what is meant by an *electric field*.

b Write the equation that defines *electric field strength*. Give the equation in words and also in symbols. State the unit of each quantity in the equation.

This diagram shows an electron placed in an electric field of strength $5000\,\text{N}\,\text{C}^{-1}$:

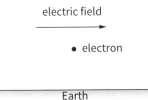

Figure 22.1: For Question 1. Diagram showing an electron in an electric field of strength 5000 N C⁻¹.

The electron is close to the Earth's surface where the gravitational field strength $g = 9.81\,\text{N}\,\text{kg}^{-1}$.

c Calculate the electric force on the electron and state its direction (electron charge $= -1.6 \times 10^{-19}\,\text{C}$).

d Calculate the gravitational force on the electron and state its direction (electron mass $= 9.11 \times 10^{-31}\,\text{kg}$).

2 As with any electric field, we can draw field lines to represent the field around a point charge. This diagram shows the electric field around a positively charged metal sphere:

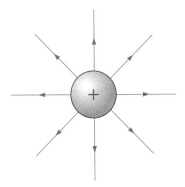

Figure 22.2: For Question 2. Diagram showing the electric field around a positively charged metal sphere.

A charged sphere can be considered to behave like a point charge where all of the charge is concentrated at the centre of the sphere.

a Draw a similar diagram to represent the electric field around a metal sphere with a negative electric charge.

b Two charged metal spheres, each of diameter 10.0 cm, are placed so that there is a gap of 20 cm between them. They can be considered to act as two point charges separated by distance d. Deduce the value of d.

3 **Coulomb's law** describes the electric force between two point charges.

This diagram shows two point charges, each of $+1.0 \times 10^{-6}$ C, separated by a distance of 1.0 cm:

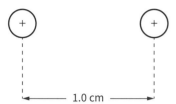

Figure 22.3: For Question 3. Diagram showing two point charges, each of $+1.0 \times 10^{-6}$ C, separated by a distance of 1.0 cm.

> **KEY WORDS**
>
> **Coulomb's law:** any two point charges exert an electrical force on each other that is proportional to the product of their charges and inversely proportional to the square of the distance between them

a Copy the diagram and add arrows to represent the force each charge exerts on the other.

b Explain how the sizes and magnitudes of the forces are an example of Newton's third law of motion.

c Describe how the forces will change if one of the charges is changed to -1.0×10^{-6} C.

d If the two charges are each increased to $+2.0 \times 10^{-6}$ C, by what factor will the force change?

e If the separation of the charges is increased to 2.0 cm, by what factor will the force change?

f If the separation of the charges is decreased to 0.5 cm, by what factor will the force change?

g Calculate the electric force between the two $+1.0 \times 10^{-6}$ C charges when they are separated by 1.0 cm. ($\varepsilon_0 = 8.85 \times 10^{-12}$ F m^{-1})

4 To calculate the electric field strength due to a point charge, we can consider a 'test' charge of +1 C placed in the field.

a A charge of +1 C is placed at some distance from a positive charge $+Q$. The electric force on it is 24 N. Calculate the field strength at this point. Give its magnitude and direction.

b Calculate the force on a charge of -5 C placed at the same point.

5 Consider a $+5.0 \times 10^{-6}$ C point charge which is far from other charges.

a Sketch a diagram to show the field lines around the charge.

b State whether the field due to the charge is uniform. Explain your answer by referring to your diagram.

c Calculate the field strength at a distance of 4.0 cm from the charge.

d Sketch a graph to show how the field strength E depends on the distance r from the charge. (There is no need to include values on the graph axes.)

6 When there are two or more charges present, we can calculate the electric force (or the field strength) by working out the forces due to each charge separately and adding them together.

Remember, force and field strength are vector quantities so it is necessary to take account of their directions.

This diagram shows two point charges, $+4.0 \times 10^{-6}$ C and $+1.0 \times 10^{-6}$ C, separated by 3.0 cm:

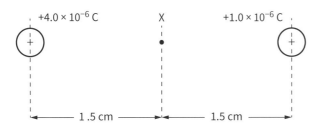

Figure 22.4: For Question 6. Diagram showing two point charges, $+4.0 \times 10^{-6}$ C and $+1.0 \times 10^{-6}$ C, separated by 3.0 cm.

a Consider a positive 'test' charge placed at point X. It is repelled by both charges. Which of the two charges exerts a greater force on it? Explain your answer.

b State the direction in which the resultant electric force acts on the test charge placed at X.

c Suggest a point at which the test charge can be placed so that the resultant electric force on it is zero. Justify your answer.

Exercise 22.2 Electric potential

Work must be done to push an electric charge to a higher **electric potential**. This energy can be changed to other forms when the charge is moved back to its starting point – that is what happens in an electric circuit when charges move around from the positive terminal to the negative. This exercise will give you practice in calculating electric forces, work done and electric potential.

KEY WORDS

electric potential at a point: the work done per unit charge in bringing a positive charge from infinity to that point

1 This question compares movement in gravitational and electric fields.

Look at these diagrams:

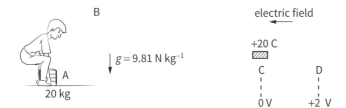

Figure 22.5: For Question 1. In the left-hand diagram, a heavy load is being lifted up from the ground at point A to a point B. In the right-hand diagram, a positive charge of +20 C is being pushed from C to D through a potential difference of 2.0 V.

a In the left-hand diagram, a heavy load is being lifted up from the ground at point A. If its mass is 20 kg, by how much has its gravitational potential energy increased when it is lifted to point B, 2.0 m above the ground? State the difference in gravitational potential between A and B. ($g = 9.81$ N kg^{-1})

b In the right-hand diagram, a positive charge of +20 C is being pushed from C to D through a potential difference of 2.0 V. Describe how you can tell from the diagram that work must be done to achieve this.

c Calculate the increase in electrical potential energy when the +20 C charge is pushed from C to D. State the difference in electric potential between C and D.

d If a negative charge of –20 C moves from C to D, deduce the change in its electrical potential energy. Explain your answer.

2 This question is about the electric potential near a point charge.

This diagram shows the electric field around a point charge +Q. A second point charge –q is placed near it:

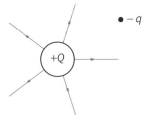

Figure 22.6: For Question 2. Diagram showing the electric field around a point charge +Q. A second point charge –q is placed near it.

a State whether the two charges attract or repel. Explain your answer.

b The second charge –q is moved further away from +Q. State whether work is done or energy is released. Explain your answer.

c If charge +Q = 0.010 C, calculate the electric potential at a distance of 0.010 m from it.

d If charge –q = –0.0050 C, calculate its electric potential energy at a distance of 0.010 m from +Q.

3 The electric field strength is equal to the negative of the potential gradient. We can write this as $-\frac{V}{d}$ for a uniform field, and more generally as $E = -\frac{\Delta V}{\Delta d}$.

These diagrams show field lines together with graphs of potential V against distance d for a uniform field and for a spherical field (the field around a point charge):

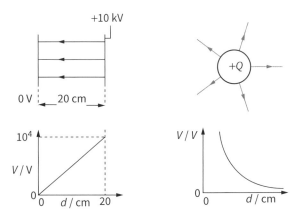

Figure 22.7: For Question 3. Diagrams showing field lines together with graphs of potential V against distance d for a uniform field (left) and for a spherical field (right).

Look at the diagrams on the left of Figure 22.7 for the uniform field.

a   Explain how you can tell from the pattern of field lines that this is a uniform field.

b   Calculate the field strength in the space between the two plates using

$$E = -\frac{\Delta V}{\Delta d}$$

Your answer should contain a negative sign and that means the field is in the opposite direction to that in which *d increases*.

c   Look at the graph of *V* against *d*. Describe the shape of the graph.

d   Explain how can you tell from this graph that the field is uniform.

Now look at the diagrams on the right of Figure 22.7 for the spherical field.

e   Explain how you can tell from the pattern of field lines that this is *not* a uniform field.

f   Look at the graph of *V* against *d*. State where the gradient is greatest (steepest).

g   State where the field is strongest.

h   Where is the field weakest? Explain your answer.

i   Think about the gravitational field around the Earth. Where is the field strongest? Describe how an object could be moved to reach a place where the field is weaker.

4   This graph shows how the potential *V* varies with distance *d* close to a positive charge:

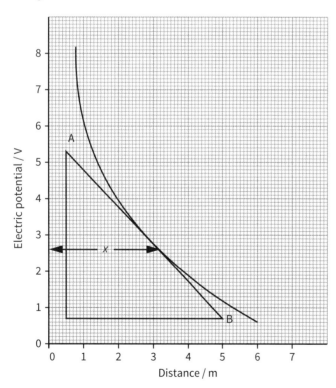

Figure 22.8: For Question 4. Graph showing how the potential *V* varies with distance *d* close to a positive charge.

The triangle under the graph is used to find the field strength at a point in the field.

The line AB is a tangent to the curve. It touches the curve at the point where we want to know the field strength.

a   State the distance x at which AB touches the curve.

b   Find the gradient of AB. This is the value of the field strength at x. Include the appropriate units in your answer.

c   State whether the gradient is positive or negative. Explain what this tells you about the force on a positive 'test' charge placed a distance x from the charge – is it attractive or repulsive?

EXAM-STYLE QUESTIONS

1   a   State Coulomb's law.   [2]

    In a carbon atom, an electron (charge $-e$) orbits the nucleus (charge $+6e$). The diameter of its orbit is 1.4×10^{-10} m. ($e = 1.6 \times 10^{-19}$ C)

    b   Calculate the electric force on the electron due to the nucleus.   [2]

    c   State the value of the electric force exerted by the electron on the nucleus   [1]

    d   The electron moves to an orbit with a greater diameter. Explain whether its electric potential energy has increased or decreased.   [2]

                                                                    [Total: 7]

2   a   State what is meant by the *electric potential* at a point.   [2]

    This diagram shows two parallel metal plates separated by a distance of 8.0 cm:

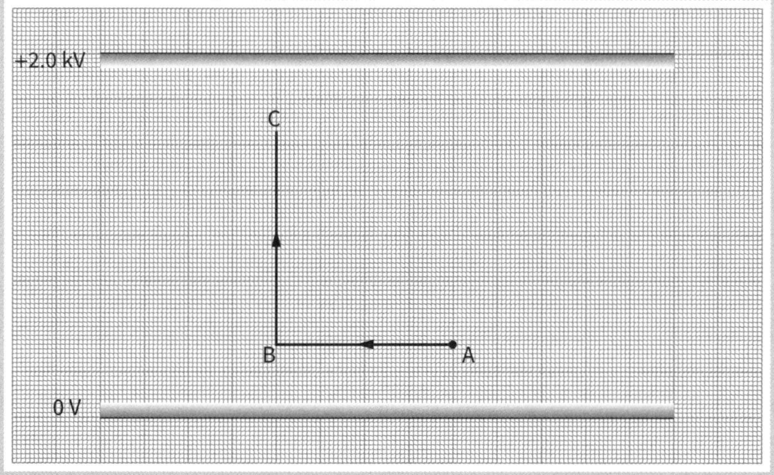

Figure 22.9

The upper plate is held at a potential of +2.0 kV. The lower plate is connected to earth so that its potential is 0 V.

CONTINUED

b Calculate the work done in transferring a single electron from the upper plate to the lower plate. ($e = 1.6 \times 10^{-19}$ C) **[2]**

c Draw a graph to show how the electric potential varies with distance between the plates. **[2]**

d Calculate the electric field strength between the plates. **[2]**

e An electron is moved along the path ABC shown in the diagram. Determine the electrical work done in moving the charge. AB = 4.0 cm and BC = 5.0 cm in length. **[3]**

[Total: 11]

TIP

You need to work out the potential difference between two points knowing that the plates are 8.0 cm apart.

3 The diagram shows three equipotential surfaces around a 250 kV transmission cable. An equipotential surface is a surface on which all points have the same potential.

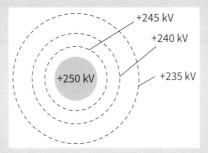

+245 kV
+240 kV
+250 kV
+235 kV

Figure 22.10

a On a copy of the diagram, draw the pattern of the electric field caused by the charge on the transmission cable. Show the direction of the electric field. **[2]**

b State and explain how the diagram shows that the electric field strength is largest near the transmission cable. **[2]**

c The distance between the surface of the cable and the 245 kV equipotential is 8.0 mm. Use this information to estimate the magnitude of the electric field strength at the surface of the cable. **[2]**

[Total: 6]

TIP

Use the idea in the equation $E = -\Delta V/\Delta d$

> Chapter 23

Capacitance

CHAPTER OUTLINE

- define capacitance and use the formula for capacitance

- solve problems involving charge, voltage and capacitance

- derive and use formulae for the energy stored in a capacitor

- derive and use formulae for the total capacitance of capacitors in series and in parallel

- analyse graphs of the variation with time of voltage, charge and current for a capacitor discharging through a resistor

- use the time constant and equations specifying how current, charge or voltage vary with time during discharge of a capacitor through a resistor

KEY EQUATIONS

$$\text{capacitance} = \frac{\text{charge}}{\text{potential difference}}; C = \frac{Q}{V}$$

$$\text{work done} = \text{charge} \times \text{potential difference}; W = QV$$

$$\text{energy stored} = \frac{1}{2}\text{charge} \times \text{potential difference}; W = \frac{1}{2}QV = \frac{1}{2}CV^2$$

$$\text{capacitors in series: } \frac{1}{C_{\text{total}}} = \frac{1}{C_1} + \frac{1}{C_2} + \frac{1}{C_3} + \dots$$

$$\text{capacitors in parallel: } C_{\text{total}} = C_1 + C_2 + C_3 + \dots$$

time constant $\tau = RC$

exponential decay for a capacitor: $x = x_0 \exp(-t/RC)$, where x represents current, charge or potential difference

Exercise 23.1 Charge, voltage and capacitance

This exercise helps you understand the basic ideas of **capacitance**.

1   This question is about the definition of capacitance. The equation that defines capacitance is:

$$C = \frac{Q}{V}$$

KEY WORDS

capacitance (of a capacitor): the charge stored on one plate per unit potential difference between the plates

a State the quantities represented by each symbol and give their units (name and symbol).

b Write down an equation relating the farad, coulomb and volt.

You can think of capacitance as telling you how many coulombs of charge are on each plate per volt of potential difference between them.

c A capacitor is marked with the value $10\,000\,\mu F$. State this in F.

d Determine the charge on a plate of the capacitor when the p.d. across it is 1 V.

e Determine the charge on a plate of the capacitor when the p.d. across it is 50 V.

2 Capacitors are usually labelled with their capacitance either in µF or pF.

a What does the prefix 'p' stand for in the SI system? State the power of 10 that it represents.

b Write these capacitance values in standard form (in other words, in scientific notation, using powers of 10):

   i $20\,\mu F$

   ii $10\,000\,\mu F$

   iii $20\,pF$

   iv $5000\,pF$.

3 This question is about how capacitors work. This circuit diagram shows a capacitor that has been connected into a circuit with a cell and a resistor:

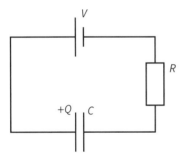

Figure 23.1: For Question 3. Circuit diagram of a capacitor, a cell and a resistor.

At first there is a current in the circuit, but eventually the capacitor is fully charged.

a When the capacitor is fully charged, state what happens to the current in the circuit.

b State the potential difference across the capacitor. State the p.d. across the resistor.

c The diagram shows that there is charge $+Q$ on one plate of the capacitor. State the charge on the other plate.

d Determine how much charge has passed around the circuit during the charging process.

e Name the type of field found between the plates of the capacitor.

Now think about the circuit at the start of the charging process, when the capacitor was first connected to the cell and the resistor.

f The plates of the capacitor were uncharged. State the p.d. across the capacitor at this time.

g State the p.d. across the resistor at this time.

h Describe how you could calculate the initial current in the circuit. Include the equation you would use.

4 If a capacitor is charged and then connected across a resistor, a current will be established in the circuit. This diagram shows one way in which this can be investigated:

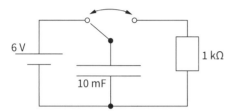

Figure 23.2: For Question 4. Circuit diagram showing one way to investigate the current.

With the switch to the left, the plates of the capacitor become charged. There is no resistance in the circuit, so this will happen instantly.

a Determine the p.d. across the capacitor when it is charged.

b Calculate the charge on each plate of the capacitor.

Now the switch is moved to the right. The circuit consists of the capacitor and a resistor.

c State the initial potential difference across the resistor.

d Determine the current in the circuit at the instant the connection is made.

e How much charge leaves the capacitor in 1.0 s? Calculate the new charge stored.

f Use your answer to **e** to calculate the p.d. across the capacitor after 1.0 s.

g Use your answer to **f** to calculate the current present in the circuit after 1.0 s.

h Explain why the current has decreased.

5 It can help to think of a capacitor as being similar to a rechargeable battery. Once it has been charged up, a capacitor can provide a source of voltage in a circuit, releasing charge to form a current. However, there is a very important difference between a capacitor and a rechargeable battery.

These graphs show how the voltage across a capacitor and a rechargeable battery change with time when they are connected across a resistor. But there is no indication of which is which.

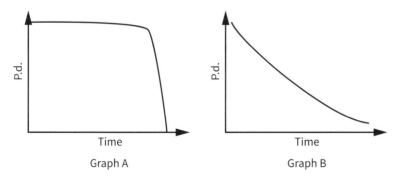

Figure 23.3: For Question 5. Two graphs of voltage against time.

a State which graph, A or B, represents the behaviour of a capacitor. Explain your answer.

b If a capacitor is connected across a large resistor, will it discharge more or less slowly? Explain your answer.

Exercise 23.2 Energy stored by a charged capacitor

Work must be done to charge up a capacitor. This means that the capacitor is a store of energy, which can be recovered when the capacitor discharges. This exercise provides practice in calculating charge, potential difference and the energy stored by a capacitor.

1 This graph shows how the p.d. V across a 0.50 mF capacitor increases as the charge Q on each of its plates increases:

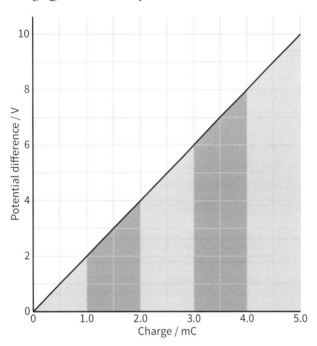

Figure 23.4: For Question 1. Graph showing how the p.d. V across a 0.50 mF capacitor increases as the charge Q on each of its plates increases.

a The graph is a straight line. Think about the equation:

$$C = \frac{Q}{V}$$

State which quantity is represented by the gradient of the graph.

b The graph is divided into strips. The area of each strip represents the work done in transferring 1 mC of charge to the capacitor. The first 'strip' is a triangle. Its area tells us the work done in transferring the first 1 mC to the capacitor. Calculate the area of this strip. (Note: the answer will be in mJ since Q is in mC.)

c   Calculate the area of the second strip. How many times bigger is this strip than the first strip?

d   Explain what the area of the second strip represents.

e   Explain why more work must be done in pushing the second 1 mC on to the capacitor.

f   From the graph, deduce the amount of work done in charging the capacitor to a p.d. of 8.0 V. Explain your method.

2   The energy stored by a capacitor C when the p.d. across it is V is given by

$$W = \frac{1}{2}QV$$

(This is the area under the graph of V against Q.)

a   A capacitor is charged to a p.d. of 6.0 V. The charge stored on each of its plates is 300 µC. Calculate the capacitance of the capacitor and the energy it stores.

b   The equation that defines capacitance is:

$$C = \frac{Q}{V}$$

Use this to show that we can write:

$$W = \frac{1}{2}CV^2$$

c   A 20 µF capacitor is charged to 240 V. Calculate the energy stored.

d   200 mJ of work is done in charging a capacitor to a p.d. of 120 V. Calculate its capacitance.

3   A metal sphere can be charged – the dome of a Van de Graaff generator is an example of this. Because it can be charged, we can say that it has a capacitance.

The charge stored Q and the potential V are related by the equation for the potential near a point charge (Chapter 22):

electric potential: $V = \dfrac{kQ}{r}$, where $k = \dfrac{1}{4\pi\varepsilon_0}$

a   Recall that capacitance is $C = \dfrac{Q}{V}$.

Rearrange the equation for V given to find an expression for C in terms of r and k.

b   State which has the greater capacitance: a sphere with a larger radius or a sphere with a smaller radius.

A metal sphere has a diameter of 40 cm.

c   Calculate the capacitance of the sphere. ($\varepsilon_0 = 8.85 \times 10^{-12}\,\mathrm{F\,m^{-1}}$)

d   Calculate the charge on the sphere when it is at a potential of 20 kV relative to earth.

e   Calculate the energy the sphere stores at this potential.

Exercise 23.3 Capacitors in series and in parallel

Two capacitors may be connected together, so it is useful to be able to calculate their combined capacitance. Alternatively, you may wish to connect two or more capacitors together to give a combined capacitance of a desired value. This is an exercise in combining capacitances in different ways.

1   Here are some calculations that make use of the formulae for combined capacitance:

capacitors in series: $\dfrac{1}{C_{total}} = \dfrac{1}{C_1} + \dfrac{1}{C_2} + \dfrac{1}{C_3} + \ldots$

capacitors in parallel: $C_{total} = C_1 + C_2 + C_3 + \ldots$

Don't forget that the equations work in the opposite way to those for resistors: you use the reciprocal formula for resistors in parallel but for capacitors in series.

a   State the total capacitance of two 10 pF capacitors connected together in parallel.

b   Calculate the total capacitance of two 10 pF capacitors connected together in series.

c   Determine the number of 10 pF capacitors that must be connected in parallel to give a total capacitance of 50 pF.

d   Now calculate the total capacitance of the number of 10 pF capacitors from part c if they were connected in series.

e   Capacitors of values 10 pF, 50 pF and 200 pF are connected in parallel. Calculate their total capacitance.

f   The capacitors from part e are connected in series. Calculate their total capacitance.

> **TIP**
>
> When capacitors are being connected in parallel, check that that your answer is greater than the value of the largest of the capacitances being connected.

2   Each of these diagrams shows three capacitors connected together. You have to find the total capacitance between A and B.

> **TIP**
>
> When capacitors are being connected in series, check that your answer is less than the value of the smallest of the capacitances being connected.

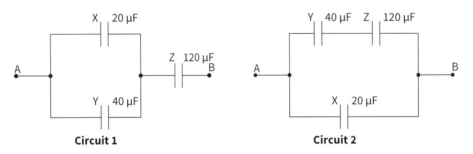

Figure 23.5: For Question 2. Two circuit diagrams showing three capacitors connected together.

a   For Circuit 1, you must first calculate the combined capacitance of X and Y. Notice whether they are connected in series or parallel and deduce their total capacitance.

b Now decide whether the pair of X and Y is in series or parallel with Z and calculate the total capacitance between A and B.

Now look at Circuit 2. The same three capacitors have been connected together, but in a different way.

c Deduce the total capacitance between A and B.

Follow the same logic as in parts **a** and **b**.

3 This question is related to the way in which the equations for capacitors in series and parallel are derived.

These diagrams show two capacitors, C_1 and C_2, connected in parallel and in series.

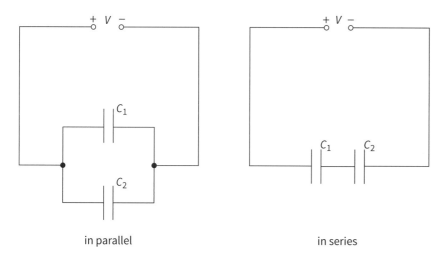

Figure 23.6: For Question 3. Two circuit diagrams showing two capacitors, C_1 and C_2, connected in parallel and in series.

For the capacitors in parallel:

a Which is the same for the two capacitors, the p.d. V across them or the charge Q on their plates? Explain your answer.

b Deduce an expression for the total charge on the capacitors.

c Hence deduce an expression for their total capacitance.

For the capacitors in series:

d Which is the same for the two capacitors, the p.d. V across them or the charge Q on them? Explain your answer.

e Deduce an expression for the p.d. across the capacitors.

f Hence deduce an expression for their total capacitance.

4 The following statements relate to combinations of two capacitors. For each, state whether the capacitors are connected in series or in parallel:

a The total capacitance is less than either of the individual capacitances.

b The total capacitance is greater than either of the individual capacitances.

c The p.d. of the supply is shared between them.

d The p.d. across one capacitor is greater than the p.d. across the other.

e One capacitor has less charge on its plates than the other.

Exercise 23.4 Discharging a capacitor

In this exercise you look at the graphs obtained when a capacitor discharges through a resistor. This is a useful method of determining the capacitance of a capacitor. This exercise provides practice in using the exponential function in the equation showing how current, voltage and charge decay with time.

1   The graph shows how the voltage across a capacitor varies with time when it is connected to a 10 000 Ω resistor.

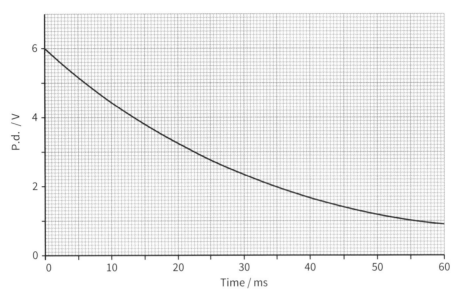

Figure 23.7: For Question 1. Graph showing how the voltage across a capacitor varies with time when it is connected to a 10 000 Ω resistor.

a   Determine the initial current in the resistor, the current at time $t = 5.0$ ms and the average current in the resistor between time $t = 0$ and $t = 5.0$ ms.

b   Using your answer for the average current in **a**, calculate the amount of charge that flows through the resistor in a time of 5.0 ms.

c   The fall in voltage in the first 5.0 ms is approximately 0.8 V. Use this value and your answer to **b** to estimate a value for the capacitance of the capacitor.

d   Determine the **time constant** of the circuit.

e   Use your answer to **d** and that the time constant of the circuit $\tau = RC$ to calculate the capacitance of the capacitor.

f   Sketch graphs to show how the charge on the capacitor and the current in the resistor vary with time.

2   A 2000 µF capacitor is charged to 9.0 V and then discharged through a 100 kΩ resistor.

Calculate:

a   the initial charge stored by the capacitor

b   the initial discharge current

c   the time constant of the circuit

d   the voltage across the capacitor after a time equal to the time constant

> **TIP**
>
> For part **d**, use the idea that in this time the voltage falls to $1/e$ or 37% of its initial value. Note: the time axis is in ms.

> **KEY WORDS**
>
> **time constant:** the time taken for the charge (or current or voltage) on a capacitor to decay to $1/e$ of its initial value, where $e = 2.718$

e   the current in the resistor after a time equal to the time constant

f   the charge stored by the capacitor after a time equal to the time constant.

3   A 400 μF capacitor is charged to a voltage of 10 V and then discharged through a 100 kΩ resistor. In this question, use the formula $x = x_0 \exp(-t/RC)$, where x and x_0 must both be charge, voltage or current.

Calculate:

a   the voltage across the plates after 20 s

b   the current after 20 s

c   the voltage across the plates after 60 s

d   the charge on the plates after 60 s

e   the time taken for the voltage to fall to 5.0 V.

> **TIP**
>
> You have to use logs to base e and then $\ln(x/x_0) = -t/RC$.

EXAM-STYLE QUESTIONS

1   a   Define *capacitance*.   [1]

A 200 μF capacitor is connected in series with a 4.0 kΩ resistor and a 240 V power supply.

b   Determine the initial current in the circuit.   [2]

c   Calculate the charge on each plate of the capacitor when the current in the circuit has fallen to 0 A.   [2]

d   Calculate the work done in charging the capacitor.   [2]

e   Sketch a graph to show how the potential changes as the charge on the capacitor increases.   [2]

[Total: 9]

2   The circuit diagram shows two capacitors, C_1 and C_2, connected to a power supply:

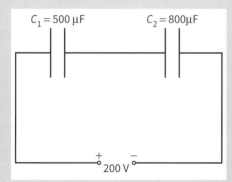

Figure 23.8

Calculate:

a   the total capacitance of C_1 and C_2 when connected in this way   [3]

b   the charge on each plate of each capacitor.   [3]

[Total: 6]

CONTINUED

3   The lamp in a torch flashes when it is connected to a charged 470 µF capacitor. The capacitor is initially connected to a p.d. of 30 V but is disconnected from the supply voltage before being connected to the lamp. The resistance of the lamp during the discharge is 1.4 Ω. Emission of light from the lamp stops when the p.d. across the capacitor falls to 2.0 V.

   a Calculate the energy released by the capacitor when the p.d. across it falls from 30 V to 2.0 V.   **[2]**

   b Calculate the time taken by the light flash.   **[3]**

   c Determine the average electrical power input to the lamp during the flash.   **[2]**

                                        [Total: 7]

4   A student measures the contact time of a metal ball that bounces on a metal plate using the apparatus shown.

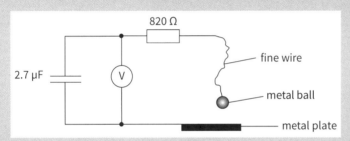

Figure 23.9

The capacitor is first charged by connecting it briefly to a battery. The student then releases the ball and records the voltmeter reading just before and just after the ball has rebounded from the plate.

   a **i** Explain what is meant by the *time constant* for a capacitor discharging through a resistor.   **[1]**

       ii Calculate the time constant for the circuit shown.   **[1]**

   b Explain why the voltmeter reading falls but does not reach zero.   **[2]**

   c During one experiment, the voltmeter reading is 5.0 V just before the ball hits the plate and 2.5 V just after it rebounds. Calculate the time for which the ball is in contact with the plate.   **[3]**

   d In order to measure longer contact times, the student uses a capacitor of capacitance 2.2 µF in addition to the 2.7 µF capacitor.

       i Calculate the total capacitance of the two capacitors in series and in parallel.   **[3]**

       ii State and explain, using ideas about time constant, which combination of the two capacitors, in series or in parallel, enables longer contact times to be measured.   **[2]**

                                     [Total: 12]

Chapter 24

Magnetic fields and electromagnetism

CHAPTER OUTLINE

- use the idea of a magnetic field as a field of force, represented by field lines

- sketch the magnetic field patterns due to a long straight wire, a flat circular coil and a long solenoid

- determine the size and direction of the force on a current-carrying conductor in a magnetic field, including the magnetic field produced by another current-carrying conductor

- define magnetic flux density

- describe how the force on a current-carrying conductor in a magnetic field can be measured

- describe the effect of a ferrous core on the magnetic field due to a solenoid

KEY EQUATIONS

$$\text{magnetic flux density} = \frac{\text{force}}{(\text{current} \times \text{length})}; \ B = \frac{F}{Il}$$

Exercise 24.1 Magnetic field lines

We use magnetic field lines to represent the strength and direction of a magnetic field. This is an exercise in drawing and interpreting magnetic field lines.

1   Any wire carrying an electric current is surrounded by a magnetic field. This diagram shows a long straight wire carrying a current upwards from B to A:

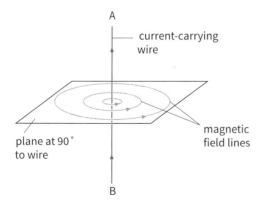

Figure 24.1: For Question 1. Diagram showing a long straight wire carrying a current upwards from B to A.

    a   Describe the shape of the magnetic field lines.

    b   State whether the field lines, as viewed from A, go around clockwise or anticlockwise.

    c   Where is the field strongest? Describe how this is represented in the diagram.

    d   Describe how the diagram would change if the direction of the current was reversed.

    e   Describe how the diagram would change if the strength of the current was increased.

2   The direction of the magnetic field lines around a current-carrying conductor can be determined as follows:

        •   Imagine that you grip the wire, curling four fingers around the wire.

        •   Point the thumb along the wire.

    a   State which hand must be used for this.

    b   State what the direction of the thumb indicates.

    c   State what the direction of the curled fingers indicates.

3   A stronger magnetic field can be created by winding a wire to form a solenoid. This diagram shows how to find the direction of the magnetic field lines:

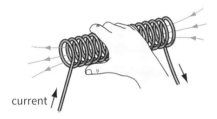

current

Figure 24.2: For Question 2. Diagram showing how to find the direction of the magnetic field lines through a solenoid.

    a   State which hand must be used for this.

    b   State what the direction of the thumb indicates.

    c   State what the direction of the curled fingers indicates.

    d   State three ways in which you could increase the strength of the magnetic field.

    e   If a second, identical solenoid is placed immediately to the left of the one shown, will the two solenoids attract or repel each other? Explain your answer.

    f   Explain how you could reverse the force that acts between the two solenoids.

Exercise 24.2 Force on a current-carrying conductor

There is a magnetic field around an electric current. When the direction of a current is across a magnetic field, the two fields interact to produce a force on the current. This exercise will give you practice in calculating magnetic forces and determining their directions.

1 This diagram shows a wire carrying a current (directed into the page):

N

 I

S

Figure 24.3: For Question 1. Diagram showing a wire carrying a current (directed into the page).

KEY WORDS

Fleming's left-hand rule: if the first finger of the left hand is pointed in the direction of the magnetic field and the second finger in the direction of the conventional current, then the thumb points in the direction of the force or motion produced

The wire is in a magnetic field due to the two magnets.

a Copy the diagram and add the field lines between the two magnets.

b Add the field lines around the current.

c Add an arrow to show the direction of the force on the conductor.

d Use your diagram to explain why the force acts in the direction you have shown.

2 To find the direction of the force, it is simpler to use **Fleming's left-hand rule**:

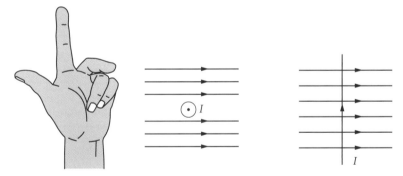

Figure 24.4: For Question 2. Diagram showing use of Fleming's left-hand rule.

a State what the thumb and first two fingers represent in this rule.

b Look at the two diagrams on the right in Figure 24.4. For each, decide whether there will be a force on the current-carrying conductor and state its direction.

3 The magnetic force on a current-carrying conductor is calculated using:

$F = BIl$

a State the quantity represented by each symbol in this equation. For each, state the SI unit (name and symbol).

b The equation is used to define the tesla. Rearrange the equation and use it to express the tesla in SI base units.

c State which quantities in this equation are vector quantities.

d Show how the equation must be modified if there is an angle θ between the current and the magnetic flux.

e Calculate the force on a wire of length 0.40 m carrying a current of 0.30 A which is at right angles to a magnetic field of **magnetic flux density** 250 mT.

f Draw a diagram to show how the wire could be positioned in the magnetic field so that the resultant force on it was zero.

> **KEY WORDS**
>
> **magnetic flux density:** the force acting per unit current per unit length on a wire placed at right-angles to the magnetic field

4 The flux density of a magnetic field can be determined by measuring the force on a current-carrying conductor placed in the field.

a A 10 cm length of copper wire carries a current of 200 mA and is directed at right angles to a magnetic field. The force on the conductor is found to be 8.0×10^{-3} N. Calculate the flux density of the field.

The flux density of the Earth's magnetic field is about 32 μT.

b Calculate the force on a wire of length 1.0 m carrying a current of 5.0 A placed in the Earth's field.

c The wire has a mass of 20 g. Explain why the magnetic force on the wire is unlikely to be noticed in normal circumstances.

5 This diagram shows apparatus that can be used to show that there is a force on a current-carrying conductor in a magnetic field.

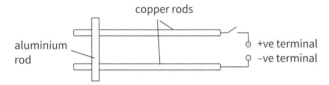

Figure 24.5: For Question 5. Diagram showing two copper rods, with an aluminium rod lying across them at right angles, a switch and terminals to a power supply.

When the switch is closed, the aluminium rod rolls to the right along the copper rods.

a State the direction of the electric current in the aluminium rod.

b State the direction of the magnetic field that acts on the aluminium rod. Explain how you arrived at your answer.

EXAM-STYLE QUESTIONS

1   **a**   Define *magnetic flux density*.   [1]

This diagram shows two identical solenoids, with a current present in each, placed side by side:

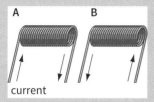

Figure 24.6

b   Consider solenoid A. State the type of magnetic pole that it will have at its left-hand end.   [1]

c   Each solenoid exerts a magnetic force on the other. State whether they will attract or repel each other. **Justify** your answer.   [2]

d   The current in solenoid A is 2 A; the current in solenoid B is 1 A. What can you say about the magnitudes of the forces the magnets exert on each other? Explain your answer.   [2]

[Total: 6]

> **COMMAND WORD**
>
> **Justify:** support a case with evidence / argument

2   This diagram shows a triangle ABC formed of copper wire, placed in a magnetic field of flux density 2.8×10^{-4} T:

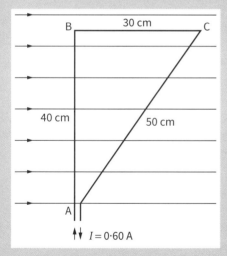

Figure 24.7

There is a current of 0.60 A in the wire.

a   Calculate the force on side AB and state its direction.   [3]

b   Calculate the force on side CA and state its direction.   [2]

c   Explain why there is no force on side BC.   [2]

[Total: 7]

CONTINUED

3   Two wires P and Q carry a current downwards through holes in a piece of card, as shown in the diagram. The current in wire P is larger than the current in wire Q.

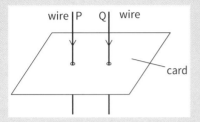

Figure 24.8

a   Copy the diagram and sketch the magnetic field pattern that exists on the card close to wire P. [2]

b   i   On the copy of your diagram, draw an arrow to show the direction of the force on wire P due to the magnetic field produced by the current in Q. [1]

ii   There is a force on wire Q due to the magnetic field produced by the current in wire P. **Compare** the force on wire P with the force on wire Q. [2]

[Total: 5]

COMMAND WORD

Compare: identify/ comment on similarities and/or differences

4   A wire carrying a current is placed in the space between the poles of a magnet. The magnet is on top of an electronic balance, as shown:

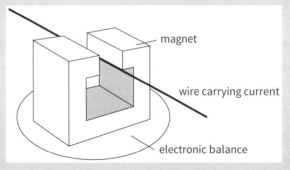

Figure 24.9

The wire is at right angles to the magnetic field produced by the magnet and has a length of 5.6 cm between the poles of the magnet. When the current is switched on, the reading on the electronic balance increases by 2.6 g when the current is 3.4 A.

a   State and explain the direction of the force on the wire due to the current. [2]

b   Calculate the average magnetic flux density between the poles of the magnet. [2]

c   State and explain what happens if the wire is rotated through an angle of 30° so that the wire is now at 60° to the magnetic field. [2]

[Total: 6]

TIP

Remember, in Newton's third law, that the force on the wire is opposite to the force on the magnet (and balance).

› Chapter 25
Motion of charged particles

CHAPTER OUTLINE

- determine the size and the direction of the force on a charge moving in a magnetic field
- understand and derive the expression $V_H = \dfrac{BI}{ntq}$ for the Hall voltage
- describe and analyse the deflection of beams of charged particles by uniform electric and uniform magnetic fields
- explain how electric and magnetic fields can be used in velocity selection

KEY EQUATIONS

magnetic force experienced by a charged particle $F = BQv\sin\theta$

force acting on a positive charge = charge × electric field strength; $F = qE$

electric field strength in a uniform field $E = \dfrac{V}{d}$

acceleration in a circle $a = \dfrac{v^2}{r} = \omega^2 r$

speed = radius × angular velocity; $v = r\omega$

force = mass × acceleration; $F = ma$

Hall voltage $V_H = \dfrac{BI}{ntq}$

current = area × number density × mean drift velocity × charge; $I = Anvq$

Exercise 25.1 Magnetic forces on particles

In this exercise, you need to equate the formula for the magnetic force to the centripetal force. You also need to understand the various directions of fields and movement for particles of positive and negative charge.

charge on an electron $= -1.6 \times 10^{-19}\,\text{C}$

mass of an electron $= 9.1 \times 10^{-31}\,\text{kg}$

mass of a proton $= 1.7 \times 10^{-27}\,\text{kg}$

1 Look at this formula for the force F acting on a charged particle in a magnetic field of flux density B:

$F = BQv \sin\theta$

   a State the meaning of the symbols Q, v and θ.

   b Describe what a charged particle must do to experience a force in a magnetic field.

   c State two situations in which there is *no* magnetic force on a charged particle, even though it is in a magnetic field.

2 A particle with charge q and mass m moves in a circular path with velocity v at right angles to a magnetic field B.

   a Show that the radius R of the path is given by: $R = \dfrac{mv}{Bq}$

   b Show that the time T for one revolution of the particle is given by: $T = \dfrac{2\pi m}{Bq}$

    (Remember, the particle is travelling in a circle of circumference $2\pi r$ with speed v.)

   c Derive an expression for the angular speed ω of the charged particle in terms of B, q and m.

3 This diagram shows the circular path of an electron moving in a uniform magnetic field that is at right angles to the circle:

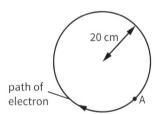

Figure 25.1: For Question 1. Diagram showing the circular path of an electron moving in a uniform magnetic field that is at right angles to the circle.

   a State the direction of the force acting on the electron when it is at point A.

   b Use **Fleming's left-hand rule** to find the direction of the magnetic field. (Remember, an electron is negative and so conventional current is opposite to its motion.)

   c Explain why the force on the electron does no work on the electron.

The speed of the electron is $1.5 \times 10^6\,\mathrm{m\,s^{-1}}$. The mass of an electron = $9.1 \times 10^{-31}\,\mathrm{kg}$.

   d Calculate the size of the force acting on the electron.

   e Calculate the magnetic flux density of the field.

   f Calculate the time taken for the electron to travel once around the circle.

KEY WORDS

Fleming's left-hand rule: if the first finger of the left hand is pointed in the direction of the magnetic field and the second finger in the direction of the conventional current, then the thumb points in the direction of the force or motion produced

4 This diagram shows a proton entering and leaving a magnetic field:

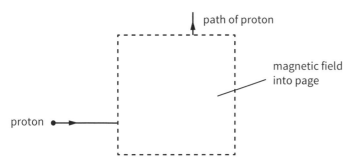

Figure 25.2: For Question 4. Diagram showing a proton entering and leaving a magnetic field.

The field is at right angles to the page, directed into the page, and is uniform inside the square shown and zero outside it.

a Describe the path of the proton through the magnetic field.

b State the direction of the magnetic force on the proton just after the proton enters the square.

c State the direction of the magnetic force on the proton just before the proton leaves the square.

d Use Fleming's left-hand rule to find the direction of the magnetic field.

e The speed of the proton is $2.5 \times 10^6 \, \text{m s}^{-1}$ and the magnetic flux density is $0.40 \, \text{T}$. Calculate the size of the magnetic force on the proton. (The charge on a proton = −charge on an electron.)

An electron with the same velocity as the proton is used instead of the proton.

f State *two* differences in the paths taken by the proton and the electron.

g State *two* changes that can be made for the electron to follow the same path as the proton.

5 A proton travelling at a speed of $4.0 \times 10^6 \, \text{m s}^{-1}$ enters a region of uniform magnetic field, of flux density $0.15 \, \text{T}$. The magnetic field is at right angles to the velocity of the proton. Calculate the radius of the circular track produced.

6 This diagram shows the path of a positive ion:

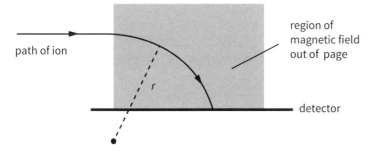

Figure 25.3: For Question 6. The path of a positive ion in a magnetic field.

The ion enters the magnetic field with a speed of $4.0 \times 10^6 \, \text{m s}^{-1}$. When the ion is within the field of flux density $0.15 \, \text{T}$, the force on the ion is $1.9 \times 10^{-13} \, \text{N}$. The mass of the ion is $2.0 \times 10^{-26} \, \text{kg}$.

   a   Calculate the charge on the ion.

   b   Calculate the radius *r* of the circular path.

   c   Another ion, with the same speed as the original ion, describes a circular arc with a larger value of *r*. Explain how this is possible.

Exercise 25.2 Electric forces on charged particles

This exercise provides practice in understanding the difference between electric and magnetic forces.

1   **a**   State which of these factors do not affect the size of the force on a charged particle in an electric field:

- amount of charge

- speed of movement

- direction of movement

- strength of electric field.

   b   A positively charged particle, travelling horizontally, enters a region with a horizontal magnetic field and then a region with a horizontal electric field. Compare the direction of the force on the particle and its path in the two fields.

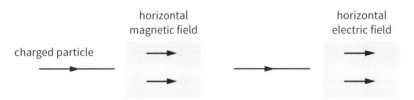

Figure 25.4: For Question 1b. Diagram showing a positively charged particle entering a region with a horizontal magnetic field and then a region with a horizontal electric field.

   c   A positively charged particle, travelling horizontally, enters a vertical magnetic field and then a vertical electric field. Compare the direction of the force on the particle and its path in the two fields.

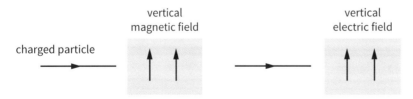

Figure 25.5: For Question 1c. Diagram showing a positively charged particle entering a vertical magnetic field and then a vertical electric field.

2   A charged particle of mass 6.6×10^{-27} kg and charge $+3.2 \times 10^{-19}$ C enters the uniform electric field between two parallel plates in a vacuum, as shown:

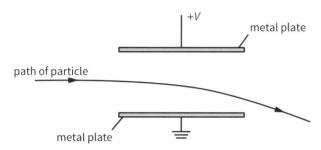

Figure 25.6: For Question 2. Diagram showing a charged particle passing through a uniform electric field between two parallel plates in a vacuum.

The electric field between the plates has magnitude 2.0×10^4 V m^{-1} and is zero outside the plates.

a   Describe what happens to the horizontal speed of the particle as it moves between the plates.

b   Describe what happens to the vertical speed of the particle as it moves between the plates.

c   Describe what happens to the direction of the acceleration of the particle as it moves between the plates.

d   Explain why the path of the particle in the electric field is not circular.

e   Calculate the vertical acceleration of the particle due to the electric field.

f   Suggest why gravity has little effect on the particle in the experiment.

Another particle with the same charge but with twice the mass enters the parallel plates with the same speed as the original particle.

g   Describe the path taken by the new particle.

h   State two ways in which the apparatus can be modified so that the new particle has the same track as the original particle.

i   Explain how your modifications in **h** produce the same acceleration for the more massive particle.

Exercise 25.3 The Hall effect

This exercise develops your understanding of the idea of an electron passing undeviated through a field, and of the formula that involves mean drift velocity.

The charge on the electron, $e = -1.6 \times 10^{-19}$ C.

1   Explain how the **Hall effect** is produced.

> **KEY WORDS**
>
> **Hall effect:** the production of a potential difference across an electrical conductor when an external magnetic field is applied in a direction perpendicular to the direction of the current

2   A conventional current enters face P of a thin slice of a semiconductor. Only electrons flow in the thin slice. A magnetic field B acts downwards.

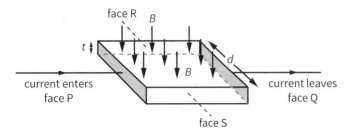

Figure 25.7: For Question 2. Diagram showing a conventional current entering face P of a thin slice of a semiconductor. A magnetic field B acts downwards.

a   State the direction of movement of the electrons as the current enters face P.

b   Use Fleming's left-hand rule to find the direction of the magnetic force on the electrons.

c   Explain which face becomes negatively charged due to the Hall effect.

d   State where a voltmeter should be connected to measure the **Hall voltage**.

e   The equation $qE = Bqv$ is used in explaining the Hall effect. State the meaning of the two terms qE and Bqv.

f   Explain why the two terms are equal.

g   Show how the equation $qE = Bqv$ is used to derive the expression for V_H the Hall voltage, given by $V_H = \frac{BI}{ntq}$, where t is the thickness of the slice.

h   The current in the film is $0.042\,A$, $t = 0.90\,mm$, $d = 10\,mm$, the Hall voltage is $2.0 \times 10^{-4}\,V$ and the concentration of free electrons in the semiconductor is $1.5 \times 10^{23}\,m^{-3}$. Calculate the magnetic field strength, B.

i   Calculate the electric field strength in the slice due to the Hall effect voltage.

j   Calculate the mean drift velocity of the electrons.

3   This diagram shows a Hall probe placed near a wire carrying a direct current:

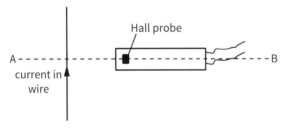

Figure 25.8: For Question 3. Diagram showing a Hall probe placed near a wire carrying a direct current.

The Hall voltage is +1.6 mV.

a   State the cause of the magnetic field that produces the Hall voltage in the probe.

b   Explain why the Hall voltage is zero when the coil rotates 90° about the axis AB from the position shown.

c   Explain why the Hall voltage is −1.6 mV when the coil rotates 180° about the axis AB from the position shown.

KEY WORDS

Hall voltage: potential difference produced across the sides of a conductor when an external magnetic field is applied perpendicular to the direction of the current. The Hall voltage V_H is directly proportional to the magnetic flux density B

TIP

For part **h**, you will need to use the electric field formula for parallel plates and the formula for current in terms of the mean drift velocity of the electrons, as well as recognising that the area $A = dt$.

d Explain why the Hall voltage decreases when the probe is moved towards B along the line AB.

Other measurements made with the probe were:

- current in the Hall probe = 100 mA
- thickness, $t = 1.0$ mm
- width, $d = 6.0$ mm
- flux density of magnetic field at B = 0.080 T.

e Calculate the number density of free electrons in the Hall slice. Remember to give the unit.

f Calculate the mean drift velocity of the free electrons in the Hall slice.

g Calculate the mean value of the magnetic force on a free electron at it moves through the slice.

h Calculate the value of the electric force on each free electron at it moves through the slice.

4 The Hall effect can be shown with a thin strip of metal. A copper strip of thickness 1.0 mm carries a current of 25 A at right angles to a magnetic field of 2.5 T. The Hall effect voltage is 6.0×10^{-6} V.

a Calculate the number density of free electrons in copper.

b Explain why Hall voltages obtained with metals are smaller than with semiconductors of the same dimensions and with the same current. Use ideas about the number density of free electrons and the velocity of the charge carriers.

> **TIP**
>
> Remember,
> 1 mm = 10^{-3} m and
> 1 mA = 10^{-3} A.

Exercise 25.4 The velocity selector

The questions in this exercise about the velocity selector always involve an electric field and a magnetic field, both at right angles to a particle's velocity. Think carefully about the directions of the forces of the fields on the charged particle.

1 This diagram shows a source of ions. The ions accelerate and pass through a velocity selector:

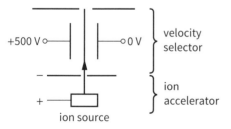

Figure 25.9: For Question 1. Diagram showing ions from a source which accelerate and pass through a velocity selector.

Between the parallel plates, both the magnetic field and the electric field are uniform. The magnetic flux density is 0.12 T and the electric field strength is 2.4×10^4 V m^{-1}.

Positive ions flow upwards from the source. The deflection of the ions due to the electric field between the plates is cancelled by the deflection caused by the magnetic field in the same region.

a State the direction of the magnetic force on the ions in the magnetic field.

b State the direction of the magnetic field within the plates.

c The ions are not deflected between the plates if they have speed v. Write down an equation relating the speed of the electrons v to the electric field E between the plates and the magnetic flux density B.

d Calculate the velocity v that is selected.

e Calculate the separation of the plates. The p.d. across the plates is shown on the diagram.

f Explain, in terms of the magnetic force and the electric force on the ion, what happens when an ion of larger speed than the value in **d** passes into the velocity selector.

2 Electrons with speed v and charge e travel in a vacuum between two narrow slits S_1 and S_2.

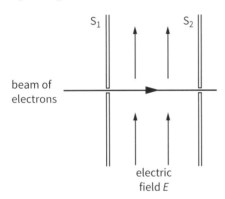

Figure 25.10: For Question 2. Diagram showing electrons travelling in a vacuum between two narrow slits S_1 and S_2. Between the slits, there is a magnetic field B (not shown) and an electric field E, both of which are uniform.

Between the slits, there is a magnetic field B and an electric field E, both of which are uniform. Only the electric field direction is shown in the diagram. The electron passes in a straight line between the slits.

a State the expression for the force F acting on an electron of charge e due to the electric field.

b State the expression for the force F acting on an electron due to the magnetic field.

The electric field acts upwards in the plane of the paper, as shown in the diagram. The electrons pass undeflected through the region between the slits.

c State the direction of the electric force on the electron.

d State the direction of the magnetic field.

e Explain how it is possible for the electron to be undeflected.

An alpha-particle with speed v passes along the same path as the electron.

f Explain, in terms of the forces acting, why the alpha-particle is also undeflected. Remember, an alpha-particle has charge $+2e$.

The magnetic flux density is increased further. The electric field strength is unchanged.

g   Explain why the electrons do not pass in a straight line between the slits.

EXAM-STYLE QUESTIONS

1   A charged particle of mass m and charge q travels in a vacuum at constant speed v. It enters a magnetic field of flux density B. The initial angle between the direction of the magnetic field and the motion of the particle is 90°.

   a   Explain why the path of the particle is a circle in the magnetic field.   **[2]**

   b   The radius of the circular path is r. **Show that** the ratio $\frac{q}{m}$ is given by the expression $\frac{q}{m} = \frac{V}{Br}$.   **[2]**

   c   A beam of electrons enters a uniform electric field produced by a p.d. of 800 V applied across two parallel plates 40 mm apart. The beam is deflected by the electric field until a uniform magnetic field of 0.80 mT perpendicular to the beam is applied, which cancels the deflection and the beam then passes in a straight line. Calculate the speed of the electrons.   **[2]**

   [Total: 6]

> **COMMAND WORD**
>
> **Show (that):** provide structured evidence that leads to a given result

2   When a gamma ray photon passes close to a nucleus, a positron and an electron can be formed. This diagram shows the tracks of the electron and positron in a magnetic field at right angles to the plane that contains their movement:

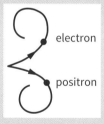

Figure 25.11

The speed of the electron is known to be equal to the speed of the positron. The tracks start as circles but become spirals.

   a   Explain how the diagram shows that the charge on the positron is positive.   **[2]**

   b   Explain how the diagram shows that the ratio of charge to mass (q/m) of the two particles is equal.   **[2]**

   c   Suggest what is happening to the speed of the particles to cause the paths to be spirals rather than circles. **Give** a reason for your answer.   **[2]**

   [Total: 6]

> **COMMAND WORD**
>
> **Give:** produce an answer from a given source or recall/ memory

CONTINUED

3   In a Hall effect experiment, a current of 15 A passes through a thin strip of copper of thickness 0.10 mm, as shown:

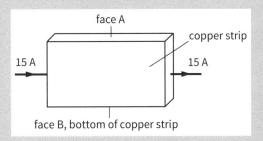

Figure 25.12

A Hall voltage of 8.8 μV occurs between the two faces, A and B, at the top and bottom of the strip. This is produced by a magnetic field of flux density 0.80 T acting on the strip. Face B is more positive than face A.

a   State the direction of the magnetic field acting on the copper strip. Explain your answer. [2]

b   Explain why:

   i   electrons pass in a straight line through the strip, even though there is a magnetic force acting on them [1]

   ii   increasing the current increases the Hall voltage. [2]

c   Calculate the number density of free electrons in the copper. [2]

[Total: 7]

4   The diagram shows part of a type of mass spectrometer used for measuring the masses of isotopes. Ions enter a velocity selector and then pass into an ion separator.

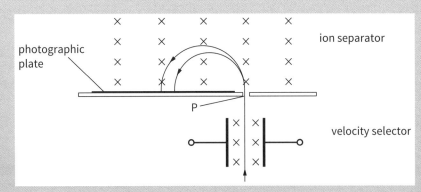

Figure 25.13

CONTINUED

a The magnetic field strength in the velocity selector is 0.18 T and the electric field strength is 30 000 V m^{-1}. The magnetic field is into the paper in both the velocity selector and the separator.

    i Explain why the velocity of the ions leaving the velocity selector is independent of the charge on the ion. **[3]**

    ii Calculate the velocity of the ions selected. **[1]**

b A sample of tin is analysed in the spectrometer. The tin contains two isotopes, tin-118 and tin-120. Each ion of tin carries a single charge of +1.60 × 10^{-19} C.

The mass of a proton or a neutron = 1.67 × 10^{-27} kg.

The tin-118 ion moves in a circle of radius 0.130 m within the ion separator and strikes the photographic plate 0.260 m from the point P at which the ion beam enters the ion separator.

Calculate:

    i the magnetic flux density of the field in the ion separator **[3]**

    ii the radius of the circular orbit of a tin-120 ion in the ion separator **[2]**

    iii the separation on the photographic plate of the positions where the two isotopes hit the plate. **[1]**

[Total: 10]

> Chapter 26

Electromagnetic induction

CHAPTER OUTLINE

- define magnetic flux and magnetic flux linkage

- recall and use $\Phi = BA$

- infer from appropriate experiments on electromagnetic induction:

    - that a changing magnetic flux can induce an e.m.f. in a circuit

    - that the direction of the induced e.m.f. opposes the change producing it

    - the factors affecting the magnitude of the induced e.m.f.

- recall and solve problems using Faraday's law of electromagnetic induction and Lenz's law

- explain simple applications of electromagnetic induction

KEY EQUATIONS

magnetic flux $\Phi = BA$

flux linkage $= N\Phi = NBA$

induced e.m.f. $E = \dfrac{-\Delta(N\Phi)}{\Delta t}$

Exercise 26.1 Flux, flux density and flux linkage

This exercise explores the meanings of the terms *flux*, *flux density* and *flux linkage*, and some of their applications. You will need to think clearly about the angle between a coil and a magnetic field. This angle may be the angle between the plane of the coil and the field or between the normal to the plane of the coil (the axis of the coil) and the field. These angles are not the same.

1 Match the terms with the correct definitions:

Term	Definition
magnetic flux	the magnetic flux that passes through an area of $1\,m^2$ when the magnetic flux density is $1\,T$
magnetic flux linkage	magnetic flux through a circuit times the number of turns
magnetic flux density	the magnetic flux density perpendicular to a circuit multiplied by the cross-sectional area of the circuit
the weber	the force acting per unit current per unit length on a wire placed at right-angles to the magnetic field

Table 26.1: For Question 1.

2 Magnetic fields are drawn with magnetic field lines that pass through coils. The field lines are sometimes close together and sometimes far apart.

    a Describe briefly the difference between *magnetic flux density*, *magnetic flux* and *magnetic flux linkage* in terms of magnetic field lines.

    b State the units of magnetic flux, magnetic flux density and magnetic flux linkage.

    c The primary coil of an ideal transformer is connected to a direct current supply. Suggest why the magnetic flux through the primary and secondary coils is the same but the magnetic flux linkage is different.

3 A physicist has a ring of area $1.8 \times 10^{-4}\,m^2$. The Earth's magnetic field is $5.0 \times 10^{-5}\,T$.

    a Describe how she places the ring so that the **magnetic flux** through the ring is as large as possible.

    b Calculate the maximum value of the magnetic flux through the ring.

    c Explain why the **magnetic flux linkage** and the magnetic flux through the ring are the same.

4 A flat coil of N turns has area A. The coil is placed so that the plane of the coil is at an angle θ to a magnetic field of magnetic flux density B:

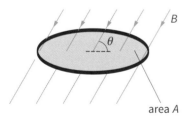

area A

Figure 26.1: For Question 1. Diagram showing a coil placed so that the plane of the coil is at an angle to a magnetic field of magnetic flux density B.

Use the definition of magnetic flux and magnetic flux linkage to show that the magnetic flux linkage through the coil is $NBA \sin \theta$.

5   A coil of cross-sectional area 2.5×10^{-4} m^2 is placed in a magnetic field of magnetic flux density 0.028 T. Calculate the magnetic flux through the coil when the plane of the coil is:

   a   perpendicular to the field (in this case $\theta = 90°$)

   b   at 0° to the field

   c   at 30° to the field.

6   A square coil of side 2.0 cm has 50 turns. It is placed in a magnetic field of magnetic flux density 2.8×10^{-2} T. Calculate the flux linkage through the coil when the angle between the plane of the coil and the field is 35°.

TIP

Take care: the units of area have to be in m^2.

7   A coil of cross-sectional area 2.0×10^{-4} m^2 is placed in a field of magnetic flux density 0.010 T. The magnetic flux linkage through the coil is 3.0×10^{-5} T. Calculate:

   a   the magnetic flux through the coil

   b   the number of turns in the coil.

Exercise 26.2 Faraday's law and Lenz's law

This exercise provides practice in recalling and solving problems using Faraday's law of electromagnetic induction and Lenz's law.

1   Describe an experiment in which **Faraday's law of electromagnetic induction** is demonstrated. You should include:

   a   a labelled diagram of the apparatus

   b   an explanation as to how the results or observations demonstrate Faraday's law.

2   A magnet is dropped vertically through a coil of wire. This diagram shows how the current induced in the coil varies with time:

KEY WORDS

Faraday's law of electromagnetic induction: the induced e.m.f. is proportional to the rate of change of magnetic flux linkage

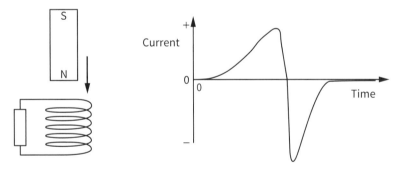

Figure 26.2: For Question 2. A magnet being dropped through a coil and a graph showing how the current induced in the coil varies with time.

The current in the coil makes the coil into an electromagnet.

   a   State why there is a current caused by an induced e.m.f. in the coil.

   b   As the N-pole approaches the top of the coil, state whether the top of the coil is a N-pole or a S-pole. Explain your idea using **Lenz's law**.

   c   As the S-pole leaves the bottom of the coil, state whether the bottom of the coil is a N-pole or a S-pole. Explain your idea using Lenz's law.

KEY WORDS

Lenz's law: an induced e.m.f. acts in such a direction so as to produce effects which oppose the change producing it

d Use Faraday's law to explain why the negative peak in current is larger in value than the positive peak.

e State two changes that could be made to the experiment to increase the current caused by the induced e.m.f.

3 A generator contains a coil rotating in a magnetic field, as shown:

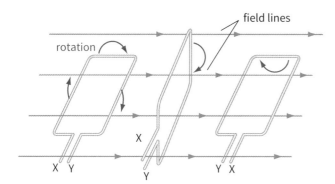

Figure 26.3: For Question 3. Diagram showing a generator which contains a coil rotating in a magnetic field.

a Use ideas about the magnetic flux through the coil to explain why there is an induced e.m.f. in the coil.

b Use Faraday's law to explain why the induced e.m.f. is a maximum when the coils are horizontal in the diagram.

c State two ways in which the size of the induced e.m.f. can be increased. Explain your answer using ideas about flux linkage and Faraday's law.

Exercise 26.3 Faraday's law in more detail

This exercise provides more practice in performing calculations using Faraday's law.

1 Which three of these units are equivalent to $Wb\,s^{-1}$, the rate of change of flux linkage?

$J\,s^{-1}$ $J\,C^{-1}$ $V\,s^{-1}$ V $T\,m^2\,s^{-1}$ $T\,m^2$

2 A coil has 50 turns and an area of $8.0 \times 10^{-4}\,m^2$. The coil is placed perpendicular to a uniform magnetic field of $0.20\,T$.

a Calculate the total flux linkage through the coil.

b Calculate the induced e.m.f. if the magnetic field is reduced to zero in $50\,ms$. ($1\,ms = 10^{-3}\,s$)

c Calculate the induced e.m.f. if the magnetic field is *reversed* in $50\,ms$.

3 A coil has 3000 turns and a cross-sectional area of $2.0 \times 10^{-4}\,m^2$. Calculate the change in magnetic flux density every second that causes an induced e.m.f. of $12\,V$ in the coil.

4   A coil with 200 turns and cross-sectional area $1.6 \times 10^{-3}\,\text{m}^2$ is placed in a uniform magnetic field of flux density $0.090\,\text{T}$. When the coil is pulled out of the magnetic field, the average e.m.f. induced in the coil is $15\,\text{V}$. Estimate the time taken to pull the coil out of the magnetic field.

5   A single loop of wire is placed perpendicular to the uniform magnetic field produced by an electromagnet. The loop of wire has resistance of $3.6\,\Omega$ and area of $6.0 \times 10^{-4}\,\text{m}^2$. When the electromagnet is switched on, it takes $0.60\,\text{s}$ to reach a magnetic flux density of $5.0 \times 10^{-4}\,\text{T}$ within the coil.

    a   Calculate the average current that flows in the wire during the $0.60\,\text{s}$ after the electromagnet is switched on.

    b   Explain why the current is zero in the loop of wire when there is a steady current in the electromagnet.

6   The magnetic flux through a coil varies regularly with time as a sine wave. The maximum value of the flux through the coil is $+\Phi_0$. Explain why:

    a   the induced e.m.f. in the coil is zero when the flux has the value $+\Phi_0$

    b   the induced e.m.f has the largest value when the flux is zero.

7   This diagram shows how the magnetic flux linkage through a coil varies with time:

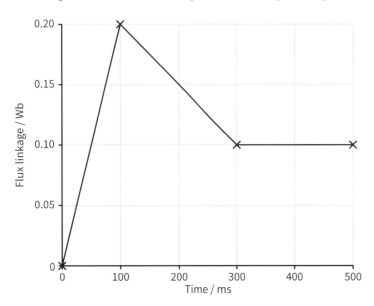

Figure 26.4: For Question 7. Diagram showing how the magnetic flux linkage through a coil varies with time.

Calculate the magnitude of the induced e.m.f. between:

    a   0 and 100 ms

    b   100 and 300 ms

    c   300 and 500 ms.

8 This graph shows the variation of flux linkage through a coil with time:

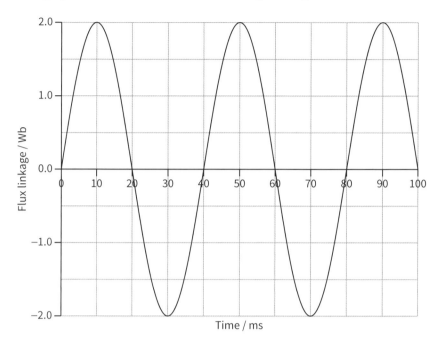

Figure 26.5: For Question 8. Graph showing the variation of flux linkage through a coil with time.

a State a time at which the e.m.f. induced in the coil has a maximum value.

b State a time at which the e.m.f. induced in the coil is zero.

c State the physical quantity that is equal to the gradient of the graph.

d Take readings from the graph to estimate the maximum value of the e.m.f. induced in the coil.

e If the cross-sectional area of the coil is $1.6 \times 10^{-2}\,\text{m}^2$ and it contains 500 turns, calculate the maximum value of the magnetic flux density.

> **TIP**
>
> You can place a ruler along the curve at the point where the e.m.f. is largest.

EXAM-STYLE QUESTIONS

1 a i State Lenz's law. [2]

   ii You have available a coil of wire, a sensitive ammeter and a bar magnet. Describe a simple experiment using this apparatus to illustrate Lenz's law. [2]

  b An electromagnet produces a uniform field from left to right and only in the gap between its poles. The gap has sides 0.050 m × 0.080 m and there is no field outside the gap. A circular coil of 40 turns surrounds all of the magnetic flux, as shown in the diagram.

CONTINUED

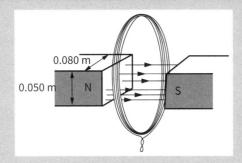

Figure 26.6

The ends of the coil are connected together so that an induced e.m.f. in the coil produces a current in the coil.

The magnetic field of the electromagnet falls linearly from 0.15 T to zero in a time of 3.0 s.

i   Calculate the initial flux linkage through the coil.   [2]

ii Calculate the induced e.m.f. in the coil as the magnetic field
    decreases.   [2]

iii State and explain the direction of the magnetic field created
    by the current in the coil when the field of the electromagnet
    decreases.   [2]

[Total: 10]

2   a   State Faraday's law of electromagnetic induction.   [2]

    b   A coil is connected to a sensitive voltmeter with an analogue display.
        A bar magnet is pushed into the coil, stopped and then removed at the
        same speed.

        i   State the effect this action has on the voltmeter reading.   [2]

        ii   Explain these observations, using Faraday's law.   [2]

        iii The action is repeated at a higher speed. State and explain
             what difference you would expect to see in the response of the
             voltmeter.   [2]

    c   A rectangular coil is rotating at constant angular speed with its axle
        perpendicular to a uniform magnetic field of 0.15 T:

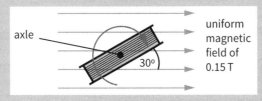

Figure 26.7

At the instant shown, the angle between the plane of the coil and the magnetic field is 30°.

CONTINUED

The coil has 50 turns and has a cross-sectional area of $4.0 \times 10^{-4}\,\mathrm{m}^2$.

i   Calculate the flux through the coil in the position shown.   [2]

ii   The coil moves from the position shown to a position where the flux through the coil is zero. The change takes a time of 0.25 s. Calculate the average value of the induced e.m.f. in the coil.   [2]

iii Explain why the induced e.m.f. is not constant even though the coil is turning at a constant angular speed.   [2]

[Total: 14]

3   An aluminium window frame is suspended from two hinges as shown.

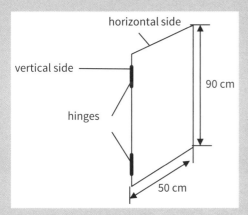

Figure 26.8: For Question 3.

The horizontal component B_{H} of the Earth's magnetic field is $2.0 \times 10^{-5}\,\mathrm{T}$. When the window is closed the frame is perpendicular to B_{H}. The window is opened in a time of 0.40 s, and in this time the plane of the window rotates through 90°.

a   When the window is closed, calculate the magnetic flux linkage through the window.   [2]

b   Explain why an e.m.f. is induced in the frame when the window is opened, stating the sides of the frame in which the e.m.f. is induced.   [2]

c   Calculate the average e.m.f. induced in the window frame as the window is opened.   [2]

[Total: 6]

Chapter 27

Alternating currents

CHAPTER OUTLINE

- understand and use the terms period, frequency, peak value and root-mean-square value

- recall that the mean power in a resistive load is half the maximum power

- represent a sinusoidally alternating current or voltage by an equation of the form $x = x_0 \sin \omega t$

- distinguish between root-mean-square (r.m.s.) and peak values and recall and use the relationships $I_{\text{r.m.s.}} = \frac{I_0}{\sqrt{2}}$ and $V_{\text{r.m.s.}} = \frac{V_0}{\sqrt{2}}$ for a sinusoidal alternating current

- explain and distinguish between half-wave rectification and full-wave rectification, and describe the use of a capacitor in smoothing

KEY EQUATIONS

root-mean-square value of an alternating current $I_{\text{r.m.s.}} = \dfrac{I_0}{\sqrt{2}}$

root-mean-square value of voltage $V_{\text{r.m.s.}} = \dfrac{V_0}{\sqrt{2}}$

sinusoidally alternating current or voltage: $x = x_0 \sin \omega t$

power = potential difference × current = current^2 × resistance; $P = VI = I^2 R$

Exercise 27.1 Understanding the terms used for alternating current and power

This exercise gives you practice in using the terms **root-mean-square (r.m.s.) current and voltage** which are used to describe alternating current. You will also gain understanding of the differences between alternating and direct current.

1   Distinguish between *direct current* and *alternating current*.

2   An alternating voltage is connected to a resistor. Explain how heat is produced in the resistor, even though the average current is zero and there is a current in both directions.

3   Explain what is meant by the r.m.s. value of an alternating current. Include in your ideas the heating effect of the alternating current.

4   Using the formula $I_{r.m.s.} = \frac{I_0}{\sqrt{2}}$, show that:

for a.c., $\dfrac{\text{maximum power converted in resistor}}{\text{average power converted in resistor}} = 2$

5   This graph shows the alternating p.d. (voltage) across a resistor:

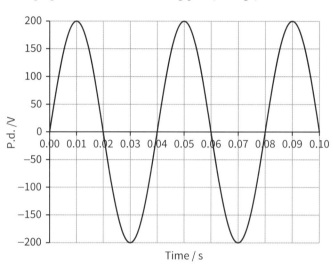

Figure 27.1: For Question 5. Graph showing the alternating p.d. (voltage) across a resistor.

> **TIP**
>
> When you use $P = VI$, if you use maximum values for V and I then you get the maximum power, and when you use r.m.s. values you get the average power.

The resistance of the resistor is 50 Ω.

Use the graph to calculate:

a   the period of the alternating voltage

b   the frequency of the supply

c   the peak voltage

d   the r.m.s. voltage

e   the average voltage

f   the peak current

g   the r.m.s. current

h   the peak power

i   the average power.

6   An electrical device is rated at 250 V, 1000 W.

Calculate:

a   the peak voltage

b   the r.m.s. current

c   the peak current

d   the peak power.

> **TIP**
>
> Unless stated otherwise, electrical ratings are r.m.s. values.

Exercise 27.2 Using the equation $x = x_0 \sin \omega t$

In this exercise you will look at a number of different examples of the use of the equation $x = x_0 \sin \omega t$.

1 An alternating current I is defined by the equation $I = I_0 \sin \omega t$, where I_0 is the peak current and ω is the angular frequency of the supply.

For a particular circuit, $I = 4.0 \sin 200t$ where I is measured in A and t in s.

Calculate:

a the peak value of the current

b the r.m.s. value of the current

c the frequency of the supply.

2 The diagram shows the variation with time of the alternating voltage from a power supply.

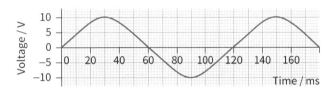

Figure 27.2: For Question 2. Graph showing the variation of the alternating voltage from a power supply over time.

a State the time taken for one complete cycle of the alternating voltage.

b Calculate the frequency of the alternating voltage.

c Determine the equation of the alternating voltage in the form $V = V_0 \sin \omega t$, giving your value for ω to three significant figures.

d Use of ωt in the formula $V = V_0 \sin \omega t$ gives, effectively, an angle in radians. When you calculate $\sin \omega t$ you need to either convert the 'angle' in radians to degrees or set your calculator to work with an *angle in radians* and not in degrees.

Use your equation to show that the voltage:

i at $t = 60\,\text{ms}$ is $0\,\text{V}$

ii at $t = 30\,\text{ms}$ is $10\,\text{V}$.

e Using your equation in part **c**, determine during which fraction of a complete cycle the voltage changes from 0 to $5.0\,\text{V}$.

3 Two sinusoidal alternating currents are represented by the equations:

$V_1 = 10 \sin 400t$ and $V_2 = 5.0 \sin 100t$

Calculate:

a the ratio of the amplitude of the two voltages, V_1 to V_2

b the ratio of the frequencies of the two voltages, V_1 to V_2.

Exercise 27.3 Rectification

Many applications of alternating current require its transformation to direct current. This exercise gives practice in understanding **full-wave** and **half-wave rectification**.

1 Describe the process of half-wave rectification using a single diode.

2 An alternating signal of peak voltage 6.0 V is connected in series to an ideal diode and a pure resistor. An ideal diode has infinite resistance when not conducting and no p.d. across it when conducting.

   a State the maximum voltage across the diode during one cycle.

   b State the voltage across the resistor when there is the maximum voltage across the diode.

3 This diagram shows a full-wave bridge rectifier:

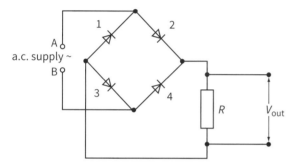

Figure 27.3: For Question 3. Circuit diagram of a full-wave bridge rectifier.

Complete these sentences to explain which diodes the current passes through:

   a When the a.c. supply makes A positive and B negative, the current flows in diodes __ and __.

   b When the a.c. supply makes B positive and A negative, the current flows in diodes __ and __.

   c The current from the supply is _____ but the current in R is _____.

4 a Describe the difference between the voltage obtained after half-wave rectification and after full-wave rectification.

   b State one advantage of full-wave rectification when compared to half-wave rectification.

   c Explain what is meant by *smoothing* the voltage obtained after rectification.

   d Explain how a capacitor is used to smooth the voltage obtained after rectification.

5 An alternating signal is connected to an ideal full-wave rectifier. The following diagram shows the voltage across a load resistor connected to the output.

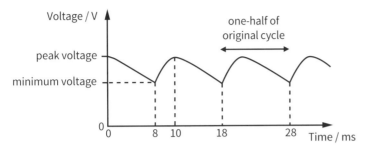

Figure 27.4: For Question 5. Diagram showing the voltage across a load resistor connected to an ideal full-wave rectifier.

The voltage is partially smoothed by a capacitor across the resistor.

Remember 1 ms = 0.001 s.

a   Determine the length of time in each half-cycle during which the capacitor is charging.

b   Determine the length of time in each half-cycle during which the capacitor is discharging.

c   Calculate the frequency of the original alternating supply. As the original waveform is full-wave rectified, you need to work out the time for the whole of an original cycle and then calculate frequency.

The resistance of the resistor is increased and the output is smoother.

d   State what happens to the peak voltage reached.

e   State what happens to the minimum voltage during one cycle.

f   State what happens to the time taken to charge the capacitor in each half-cycle.

g   State what happens to the time taken to discharge the capacitor in each half-cycle.

h   State what change in the capacitor would produce the same change as increasing the resistance of the resistor.

EXAM-STYLE QUESTIONS

1   The alternating mains electricity supplied to a house has a root-mean-square voltage $V_{r.m.s.}$ of 230 V and a frequency of 50 Hz.

   a   i   State what is meant by *root-mean-square voltage*.   **[1]**

      ii   Calculate the peak value of the supply voltage V_0.   **[2]**

      iii   Calculate the mean voltage V.   **[1]**

   b   The alternating supply is connected in series with a resistor of resistance 5.9 kΩ . Calculate the peak power dissipated in the resistor.   **[2]**

   c   Sketch the graph of the supply voltage against time for two complete periods. Label the axes with appropriate values.   **[2]**

                                            [Total: 8]

CONTINUED

2   A load resistor, capacitor and four diodes used as a rectifier are connected to the output from a transformer. The diagram shows how the resulting potential difference V across the resistor varies with time t.

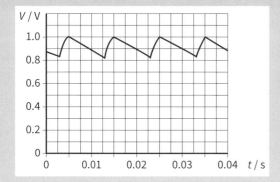

Figure 27.5

a   i   State how the diagram shows that the current in the load resistor is direct current.   [1]

     ii   State the name of the type of the rectifier used.   [1]

     iii   Draw the rectifying circuit of four diodes, load resistor and capacitor connected to the output of the transformer.   [3]

b   The diodes used in the rectifier are ideal diodes. Determine the original alternating supply's:

     i   peak voltage   [1]

     ii   root-mean-square voltage   [2]

     iii   frequency.   [2]

c   The smoothing is not good enough for some applications.

     i   Explain what is meant by *smoothing*.   [1]

     ii   Explain how the diagram shows that the smoothing is not ideal.   [2]

     iii   Suggest and explain how to increase the smoothing for the same load resistor.   [2]

d   The resistor has a resistance of $2000\,\Omega$.

     During part of each cycle shown in the diagram the capacitor discharges for a time T.

     Calculate:

     i   the mean potential difference across the resistor   [1]

     ii   the mean current in the resistor   [1]

     iii   the time T [1]

     iv   the charge passing through the resistor in the time T [2]

     v   the decrease in voltage as the capacitor discharges   [1]

     vi   the capacitance of the capacitor (use your answers to **iv** and **v**).   [2]

[Total: 23]

Chapter 28

Quantum physics

CHAPTER OUTLINE

- describe evidence for the particulate and wave nature of electromagnetic radiation

- recall and use $E = hf$

- understand that a photon has momentum and that the momentum is given by $p = \dfrac{E}{c}$

- explain the photoelectric effect in terms of photon energy, work function energy, threshold frequency and threshold wavelength, and recall, use and explain the significance of $hf = \phi + \frac{1}{2}mv_{max}^2$

- explain why the maximum photoelectric energy is independent of intensity, whereas the photoelectric current is proportional to intensity

- explain how discrete electron energy levels in isolated atoms produce spectral lines

- distinguish between emission and absorption line spectra

- recall and solve problems using the relation $hf = E_1 - E_2$

- describe and interpret the evidence provided by electron diffraction for the wave nature of particles

- recall and use the relation for the de Broglie wavelength $\lambda = \dfrac{h}{p}$

KEY EQUATIONS

speed of electromagnetic radiation in free space $c = f\lambda$

energy of a photon = Planck constant × frequency; $E = hf$

Einstein's photoelectric equation: energy of photon = work function + maximum kinetic energy of electron

$$hf = \phi + \tfrac{1}{2}mv_{max}^2$$

energy of a photon, absorbed or emitted, as a result of an electron making a transition between two energy levels E_1 and E_2: $hf = E_1 - E_2$

de Broglie wavelength $\lambda = \dfrac{h}{p}$

momentum of a photon $= \dfrac{\text{energy of photon}}{\text{speed of light in a vacuum}}$; $p = \dfrac{E}{c}$

Exercise 28.1 Light: is it a wave or a particle?

You can imagine the wave properties of light by thinking of light as an oscillating electric and magnetic field moving through space, just as a boat on the surface of water oscillates as a water wave moves through water. You can imagine the **quantum** or particle properties of light by thinking of light as many cars all moving at the same, fast speed along a road, carrying energy. This exercise is about these ideas.

The Planck constant, $h = 6.63 \times 10^{-34}$ J s.

1 Light shows wave properties such as reflection, refraction, diffraction and interference.

    a State which two of these properties best suggest that light is a wave rather than a particle.

    b Describe how the dark positions in Young's double-slit pattern can be explained if light is a wave, but cannot be explained if light is a series of particles.

2   a Describe what happens in photoelectric emission.

    b Describe an experiment that demonstrates this **photoelectric effect**.

3 The wave theory tries to explain photoelectric emission as the slow absorption of energy by electrons from the wave, eventually giving them enough energy to escape. However, various observations in photoelectric emission suggest that light has particle properties, one of which is that there is a **threshold frequency**.

    a State what is meant by *threshold frequency*.

    b Explain how it is difficult to explain a threshold frequency using wave theory.

    c Explain how threshold frequency is explained in the particle theory, if the energy of the **photon** depends on frequency.

    d State two other observations about photoelectric emission that suggest light has particle properties.

4 The light from a lamp is made brighter but the colour is kept the same.

    a Use wave theory to state what happens to the amplitude, frequency and speed of the light.

    b Use particle theory to state what happens to the energy of a photon and the number of photons emitted per second.

The light causes photoelectric emission. The light intensity is steadily increased.

    c State what happens to the maximum energy of the emitted electrons.

    d State what happens to the number of electrons emitted per second.

5 Light from a source does not cause the photoelectric effect when it hits a metal surface. A student suggests making the light brighter will then allow photoelectric emission to occur.

    a Use the particle theory to explain why this is wrong.

    b Suggest two changes that may allow photoelectric emission to occur.

KEY WORD

quantum: the smallest amount of a quantity that exists independently, particularly the photon as the smallest amount of electromagnetic radiation that can be emitted or absorbed

---

KEY WORDS

photoelectric effect: the emission of an electron from the surface of a metal when light shines on the surface

threshold frequency: the minimum frequency of electromagnetic radiation that will eject electrons from the surface of a metal

photon: a quantum of electromagnetic energy

6   a   Calculate the energy of a photon with a frequency of 6.0×10^{14} Hz.

    b   Calculate the momentum of a photon with a frequency of 6.0×10^{14} Hz.

    c   Calculate the energy of a photon with a wavelength of 4.0×10^{-7} m.

    d   Calculate the momentum of a photon with a wavelength of 4.0×10^{-7} m.

7   A lamp emits 10 J of energy each second as light of frequency 5.0×10^{14} Hz.

    a   Calculate the energy of one photon of this light.

    b   Calculate the number of photons emitted per second.

8   Light is incident on a metal surface, and causes photoelectric emission. The frequency of the light is increased, but the total amount of light energy incident on the surface each second is constant.

    a   State what happens to the energy of each photon.

    b   State what happens to the number of photons per second in the incident light.

    c   State what happens to the rate of emission of the electrons from the surface.

    d   State what happens to the maximum kinetic energy of an electron emitted from the surface.

Exercise 28.2 The photoelectric equation

This exercise provides practice in understanding and using the photoelectric equation:

energy of photon = work function energy + maximum kinetic energy of electron emitted

Speed of electromagnetic radiation, $c = 3.0 \times 10^8$ m s^{-1}.

The **Planck constant**, $h = 6.63 \times 10^{-34}$ J s.

1   a   Explain the term *photon*.

    b   State what is meant by *work function energy*.

    c   Explain why the equation gives a maximum value for the kinetic energy of the emitted electron.

    d   Suggest why only a few electrons are emitted with the maximum kinetic energy.

2   Photons with energy 1.20×10^{-18} J are incident on a metal surface. The maximum energy of electrons emitted from the surface is 5.0×10^{-19} J. Calculate the **work function** of the metal.

3   Radiation of wavelength 3.0×10^{-7} m falls on a sodium surface. Sodium has a work function of 3.6×10^{-19} J. Calculate the maximum kinetic energy of the electrons emitted.

4   In a photoelectric experiment, electrons of maximum kinetic energy 1.5×10^{-19} J are emitted from a metal surface of work function 3.2×10^{-19} J. Calculate the frequency of the incident radiation.

KEY WORDS

Planck constant (h): a fundamental constant which links the energy of a photon E and its frequency f; $E = hf$

work function: the minimum energy required by a single electron to escape from a metal surface

---

5   When light of frequency 5.3×10^{14} Hz is incident on a metal surface, electrons are emitted with almost zero kinetic energy.

   a   Calculate the **threshold wavelength** of the material of the surface.

   b   Calculate the work function of the surface.

   c   Calculate the maximum kinetic energy of electrons emitted when light of frequency 6.0×10^{14} Hz is used.

6   When electromagnetic radiation of wavelength 400 nm strikes a metal surface, the maximum kinetic energy of the emitted electrons is 1.2×10^{-19} J. Calculate the work function of the metal.

7   The work functions of sodium and zinc are 2.3 eV and 4.3 eV respectively. Explain why only one metal emits electrons when light of frequency 6.0×1014 Hz is incident on the surface.

8   This graph shows the variation with frequency f of the maximum kinetic energy E_k of the electrons emitted from the surface of a metal:

KEY WORDS

threshold wavelength: the maximum wavelength of electromagnetic radiation that will eject electrons from the surface of a metal

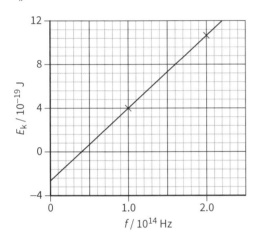

Figure 28.1: For Question 8. Graph showing the variation with frequency f of the maximum kinetic energy E_k of the electrons emitted from the surface of a metal.

   a   Use the photoelectric equation to show that the gradient of the graph is equal to the Planck constant.

   b   Obtain a value for the Planck constant from the graph.

   c   State how the work function energy ϕ can be obtained from the graph.

   d   Obtain a value for the work function energy.

Imagine that the graph is redrawn for a metal with a smaller work function.

   e   State how the gradient and intercept of the new graph compare with the old graph.

Exercise 28.3 Line spectra

This exercise tests your understanding and interpretation of line spectra, and gives you practice in calculating energies.

KEY WORDS

energy level: a quantised energy state of an electron in an atom

1 This diagram shows **energy levels** of the hydrogen atom:

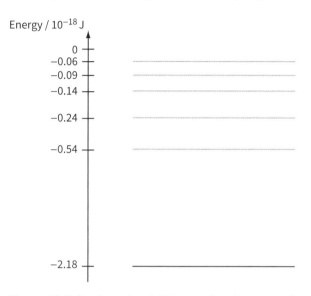

Figure 28.2: For Question 1. Diagram showing energy levels of the hydrogen atom.

An electron is in the energy level at -0.24×10^{-18} J. The electron can emit or absorb a photon to change levels.

a Complete this table to show the energy of the photon emitted if this electron moves to a new level, and state whether the atom emits or absorbs a photon for the electron to move to the new level:

Energy of new level	Energy of photon emitted or absorbed	Does the electron emit or absorb a photon to move to the new level?
-0.54×10^{-18} J		
-0.14×10^{-18} J		
-2.18×10^{-18} J		
-0.09×10^{-18} J		

Table 28.1: For Question 2a.

KEY WORDS

emission line spectrum: a series of discrete wavelengths emitted by an atom

absorption line spectrum: a pattern of dark lines or discrete wavelengths in a continuous spectrum caused by the absorption of electromagnetic radiation

b Apart from absorbing a photon, suggest two other ways in which the electron can be made to move to a higher level.

2 a Describe the difference between an *emission* line spectrum and an *absorption* line spectrum.

b Explain why the lines in an **emission line spectrum** of a gas occur at the same wavelengths as the lines in the **absorption line spectrum** of the same gas.

c   Describe how to show an emission line spectrum of a gas.

d   Describe how to show an absorption line spectrum of a gas.

3   This diagram shows four energy levels of the helium atom:

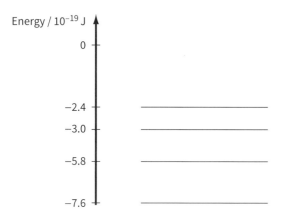

Figure 28.3: For Question 3. Diagram showing four energy levels of the helium atom.

An emission line spectrum is formed when electrons **transition** between these levels.

a   Show how six different lines are found in the spectrum involving these levels.

b   State the two levels associated with the line in the spectrum with the highest frequency.

c   For the line in the spectrum with the highest frequency, calculate the energy of the photon emitted.

d   State the two levels associated with the line in the spectrum with the longest wavelength.

Exercise 28.4 De Broglie wavelength

Electrons can be shown to have wave properties, even though they have particle properties. This exercise develops your understanding of the different particle and wave properties, and the relationships between them.

1   Explain what is meant by the **de Broglie wavelength** of an electron.

2   An electron has a mass of 9.11×10^{-31} kg. Planck's constant h is 6.63×10^{-34} J s.

a   Calculate the de Broglie wavelength of an electron if its speed is 1.6×10^{6} m s^{-1}.

b   Calculate the momentum of an electron if its kinetic energy is 4.0×10^{-16} J.

c   Calculate the de Broglie wavelength of the electron if its kinetic energy is 4.0×10^{-16} J.

3   A neutron of mass 1.7×10^{-27} kg has a de Broglie wavelength of 5.0×10^{-12} m.

a   Calculate its momentum.

b   Calculate its speed.

4 Electron energies are often given in **electronvolts (eV)**. 1 eV = 1.6×10^{-19} J.

An electron is accelerated from rest through a potential difference of 1000 V.

   a Calculate the final kinetic energy of the electron in J.

   b Determine the final speed of the electron.

   c Calculate the final momentum of the electron.

   d Calculate the de Broglie wavelength of the electron.

5 Sometimes electrons behave like particles and sometimes they behave like waves.

   a State an example of a wave behaviour of an electron.

   b State which term in the de Broglie equation $\lambda = \frac{h}{p}$ refers to wave behaviour and which term refers to particle behaviour.

   c Show that the de Broglie equation has the same units on each side of the equation.

6 A person of mass 50 kg walks at a speed of $0.20 \, \text{m s}^{-1}$.

   a Calculate their de Broglie wavelength.

   b Suggest why it is difficult to show diffraction with a wave of this wavelength but it is possible to show diffraction with a wave of the wavelength you calculated in question 4.

> KEY WORD
>
> **electronvolt (eV):** the energy gained by an electron travelling through a potential difference of 1 volt
> 1 eV = 1.60×10^{-19} J

EXAM-STYLE QUESTIONS

1 In the photoelectric effect, when electromagnetic radiation strikes the surface of a metal, electrons leave the metal surface. However, when radiation of less than a certain frequency strikes the surface, it is observed that there is no emission of electrons.

   a Explain why there is no emission of an electron if the frequency is too low. [2]

   b State two other pieces of evidence provided by the photoelectric effect which suggest that electromagnetic radiation has particle properties. [2]

   c The work function of the metal is 3.8 eV. Calculate the minimum frequency of electromagnetic radiation that causes photoelectric emission. [2]

   d An electron at the surface of the metal is emitted with a kinetic energy of 4.5×10^{-19} J. Calculate the energy of the incident photon in eV. [2]

[Total: 8]

2 Electrons are known to show wave properties, with a wavelength given by the de Broglie equation.

   a State the de Broglie equation in words. [1]

   b Show that the wavelength of an electron of kinetic energy E is given by the equation:

   $$\lambda = \frac{h}{\sqrt{(2mE)}}$$

   where m is the mass of the electron. [2]

CONTINUED

   c   Calculate the de Broglie wavelength of an electron accelerated through a p.d. of 2.0 kV.   **[2]**

   d   The electrons in part **c** are passed through a crystal structure and diffract. Explain why the electrons are diffracted.   **[1]**

                                                              [Total: 6]

3 **a**   Explain how an emission line spectrum provides evidence for the existence of discrete electron energy levels in atoms.   **[3]**

   b   Electron transitions between three levels A, B, and C in this energy diagram produce electromagnetic radiation of wavelengths 557 nm and 358 nm:

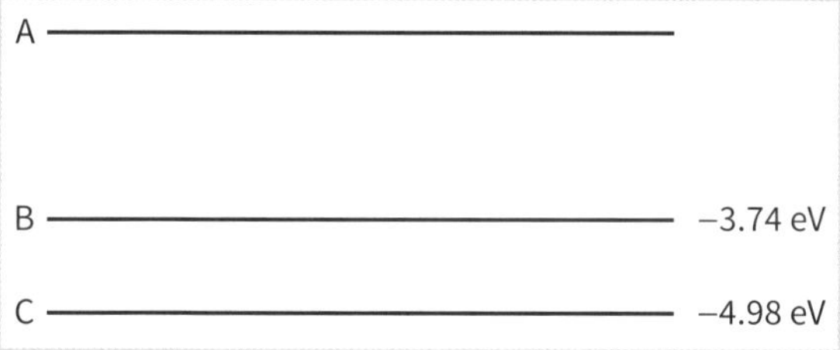

Figure 28.4

     i   Calculate the energy of photons of these two wavelengths.   **[2]**

     ii   Describe the transitions that give rise to each of these two wavelengths.   **[2]**

     iii   Calculate the value of the energy level A.   **[2]**

     iv   Calculate the wavelength of another line produced by transition between these three levels.   **[2]**

                                                             [Total: 11]

4 **a**   State an effect that provides evidence that:

     i   light acts as a particle   **[1]**

     ii   an electron acts like a wave.   **[1]**

   b   Four electron levels in an isolated atom have energy levels −0.50 eV, −0.89 eV, −1.56 eV and −3.6 eV.

     Calculate:

     i   the smallest wavelength of electromagnetic radiation emitted due to transition between these levels. Explain your working.   **[3]**

     ii   the momentum of a photon having the wavelength calculated in **i**. **[2]**

   c **i**   State what is meant by the de Broglie wavelength.   **[2]**

     ii   Calculate the speed of an electron having a de Broglie wavelength equal to the wavelength in **b**.   **[2]**

                                                             [Total: 11]

Chapter 29

Nuclear physics

CHAPTER OUTLINE

- recall and use the relationship $E = mc^2$
- define and understand the terms mass defect, binding energy, activity, half-life and decay constant
- represent simple nuclear reactions by nuclear equations of the form:

  $^{14}_{7}N + ^{4}_{2}He \rightarrow ^{17}_{8}O + ^{1}_{1}H$

- sketch the variation of binding energy per nucleon with nucleon number
- explain what is meant by nuclear fusion and nuclear fission, and the relevance of binding energy
- describe the spontaneous and random nature of nuclear decay
- recall $A = \lambda N$ and use it to solve problems
- use the relationship $x = x_0 e^{-\lambda t}$, including sketching exponential decay graphs
- solve problems using the relation $\lambda = \dfrac{0.693}{t_{1/2}}$

KEY EQUATIONS

energy = mass × speed of light in free space^2; $E = mc^2$

activity of a radioactive sample = –(decay constant of the isotope) × number of undecayed nuclei; $A = \lambda N$

radioactive decay: $x = x_0 e^{-\lambda t}$

relationship between half-life and decay constant; $\lambda = \dfrac{0.693}{t_{1/2}}$

Exercise 29.1 Balancing equations

This exercise provides practice in balancing nuclear equations, as well as recognising particles and types of reaction.

1   Determine the particle X in the nuclear reaction:

   $^{14}_{7}N + ^{1}_{0}n \rightarrow ^{14}_{6}C + X$

2   A nuclear reaction is:

   $^{235}_{92}U + ^{1}_{0}n \rightarrow ^{90}_{38}Sr + ^{144}_{54}Xe + 2^{x}_{y}X$

   a   Determine the value of x.

   b   Determine the value of y.

c State the name of the particle $_y^x X$.

d State the name of this type of nuclear reaction.

3 A nuclear reaction is written as $4_1^1 H \rightarrow {}_2^4 He + x_1^0 e + 2v$, where v is a neutrino.

a Determine the value of x.

b State the name of the particle $_1^0 e$.

c State the name of this type of nuclear reaction.

d Explain why high temperatures are needed in order for the $_1^1 H$ particles to come together.

4 A nuclear reaction is written as:

$$_{92}^{238} U \rightarrow {}_{90}^x Th + {}_2^4 He$$

a Determine the value of x.

b State the name of the particle $_2^4 He$.

c State the name of this type of nuclear reaction.

5 Helium-3 (proton number 2) absorbs a neutron to become another isotope of helium. Write down the nuclear reaction.

6 A boron-10 nucleus $\left({}_5^{10} B \right)$ absorbs a neutron and emits a nucleus of lithium-7 $\left({}_3^7 Li \right)$ and an alpha-particle. Write down the nuclear reaction.

Exercise 29.2 Mass defect and binding energy

Mass defect, **binding energy**, nucleon number and proton number are all different quantities for a particular nucleus. This exercise develops your understanding of these terms. You also need to understand that masses can be measured in kg or in terms of the unified **atomic mass unit** u, and that energy can be measured in joules or electronvolts.

1 Match each quantity with its definition:

Quantity	Definition
binding energy	the difference between the total mass of the individual, separate nucleons and the mass of the nucleus
nucleon number	the minimum external energy required to separate all the nucleons in a nucleus to infinity
mass defect	the total number of protons and neutrons in one nucleus

Table 29.1: For Question 1.

2 a Calculate the energy equivalence of $1.0\,g$ of matter.

b Show that $1.0\,u$ has an energy equivalence of $930\,MeV$.

c Explain why a neutron has no nuclear binding energy.

KEY WORDS

mass defect: the difference between the total mass of the individual, separate nucleons and the mass of the nucleus

binding energy: the minimum external energy required to completely separate all the nucleons in a nucleus to infinity

atomic mass unit: $\frac{1}{12}$ of the mass of a neutral atom of carbon-12, equal to $1.66 \times 10^{-27}\,kg$

TIP

Remember: $E = mc^2$ uses mass in kg.

---

3   The mass of a thorium-228 nucleus = 3.7857×10^{-25} kg

The rest mass of a proton = 1.6726×10^{-27} kg

The rest mass of a neutron = 1.6749×10^{-27} kg

   a   Calculate the number of protons and the number of neutrons in one $^{228}_{90}$Th nucleus.

   b   Calculate the total mass, in kg, of all the nucleons when they are separated from the nucleus. Give your answer for **b** to as many significant figures as you can so that the mass defect in **c** is accurate.

   c   Calculate the mass defect of $^{228}_{90}$Th, in kg.

   d   Calculate the binding energy of $^{228}_{90}$Th, in J.

   e   Calculate the binding energy of $^{228}_{90}$Th, in eV.

4   The masses of three particles are:

    • helium-4 nucleus = 4.0015 u

    • proton = 1.0073 u

    • neutron = 1.0087 u.

   a   Calculate the mass defect of a helium-4 nucleus, in u.

   b   Calculate the mass defect of a helium-4 nucleus, in kg.

   c   Calculate the binding energy of a helium-4 nucleus, in J.

   d   Calculate the binding energy of a helium-4 nucleus, in eV.

5   The binding energy of a $^{2}_{1}$H nucleus is 2.24 MeV. A nucleus contains one proton and one neutron.

    • rest mass of proton = $1.672\,62 \times 10^{-27}$ kg

    • rest mass of neutron = $1.674\,93 \times 10^{-27}$ kg

   a   Calculate the binding energy of the nucleus, in J.

   b   Calculate the mass defect of the nucleus, in kg.

   c   Calculate the total mass of the proton and neutron when separated to infinity, in kg. Keep all significant figures.

   d   Calculate the mass of the nucleus, in kg.

> **TIP**
>
> You will need to look up the mass of 1 u in kg, then use $E = mc^2$. This gives the energy in joules. The conversion factor between energies in J and in eV is the charge on the electron, 1 eV = 1.6×10^{-19} J.

6   One possible reaction when a neutron strikes a uranium nucleus is:

$$^{1}_{0}n + ^{235}_{92}U \rightarrow ^{90}_{36}Kr + ^{144}_{56}Ba + 2\,^{1}_{0}n$$

    • mass of $^{1}_{0}n$ = 1.009 u

    • mass of $^{235}_{92}U$ = 235.124 u

    • mass of $^{90}_{36}Kr$ = 89.920 u

    • mass of $^{144}_{56}Ba$ = 143.923 u

   a   Calculate the change in rest mass during the whole reaction, in u.

   b   Calculate the energy released, in joules, by one such reaction.

Exercise 29.3 Binding energy per nucleon, fusion and fission

In this exercise you will develop your understanding of the difference between binding energy and binding energy per nucleon, and how they are used to calculate the energy released in a nuclear reaction.

1 a Copy and complete this table:

Nuclide	Number of nucleons	Binding energy / MeV	Binding energy per nucleon / MeV
$^{235}_{92}\text{U}$			7.6
$^{56}_{26}\text{Fe}$		492	
$^{87}_{35}\text{Br}$			8.6

Table 29.2: For Question 1a.

b State which of the three nuclides in the table is most stable. Explain how the table shows this.

2 A simple **nuclear fusion** reaction is:

$$^2_1\text{H} + {}^2_1\text{H} \rightarrow {}^4_2\text{He}$$

The binding energy per nucleon for ^4_2He is 7.1 and for ^2_1H is 1.1 MeV.

a Calculate the binding energy of ^2_1H. (This is for the whole nucleus, not the binding energy per nucleon.)

b Calculate the binding energy of ^4_2He.

c Calculate the energy released in the nuclear reaction.

3 This graph shows the binding energy per nucleon plotted against nucleon number:

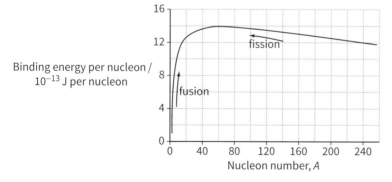

Figure 29.1: For Question 3. Graph showing the binding energy per nucleon plotted against nucleon number.

KEY WORDS

nuclear fusion: a nuclear reaction in which two light nuclei join together to form a heavier nucleus

TIP

If the total binding energy on the left of the equation is different from the total binding energy on the right, then energy must be released – the difference in the totals.

Fission and fusion are nuclear processes that give out energy.

a   Use the graph to estimate the nucleon number of the most stable isotope.

b   State the difference between fission and fusion in terms of the nuclei involved.

c   Use the graph to explain how **nuclear fission** and nuclear fusion both liberate energy.

d   Explain why the energy given out per nucleon from fusion is greater than the energy given out per nucleon from fission.

e   Explain why two nuclei of $^{110}_{48}Cd$ cannot produce energy by fusing together.

f   Use the graph to estimate the binding energy of a U-238 nucleus.

g   Use the graph to estimate the binding energy of a nucleus with nucleon number 119.

h   In fission, a nucleus of U-238 splits into two nuclei of nucleon number of about 119. Use your answers to **f** and **g** to estimate the energy emitted.

i   Use your answer to **h** to calculate the energy released in the fission of 1 g of uranium-238. Remember, 6.02×10^{23} atoms (the Avogadro constant) is contained in one mole of material; in this case, 238 g or that the mass of one nucleus is close to 238 u.

Exercise 29.4 Half-life and the decay constant

This exercise provides practice in determining **half-lives** and dealing with **exponential decay** equations. You should also recognise the difference between a **random decay** and a **spontaneous decay**.

The problem is recognising which equation to use.

Use $\lambda = \frac{0.693}{t_{1/2}}$ to find half-life from the **decay constant** or vice versa.

Use $A = \lambda N$ to relate **activity** and number of nuclei *at one instant of time*.

Use $x = x_0 e^{-\lambda t}$ to relate *the same quantity* at *different times; x* can be activity or the number of undecayed nuclei.

Watch out for the units of time. If half-life is measured in *hours* then the decay constant is in hours^{-1} and if you then use $A = \lambda N$, the activity A is in number of decays per hour.

1   Copy and complete the following table. Include the units of your answers. You can use the formula $x = x_0 e^{-\lambda t}$ to calculate the last two columns but you may be able to use simple ideas about halving in one half-life, particularly in **a** and **e**.

KEY WORDS

nuclear fission: the splitting of a nucleus into smaller nuclei

KEY WORDS

half-life: the time taken for half the number of active nuclei in a radioactive sample to decay

exponential decay: describes the decrease of a quantity where the rate of decrease is proportional to the value of the quantity

radioactive decay constant: the probability that an individual nucleus will decay per unit time interval

activity: the number of nuclei in a sample that decay per unit time interval

	Half-life	Decay constant	Initial number of nuclei	Initial activity	Number of undecayed nuclei left after 10 s	Activity after 10 s
a	5.0 s		1000			
b		0.0020 s⁻¹		10 Bq		
c	100 s		100			
d			10 000	1000 Bq		
e			4000		1000	

Table 29.3: For Question 1.

2 A radioactive nuclide has a half-life of 300 minutes. It initially contains 1.8×10^6 radioactive atoms.

   a Calculate the decay constant of the nuclide in min⁻¹.
   b Calculate the initial activity of the nuclide in min⁻¹.
   c Calculate the initial activity in Bq.

3 The half-life of potassium-42 is 12 hours.

   a Calculate the decay constant in h⁻¹.
   b Calculate the decay constant in s⁻¹.
   c Calculate the percentage of the original radioactive potassium present after 12 hours.
   d Calculate the percentage of the original radioactive potassium present after 20 hours.

4 A sample of bone contains 5.0×10^{-14} g of carbon-14 and has an activity of 30 Bq.

   a Use the Avogadro constant to find the number of carbon-14 atoms in the sample.
   b Calculate the decay constant.
   c Calculate the half-life.
   d Calculate the time before the activity falls to 6.0 Bq.

TIP

Remember N_A is the number of atoms in one mole, which is the nucleon number in grams; in this case, 14 g or that the mass of a single carbon-14 atom is close to 14 u.

EXAM-STYLE QUESTIONS

1 A small number of the atoms in the atmosphere are those of the isotope tritium ^3_1H. These atoms are unstable and their radioactive decay is both random and spontaneous.

   a i   Explain what is meant by *spontaneous decay*. [1]
      ii Explain what is meant by *random decay*. [1]
      iii State an experimental observation that suggests that radioactive decay is random. [1]
   b A nucleus of tritium ^3_1H decays by the emission of a beta-minus particle and an antineutrino to form an isotope of helium (He).

CONTINUED

The rest masses of a tritium nucleus, the helium nucleus formed, a beta-particle, a proton and a neutron are shown in this table. The antineutrino has negligible mass:

	Mass / u
tritium nucleus	3.016 050
helium-3 nucleus	3.014 932
beta-particle	0.000 549
proton	1.007 277
neutron	1.008 665

Table 29.4

i   Write down the nuclear equation that represents the decay of tritium.   [2]

ii   Calculate the mass defect of a tritium nucleus.   [2]

iii   Explain the term *binding energy* of a nucleus.   [2]

iv   Calculate the binding energy, in joules, of a tritium nucleus.   [3]

v   Calculate the energy released in the decay of a tritium nucleus.   [2]

[Total: 14]

2   The isotope sodium-22 $\left(^{22}_{11}\text{Na}\right)$ undergoes β^+-decay to form neon-22, which is stable.

The half-life of sodium-22 is 2.60 years.

a   Write down the nuclear equation for the decay.   [2]

b   i   Define *radioactive decay constant*.   [1]

ii   Calculate the decay constant of sodium-22.   [2]

iii   Explain, in words, why a nucleus with a small decay constant has a long half-life.   [2]

c   A pure sample of sodium-22 has an initial activity of 1.7×10^3 Bq.

i   Calculate the initial number of sodium-22 nuclei in the sample.   [2]

ii   Calculate the number of sodium-22 nuclei that remain in the sample after 5.0 years.   [3]

iii   After 5.0 years, the sample contains only sodium-22 and neon-22 nuclei. Use your answers to parts **i** and **ii** to calculate the ratio:

$$\frac{\text{number of sodium-22 nuclei after 5.0 years}}{\text{number of neon-22 nuclei after 5.0 years}}$$ [2]

[Total: 14]

CONTINUED

3 **a** Explain what is meant by the phrase *radioactivity is random*. [1]

   b Uranium-235 was present during the formation of the Earth. Of an original sample of uranium-235, only 1.1% of the original amount is present in rocks today. The half-life of uranium-235 is 7.0×10^8 years. Calculate the age of the Earth suggested by this data. [3]

   c **i** Sketch a graph of binding energy per nucleon against nucleon number for naturally occurring nuclides. [2]

      ii Use your graph to explain how energy is released when some nuclides undergo fission and when other nuclides undergo fusion. [3]

[Total: 9]

4 In 2011 an accident in a nuclear power station in Japan released radioactive iodine-131 into the environment. The half-life of iodine-131 is 8.0 days.

   a Define *activity* of radioactive material. [1]

   b The count from a sample of seaweed near the power station was measured in a laboratory far from the power station over a period of 20 minutes. The readings of the count obtained, corrected for background radiation, were 3940, 4020, 3860.

      i Explain why the readings are different from one another. [1]

      ii Estimate the count obtained in a time of 20 minutes when the same sample of seaweed is analysed 10 days later. [3]

   c Iodine-131 is formed in a nuclear reactor during nuclear fission of uranium-235.

      i Explain what is meant by the *nuclear fission* of uranium-235. [2]

      ii Explain, using ideas about binding energy per nucleon, why energy is released during nuclear fission. [2]

[Total: 9]

> Chapter 30

Medical imaging

CHAPTER OUTLINE

- explain the principles of medical imaging of internal body structures using X-rays, ultrasound and positron emission tomography (PET) scanning

- describe the main features of a modern X-ray tube

- solve problems concerning the attenuation of X-rays and ultrasound in matter

- understand the principles and purpose of computerised axial tomography (CT) scanning

- understand and use the terms specific acoustic impedance and intensity in relation to ultrasound

KEY EQUATIONS

acoustic impedance = density × speed of sound; $Z = \rho c$

fraction of ultrasound reflected $\dfrac{I_r}{I_0} = \dfrac{(Z_2 - Z_1)^2}{(Z_2 + Z_1)^2}$

attenuation of ultrasound and X-rays in matter: $I = I_0 e^{-\mu x}$

energy of a photon = Planck constant × frequency; $E = hf$

momentum of a photon = $\dfrac{\text{energy of a photon}}{\text{speed of electromagnetic radiation in a vacuum}}$; $p = \dfrac{E}{c}$

Exercise 30.1 Producing X-rays

X-rays have been used to make images of the insides of human beings for 120 years. This exercise is about the nature of X-rays and how they are produced.

1   X-rays are produced for medical imaging. This diagram shows the construction of a typical X-ray tube:

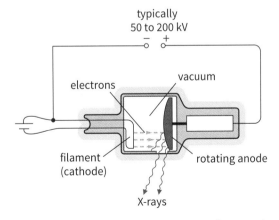

Figure 30.1: For Question 1. Diagram showing the construction of a typical X-ray tube.

a State the names of the positive and negative electrodes.

b Explain why a high voltage is needed between the two electrodes.

c Describe the type of field that exists between the two electrodes.

d Explain why a vacuum is needed in the tube.

e X-rays are emitted over a large angle. Only those emerging from the tube are shown. State the name of the thin-walled section of the tube through which they emerge.

f Describe the energy transfers which occur as electrons emerge from one electrode and strike the other.

g Explain why the anode rotates.

h State the word that describes a beam of X-rays which is roughly parallel-sided.

2 This diagram shows typical X-ray spectra produced using electrons of different energies:

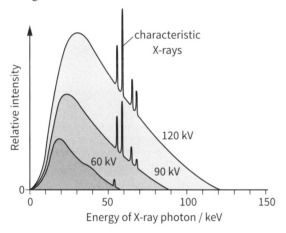

Figure 30.2: For Question 2. Diagram showing typical X-ray spectra produced using electrons of different energies.

a State the greatest accelerating voltage used to produce these spectra.

b Determine the greatest X-ray photon energy produced using an accelerating voltage of 100 kV.

Each of the three spectral curves consists of two parts: **braking radiation** and **characteristic radiation**.

c Which of these two parts has a continuous spectrum?

d State the word that describes the other spectrum.

e State the minimum X-ray energy in the braking radiation spectrum.

f Describe how the *peak energy* of the braking spectrum changes as the accelerating voltage is increased.

g Describe how the *peak intensity* of the braking spectrum changes as the accelerating voltage is increased.

Consider a single line in the characteristic X-ray spectrum.

h Describe how the *energy* of the spectral line changes as the accelerating voltage is increased.

i Describe how the *intensity* of the spectral line changes as the accelerating voltage is increased.

KEY WORDS

braking radiation: X-ray emissions produced by an electron as it collides successively with a series of atoms, giving up its kinetic energy. A whole range of different energy X-rays may be produced

characteristic radiation: X-ray radiation produced when an inner electron is knocked out of its orbital by an incident electron. The X-ray is produced when another electron drops from a higher energy orbital. Each drop produces an X-ray of a specific energy

3 This question is about energy units.

  a The energy of an electron or photon may be quoted in eV. State the full name of this unit. State the value of 1 eV in J.

  b Convert each of the following energy values to J: 100 eV, 500 keV, 2.2 MeV.

  c Convert each of the following energy values to eV: 8.0×10^{-19} J, 8.0×10^{-16} J, 2.56×10^{-14} J.

The energy E of a photon is related to its frequency f by $E = hf$, where the Planck constant $h = 6.63 \times 10^{-34}$ J s.

  d Calculate the energy of an X-ray photon of frequency 4.0×10^{18} Hz.

  e Calculate the frequency of an X-ray photon of energy 60 keV.

An electron is accelerated through a p.d. of 80 kV. Its energy is converted into a single X-ray photon.

  f Calculate the frequency of the photon.

  g Calculate the wavelength of the X-ray in free space.

    Remember, the speed of electromagnetic radiation in free space is: $c = f\lambda$, where $c = 3.0 \times 10^8$ m s^{-1}.

Exercise 30.2 X-rays and matter

This exercise is about how X-rays interact with matter and how high-quality X-ray images can be produced.

1 X-ray photons carry energy. If a beam of X-rays is spread over a large area, its **intensity** I will be low. This is represented by the equation:

$$I = \frac{P}{A}$$

  a What quantities are represented by the symbols P and A in this equation? Give their names and their SI units.

  b Calculate the intensity of an X-ray beam of power 150 W passing through an area of 60 cm². Give your answer in kW m⁻². Take care when converting cm² to m².

When a beam of X-rays enters a patient's body, its intensity is *attenuated*. This graph shows how the intensity changes as the beam passes through flesh and bone:

> **KEY WORD**
>
> **intensity:** power transmitted normally per unit cross-sectional area

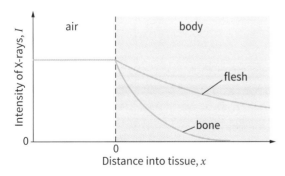

Figure 30.3: For Question 1b Graph showing attenuation of intensity of X-rays with distance in tissue.

c Explain how you can tell from the graph that the beam is **collimated** (parallel-sided) as it passes through the air.

d Of the three materials represented (air, flesh, bone), which absorbs X-rays most strongly? Explain how you can tell.

e Which material is the least absorbing? Explain how you can tell.

The intensity of the X-rays decreases exponentially as it passes through flesh and bone. This can be characterised by the *half-thickness* of the material.

f Explain what is meant by half-thickness. Include a sketch graph of intensity against distance in your answer.

g Which has a greater half-thickness: flesh or bone?

2 The intensity of an X-ray beam decreases as it passes through biological material according to the equation $I = I_0 e^{-\mu x}$, where μ is the **attenuation coefficient** of the material.

a The quantity $\frac{I}{I_0}$ is the fraction of the initial intensity that remains after the beam has passed through a thickness x of the material. Rearrange the equation for I to make $\frac{I}{I_0}$ its subject.

b Calculate the fraction of the intensity of a 250 keV X-ray beam that remains after it has passed through 4.0 cm of bone whose attenuation coefficient $\mu = 0.32$ cm^{-1}.

c Determine the fraction that has been absorbed by the bone.

d Calculate the value of $\frac{I}{I_0}$ when x = the half-thickness of the absorbing material.

e Use this idea to calculate the half-thickness of bone for 250 keV X-rays.

3 Medical physicists try to produce the best possible X-ray images while causing as little damage as possible to the patient.

They want to produce images which are as **sharp** as possible, and with as much **contrast** as possible.

a Explain why it is important to keep the radiation dose to the patient as low as possible.

b Explain how an image intensifier helps to keep the radiation dose low.

c A narrow X-ray beam can be produced by reducing the size of the window of the X-ray tube. Explain how this helps to improve the X-ray image.

d Explain what is meant by the term *contrast* in connection with X-ray images.

e Explain how a barium meal helps to improve the contrast of an X-ray image.

4 A **CT scan** is a technique that can be used to produce images of a patient's organs.

a What does 'CT' stand for?

b Explain briefly how a CT scan differs from a conventional X-ray image.

c Explain how a CT scan can help to reduce the exposure of healthy organs to damaging X-rays.

KEY WORDS

collimated beam: a beam with parallel sides (this means that the beam does not spread out)

attenuation (or absorption) coefficient: the fraction of a beam of X-rays that is absorbed per unit thickness of the absorber

TIP

Remember to calculate the value of the exponent first.

KEY WORDS

sharpness (of an image): the degree of resolution of an image, which determines the smallest item that can be seen

contrast (of an image): is the difference in brightness between the brightest and the darkest areas

CT scanning: computerised axial tomography (CT or CAT) scanning, a technique in which X-rays are used to image the body, producing a 3D image of an internal structure

Exercise 30.3 Ultrasound scanning

Ultrasound waves are mechanical waves similar to sound waves and are not thought to have any damaging side-effects for patients in normal use. This exercise looks at how they are produced and used in medicine.

KEY WORD

ultrasound: sound waves of frequencies higher than 20 kHz

1 Ultrasound waves travel at about $330\,\text{m s}^{-1}$ in air, $1500\,\text{m s}^{-1}$ in water and $1590\,\text{m s}^{-1}$ in tissue such as muscle.

    a Explain the term *ultrasound*.

    b Calculate the wavelength of ultrasound waves of frequency 40 kHz in water and in muscle tissue.

    c The speed of an ultrasound wave changes as it passes from air into tissue. State whether the frequency increases, decreases or stays the same, and whether the wavelength increases, decreases or stays the same.

    d To resolve small objects, it is necessary to use ultrasound with a wavelength comparable to the size of the objects. Suggest a suitable frequency of ultrasound if you wish to observe kidney stones of diameter 2 mm.

2 This diagram shows an ultrasound *transducer* – this means that it both produces and detects ultrasound waves:

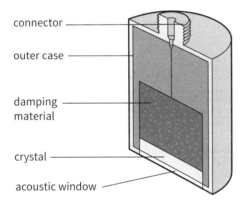

connector

outer case

damping material

crystal

acoustic window

Figure 30.4: For Question 2. Diagram showing a cross-section through an ultrasound transducer.

    a The **piezo-electric** crystal is the part which generates ultrasound waves. Describe how it is caused to vibrate.

    b Explain the function of the acoustic window.

The transducer sends pulses of ultrasound into the patient's body. It also detects ultrasound waves reflected from inside the body.

    c Describe how the crystal behaves when the reflected waves reach it.

    d Explain why the ultrasound waves are sent out in pulses.

    e Explain the function of the damping material.

The crystal is usually made of polyvinylidene difluoride. The speed of sound in this material is $2200\,\text{m s}^{-1}$.

    f Calculate the wavelength of ultrasound waves of frequency 2.2 MHz in this material.

    g The thickness of the crystal is usually one half-wavelength. Calculate this value.

KEY WORDS

piezo-electric effect: the production of an e.m.f. across a crystal by putting the crystal under stress; the opposite effect is applying a p.d. across the crystal causing it to change shape

3 This diagram shows what happens when an ultrasound wave strikes the boundary between two different materials.

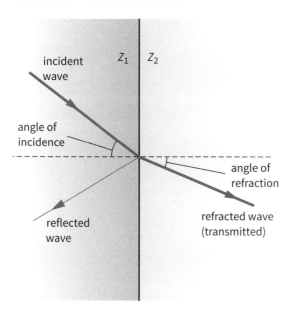

Figure 30.5: For Question 3. Diagram showing what happens when an ultrasound wave strikes the boundary between two different materials.

a Only part of the wave is transmitted. State what happens to the rest of the ultrasound.

b Explain what causes the wave to change direction.

The fraction of the intensity of the ultrasound wave reflected is given by:

$$\frac{I_r}{I_0} = \frac{(Z_2 - Z_1)^2}{(Z_2 + Z_1)^2}$$

where Z represents the **acoustic impedance** of the material.

This table gives values of Z for air and for three different tissues:

Material	Acoustic impedance Z / $\mathrm{kg\,m^{-2}\,s^{-1}}$
air	400
fat	1.34×10^6
muscle	1.71×10^6
bone	6.40×10^6

Table 30.1: For Question 3b.

c Fat and muscle have similar values for Z. Calculate the fraction of an ultrasound beam transmitted when passing from muscle to fat.

d Using data from the table, explain why a boundary between bone and muscle will give a strong reflected signal.

KEY WORDS

acoustic impedance: the product of the density of the substance and the speed of the ultrasound in the substance

TIP

Take care! The equation tells you the fraction *reflected*.

e   Air has a very low acoustic impedance. This means that very little of an ultrasound wave will pass from air into tissue. Explain how this problem may be overcome when a patient is given an ultrasound scan.

4   This diagram shows how ultrasound can be used to investigate a patient's bone:

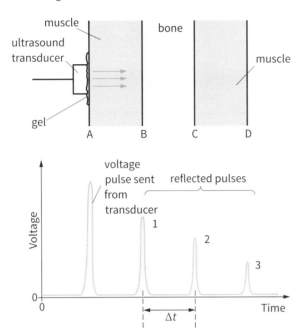

Figure 30.6: For Question 4. Diagram showing how ultrasound can be used to investigate a patient's bone and a resulting graph of transducer voltage against time.

a   Explain how the reflected ultrasound waves can provide information about the *thickness* of the bone.

b   Explain how the intensity of the reflected ultrasound waves can provide information about the nature of the tissues through which they have passed.

Exercise 30.4 PET scanning

PET scanning involves introducing a **radioactive tracer** that is absorbed in certain parts of the body. When a nucleus of the tracer decays it emits a positron which annihilates with an electron to produce two gamma ray photons. These are detected and the line between the detectors shows that the initial decay occurred on this line.

1   a   Describe what is meant by a *radioactive tracer*.

    b   State the type of decay that the tracer undergoes in PET scanning.

    c   The radioactive tracer is usually attached to a glucose molecule before being introduced into the body. State what happens to the glucose molecule after it is introduced into the body.

    d   The tracer usually has a short half-life for its decay. State one advantage and one disadvantage of having a short half-life.

KEY WORDS

PET scanning: positron emission tomography involves introducing a radioactive tracer into the body and produces images to show where the radioactive substance is concentrated

radioactive tracer: a substance that consists of radioactive material attached to a natural chemical, such as glucose

2   In an electron–positron **annihilation event**, a positron interacts with an electron. They may be taken to be initially at rest. Two gamma ray photons are formed that travel in opposite directions.

   a   Using the equation $E = mc^2$, calculate the kinetic energy of one of the gamma ray photons formed. Give your answer in J and in keV.

   b   State two quantities that are conserved during the annihilation.

   c   Explain why two gamma ray photons must be emitted rather than one, and why they must travel in opposite directions.

3   In one type of PET scanner, known as a time-of-flight scanner, the time that each of the photons reaches the ring of detectors around the patient is measured.

   If the annihilation event occurs midway between the detectors, the two photons arrive at the same time. If the event happens closer to one detector, the photon arrives sooner at that detector.

   If the time between detecting the two photons is Δt then one photon takes $\frac{1}{2}\Delta t$ more time and the other takes $\frac{1}{2}\Delta t$ less time than if they were created at the centre.

   a   The time difference between the detection of the two photons is measured as 800 ps. Calculate the distance from the position of the annihilation event to the centre of the line joining the two detectors.

   b   The uncertainty in measuring the time difference with one PET scanner is 400 ps. Calculate the uncertainty that this introduces into measuring position.

   c   Explain how using many annihilations enables an image to be built up of the position of the radioactive substance within the body.

> **KEY WORDS**
>
> **annihilation event:** a positron annihilates on contact with an electron to produce two 500 keV photons travelling in opposite directions

> **TIP**
>
> Remember 1 ps = 10^{-9} s.

EXAM-STYLE QUESTIONS

electron charge $e = -1.60 \times 10^{-19}$ C

Planck constant $h = 6.63 \times 10^{-34}$ J s

1   Ultrasound waves travel at 1590 m s^{-1} in muscle tissue. The density of muscle tissue is 1075 kg m^{-3}.

   a   Explain what is meant by *ultrasound*.   **[1]**

   b   Calculate the acoustic impedance of muscle.   **[2]**

   The acoustic impedances of two other tissue types are:

   • fat: $Z = 1.34 \times 10^6$ kg m^{-2} s^{-1}

   • bone: $Z = 6.40 \times 10^6$ kg m^{-2} s^{-1}.

   c   Use this data to explain why an ultrasound scan will give clearer images of muscle–bone boundaries than muscle–fat boundaries.   **[3]**

                                                          [Total: 6]

CONTINUED

2 X-rays are produced for medical use in an X-ray tube.

An X-ray tube has a p.d. between the anode and cathode of 115 kV.

a Calculate the maximum energy (in J) of X-ray photons produced in such a tube. [2]

b Calculate the maximum frequency of these X-rays. [2]

X-rays can be used to produce images of bones that are embedded in muscle tissue. The attenuation coefficient for bone: $\mu = 600\,\text{m}^{-1}$.

c A beam of X-rays of intensity $15\,\text{W m}^{-2}$ is directed on to a patient's arm. Calculate the intensity of the beam after it has passed through 3.0 mm of bone. [3]

d Muscle tissue has a lower attenuation coefficient than bone. Explain how this allows X-rays to be used to produce a 'shadow image' of bone embedded in tissue. [2]

[Total: 9]

3 To locate an area of increased activity within the brain using positron emission tomography (PET) a chemical, similar to glucose but containing a radioactive isotope, is injected into the body where it is absorbed by the area of increased activity.

The isotope emits a positron, which causes annihilation with an electron resulting in the emission of two gamma rays. These gamma rays can be used to locate the area of increased activity.

a i Calculate the wavelength of the emitted photons. [3]

ii Explain how momentum is conserved during annihilation. [1]

b Describe how the position of increased activity within the brain is located. [5]

[Total: 9]

Chapter 31

Astronomy and cosmology

KEY EQUATIONS

radiant flux intensity $= \dfrac{\text{power or luminosity of star}}{\text{surface area of sphere}}$; $F = \dfrac{L}{4\pi d^2}$

Wien's displacement law: $\lambda_{\max} \propto \dfrac{1}{T}$

Stefan's law: $L = 4\pi\sigma r^2 T^4$

redshift: $\dfrac{\Delta\lambda}{\lambda} \approx \dfrac{\Delta f}{f} \approx \dfrac{v}{c}$

Hubble's law: $v \approx H_0 d$

surface area of a sphere $= 4\pi r^2$

Exercise 31.1 Luminosity, standard candles and distances to galaxies

This exercise provides practice in understanding **luminosity**, **radiant flux intensity**, the inverse square law and the use of **standard candles** to determine distances to galaxies.

1   Describe what is meant by a *Cepheid variable* and a *supernova*.

2   State what common feature of Cepheid variable stars and type 1a supernovae make them suitable for measuring distances.

3   Explain why only type 1a supernovae are used as standard candles to measure distances to the most distant galaxies.

4   The luminosity of the star Canopus is 4.1×10^{30} W and its distance from the Earth is 2.9×10^{18} m. Calculate the radiant flux intensity of Canopus at the Earth. Include the unit of your answer.

5   A type 1a supernova is observed in a distant galaxy. Its radiant flux intensity at the Earth is measured to be 1.8×10^{-15} W m^{-2}. Theory predicts that it has a luminosity of 2.0×10^{36} W.

Calculate the distance of the galaxy from the Earth.

6   Two distant stars are observed through a telescope on Earth. Star A is observed to have half the radiant flux intensity of star B. Star A is known to be twice as far away as star B.

Calculate the ratio of luminosity of star A : luminosity of star B.

7   The Sun is 1.5×10^{11} m from the Earth and has a radiant flux intensity at the Earth's orbit of 1300 W m^{-2}. Another star is 7.1×10^{19} m away from the Earth, and the radiant flux intensity of its radiation reaching the Earth is 3.3×10^{-8} W m^{-2}.

Calculate:

a   the luminosity of the Sun

b   the ratio of power emitted by the other star : power emitted by the Sun.

> **TIP**
>
> Rearrange the formula for radiant flux intensity so that luminosity is the subject of the formula, and then you can see how doubling distance and flux density affects luminosity.

Exercise 31.2 Wien's displacement law

This exercise provides practice using **Wien's displacement law** to relate temperature to the peak wavelength in the continuous spectrum from a hot object.

In this exercise $\lambda_{max} T$ = constant, where the constant = 2.9×10^{-3} m K.

1   Use Wien's displacement law to explain why a piece of metal placed in the fire starts by glowing red and then becomes bluer in colour.

2   The table shows the wavelength λ_{max} of the peak energy in the spectrum of a number of stars and their surface temperatures T.

> **KEY WORDS**
>
> **Wien's displacement law:** $\lambda_{max} T$ = constant, where T is the thermodynamic temperature of the object and λ_{max} is the emitted wavelength at the peak intensity

λ_{max} / nm	580	0.10	193	145
T / K	5000	10 000	15 000	20 000

Table 31.1: For Question 2.

Show that the values in the table are consistent with Wien's displacement law

$$\lambda_{max} \propto \frac{1}{T}$$

and find the constant in the equation $\lambda_{max} T$ = constant. Include the unit of your answer.

3 Maximum energy is emitted by a star at a wavelength of 550 nm. Calculate the temperature of the star. Use the value of the constant in Wien's displacement law given at the start of this exercise.

4 The hottest stars are blue supergiants which have surface temperatures of over 40 000 K. Determine the wavelength at which such stars emit their maximum amount of energy.

5 Determine the wavelength at which a **black body** of the same temperature as the human body (37 °C) radiates its maximum energy.

6 The graph shows the spectrum of the star Proxima Centauri, the nearest star to the Sun.

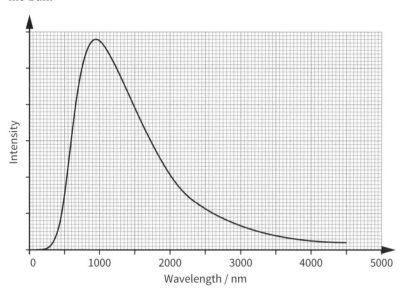

Figure 31.1: For Question 6. Graph showing the spectrum of the star Proxima Centauri.

a Use the graph to estimate the wavelength of the peak emission λ_{max}. Include a value for the uncertainty in your answer.

b Use Wien's displacement law to determine the temperature of the star. Using your uncertainty in λ_{max}, estimate the uncertainty in your answer for the temperature.

c Visible wavelengths are in the range 400–700 nm. Suggest what colour the star appears to be when observed by eye.

Exercise 31.3 Stefan's law and stellar radii

This exercise provides practice in using **Stefan's law** to relate temperature to the luminosity of an object. Stefan's law and Wien's displacement law are both used together to estimate the radius of a star.

In this exercise, luminosity L is given by $L = 4\pi\sigma r^2 T^4$, where $\sigma = 5.67 \times 10^{-8}$ W m^{-2} K^{-4}.

1 The surface temperature of the star Proxima Centauri is 3000 K.

   Its effective radius is 1.0×10^8 m. Calculate the luminosity of the star.

2 Calculate the SI base units of the Stefan–Boltzmann constant.

3 Use Stefan's law to calculate the surface area of the Sun. Assume that its power output is 3.6×10^{26} W and its surface temperature is 5700 K.

4 The maximum power emitted by a star is 9.5×10^{29} W and the peak of its spectrum occurs at a wavelength of 450 nm.

   a Use Wien's displacement law to determine the surface temperature of the star. Use the constant in the equation from Exercise 31.2.

   b Use Stefan's law to determine the radius of the star.

5 Star A and star B are similar distances from Earth.

   Star A has twice the radius of star B.

   Star B has a surface with twice the thermodynamic temperature of star A.

   The spectra from these two stars are compared.

   State and explain:

   a which star has the peak in its spectrum at the highest wavelength

   b which star has a spectrum showing higher peaks and thus emits more power.

Exercise 31.4 Hubble's law and the Big Bang theory

In this exercise you will calculate **redshifts** in the emission spectra from distant objects and use them to calculate recession speeds. You will use **Hubble's law** and explain how this is in agreement with the **Big Bang theory**.

You will use $\frac{\Delta\lambda}{\lambda} \approx \frac{\Delta f}{f} \approx \frac{v}{c}$ and $v - H_0 d$, where the Hubble constant $H_0 = 2.4 \times 10^{-18}$ s^{-1}.

The speed of light $c = 3.0 \times 10^8$ m s^{-1}.

1 Sunspots move across the face of the Sun. This indicates that the Sun rotates.

   A spectrum is obtained from one edge of the Sun, as it rotates towards the Earth. This is compared with a spectrum obtained from the centre of the Sun, which is not moving towards or away from the Earth.

   a State and explain any difference in the two spectra.

   b The edge moves towards the Earth at a speed of 2000 m s^{-1}. Calculate the percentage change in wavelength observed.

   c The wavelength of one line in the spectrum is approximately 300 nm. Estimate how accurately the wavelength must be measured to show that there is a difference in the two spectra.

KEY WORDS

redshift: the increase in the wavelength of electromagnetic waves due to recession of the source

Hubble's law: the recession speed of a star or galaxy is directly proportional to its distance from Earth

Big Bang theory: a model of the creation and evolution of the Universe from an extremely hot and dense state

2   The table shows the wavelength of a line in the calcium spectrum detected in the light from three galaxies. In the laboratory this line is known to have a wavelength of 393.7 nm.

Wavelength / nm from galaxy 1	Wavelength / nm from galaxy 2	Wavelength / nm from galaxy 3
401.0	412.9	444.5

Table 31.2: For Question 2.

a   Calculate the apparent change in wavelength of the line for each galaxy.

b   Calculate the speed of recession of each galaxy away from Earth.

c   Use Hubble's law to calculate the distance of each galaxy from Earth.

3   A galaxy is moving away from the Earth at a speed of $2.3 \times 10^7 \, \text{m s}^{-1}$. A line in the hydrogen spectrum is known to have a wavelength of 410 nm. Calculate the wavelength of this spectral line emitted by the galaxy when measured on Earth.

4   Using Hubble's law, calculate:

a   the distance from Earth of a star that is receding from the Earth at $2500 \, \text{km s}^{-1}$

b   the speed of a galaxy that is 100 Mpc away from Earth, where 1 parsec = $3.1 \times 10^{16} \, \text{m}$.

5   Explain how redshift leads to the ideas of an expanding Universe and to the Big Bang theory.

EXAM-STYLE QUESTIONS

1   The star Sirius is $8.1 \times 10^{16} \, \text{m}$ from Earth and its luminosity is $9.9 \times 10^{27} \, \text{W}$.

a   i   Describe what is meant by the *radiant flux intensity* of a star.   [2]

    ii   Calculate the radiant flux intensity of Sirius at the Earth. Include the unit in your answer.   [2]

    iii   Suggest *one* reason why the measured radiant flux intensity may be different from the value calculated in part **ii**.   [1]

b   Stefan's equation for the luminosity L of a star can be written as $L = 4\pi\sigma r^2 T^4$.

    i   State the meaning of T in the equation.   [1]

    ii   The surface temperature of Sirius is measured to be 9900 K. Estimate the effective radius of Sirius.   [2]

c   The following graph shows the continuous spectrum of the relative power emitted from Sirius and another star Beta Andromedae.

CONTINUED

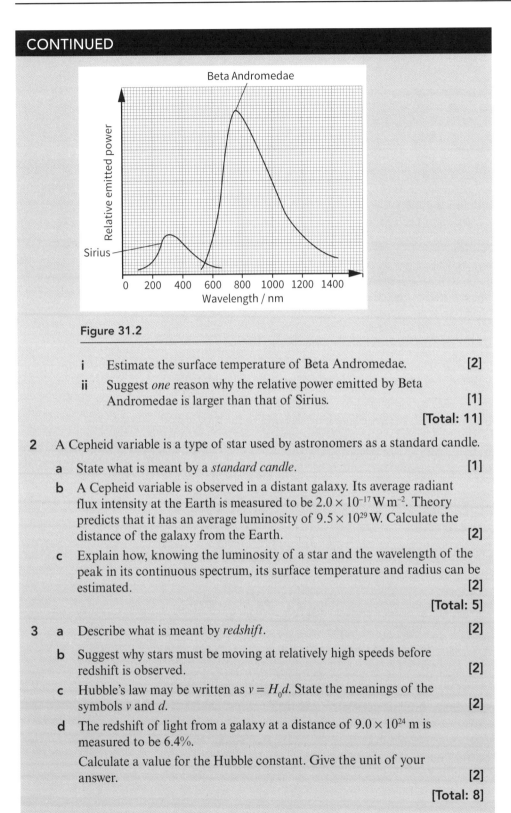

Figure 31.2

  i   Estimate the surface temperature of Beta Andromedae. [2]

  ii   Suggest *one* reason why the relative power emitted by Beta Andromedae is larger than that of Sirius. [1]

[Total: 11]

2   A Cepheid variable is a type of star used by astronomers as a standard candle.

  a   State what is meant by a *standard candle*. [1]

  b   A Cepheid variable is observed in a distant galaxy. Its average radiant flux intensity at the Earth is measured to be $2.0 \times 10^{-17}\,\mathrm{W\,m^{-2}}$. Theory predicts that it has an average luminosity of $9.5 \times 10^{29}\,\mathrm{W}$. Calculate the distance of the galaxy from the Earth. [2]

  c   Explain how, knowing the luminosity of a star and the wavelength of the peak in its continuous spectrum, its surface temperature and radius can be estimated. [2]

[Total: 5]

3   a   Describe what is meant by *redshift*. [2]

  b   Suggest why stars must be moving at relatively high speeds before redshift is observed. [2]

  c   Hubble's law may be written as $v = H_0 d$. State the meanings of the symbols v and d. [2]

  d   The redshift of light from a galaxy at a distance of $9.0 \times 10^{24}\,\mathrm{m}$ is measured to be 6.4%.

   Calculate a value for the Hubble constant. Give the unit of your answer. [2]

[Total: 8]

Practical skills at A Level

KEY EQUATIONS

absolute uncertainty in gradient = gradient of line of best fit − gradient of worst acceptable line

absolute uncertainty in y-intercept = y-intercept of line of best fit − y-intercept of worst acceptable line

Exercise P2.1 Graphs

This exercise involves the use of error bars on graphs and finding the uncertainty in a gradient, including logarithms.

1   Two quantities x and y are related by the equation $y = kx^n$ where k and n are constants.

a   By taking logarithms, find an expression for $\ln y$ in terms of $\ln x$.

This graph shows ln y plotted against ln x, for two points with error bars:

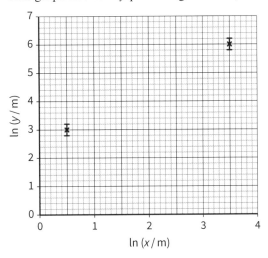

Figure P2.1: For Question 1. Graph showing ln y plotted against ln x.

b Calculate the gradient of the best line joining the two points.

c Calculate the gradient of the worst acceptable line.

d Note down the intercept of the best line on the y-axis.

e Note down the intercept of the worst acceptable line on the x-axis.

f Using your answers for the gradients state the value of n and its uncertainty.

g Using your answers for **d**, calculate the best value of k. (You will have to use the inverse of a logarithm as the intercept is ln k.)

2 In an experiment, imagine that you have measured the current I and the voltage V across a lamp and obtained the values:

$V = 1.65 \pm 0.07\,\text{V}$ and $I = 0.25 \pm 0.03\,\text{A}$

A point is plotted at (0.25, 1.65) on a graph with voltage on the y-axis and current on the x-axis. The error bars now need to be drawn.

a Describe how to plot the vertical error bar, showing the uncertainty in the voltage.

b Describe how to plot the horizontal error bar, showing the uncertainty in the current.

3 Imagine that you have measured a current as $3.6 \pm 0.2\,\text{A}$.

a Calculate:

   i ln (3.6)

   ii ln (3.8)

   iii ln (3.4)

b State the length of the error bar required above the point and below the point, when you plot a point with a y-value of ln (3.6).

c State the label that should be written on the y-axis if you were to plot the point ln (3.6).

4   This graph shows values of ln (V / V) plotted against R^{-1} / $10^{-6}\,\Omega^{-1}$:

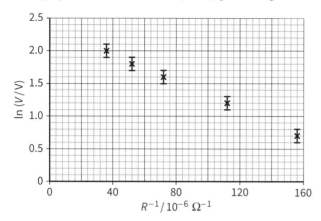

Figure P2.2: For Question 4. Graph showing values of ln V / V plotted against R^{-1} / $10^{-6}\,\Omega^{-1}$.

a   Place a ruler on the graph along the line of best fit. Read off values and obtain the gradient of this line. Take care with the 10^{-6} on the x-axis (120 really means 1.2×10^{-4}, for example).

b   Place a ruler on the graph along the worst acceptable straight line. Read off values and obtain the gradient of this line.

c   State the gradient with its uncertainty.

The formula that relates V and R is:

$V = V_0 e^{-t/RC}$

where C is a capacitance and t the time for the reading (in this case, 10 s).

d   Express the gradient of the graph in terms of C and t.

e   Using your value for the gradient, determine the value of C. Include the unit.

f   Determine the percentage uncertainty in your value for C.

Exercise P2.2 Uncertainty and using an oscilloscope

This exercise provides more practice estimating uncertainty and in using an oscilloscope.

1   This diagram shows the trace of an alternating voltage obtained on an oscilloscope screen (the grid lines on the diagram are one division apart on the screen).

a   Determine the amplitude of the trace. Give your answer as a multiple of one division. Estimate the uncertainty in your answer.

b   The Y-gain control is set at 2.0 V/division. Use your answers to **a** to determine the peak voltage and its uncertainty.

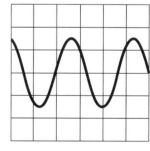

Figure P2.3: For Question 1. Diagram showing the trace of an alternating voltage obtained on an oscilloscope screen.

c   The time base (X-gain) on the oscilloscope is set at 0.5 ms/division. Determine the time for one oscillation and the uncertainty in this value.

d   Use your answer to **c** to calculate the frequency of the a.c. and the uncertainty in this value. Since your calculation involves a division, you need to use percentage uncertainties. You can assume that the oscilloscope is calibrated and that there is no uncertainty in the time base value.

> **TIP**
>
> Remember to add percentage uncertainties to find the percentage uncertainty in the speed.

2   Light gates are placed on a slope and used to time a ball rolling from rest down a slope. The distance travelled by the ball is 0.245 ± 0.002 m and a data logger connected to the light gates measures the time taken as 1.26 ± 0.01 s.

a   Calculate the average speed of the ball. Give your answer as a value, an absolute uncertainty estimate and a unit. You will need to use the formula:

$$\text{speed} = \frac{\text{distance}}{\text{time}}$$

> **TIP**
>
> Remember when finding the total percentage uncertainty that t appears twice.

b   Calculate the average acceleration of the ball. Give your answer as a value, an absolute uncertainty estimate and a unit. You will need to use the formula:

$$s = \frac{1}{2}at^2$$

Exercise P2.3 Experimental methods

Writing a method can be difficult unless you are organised and cover each aspect logically and carefully. This exercise gives you practice thinking about the different aspects.

Read through the descriptions of experiments A–I in the following table and then, for each experiment:

1   State which is the **dependent variable**, which is the **independent variable** and any quantities that should be **controlled**.

2   Draw a diagram of the apparatus and describe how the variables are measured or how they are calculated from the readings taken.

3   Describe how the independent variable is changed.

4   Give one additional detail, e.g. how to ensure there is a large change in the dependent variable.

5   State one safety precaution.

6   State what graph you would draw and how it is used to find any constants mentioned.

> **KEY WORDS**
>
> **dependent variable:** a physical quantity whose value changes as a result of the change in another quantity
>
> **independent variable:** a physical quantity whose value is controlled or selected by the experimenter
>
> **control variable:** a quantity that has to be kept constant otherwise the relationship between the other variables is not tested fairly

Experiment	Description
A	A student uses light gates to test the relationship between the distance s that a ball rolls down a slope and the time taken t, according to the formula: $$s = \tfrac{1}{2}at^2$$ where a is a constant.
B	A student tests that the resistance R of a thermistor varies with the temperature T, (measured in K) according to the formula: $$R = e^{-kt}$$ where k is a constant.
C	A student tests the relationship between V_s the output voltage from a transformer, and V_p the input voltage. He uses the formula: $$V_s = V_p \times \left(\frac{N_s}{N_p} \right)$$ where N_s and N_p are the number of turns on the output and input coils respectively.
D	A student tests the relationship between the magnetic flux density B at the centre of a circular coil and the current I in the coil. She uses the formula: $$B = \frac{\mu_0 N I}{2R}$$ where N is the number of turns in the coil, R is the radius of the coil and μ_0 is a constant.
E	A student tests the relationship between the peak alternating current I_0 and the frequency f of the applied alternating voltage. She finds the formula: $$\left(\frac{V_0}{I_0} \right)^2 = R^2 + \left(4\pi^2 f^2 C^2 \right)$$ where V_0 is the peak value of the alternating voltage, R is the resistance of the circuit and C is the capacitance.
F	A student tests that, when a burette tap is opened, the volume V of liquid changes with time t according to the formula: $$V = V_0\, e^{-\lambda t}$$ where V_0 is the initial volume and λ is a constant.
G	A student tests that the terminal velocity v of a steel ball falling through oil depends upon the radius R of the ball according to the formula: $$v = AR^2$$ where A is a constant.

Table P2.1: For Question 6 (continues).

Experiment	Description
H	One end of a metre rule is clamped horizontally and the other end has a mass attached. The distance between the clamp and the centre of the mass is l. A student tests that the period T, when the rule oscillates up and down, depends upon l according to the formula: $T^2 = kl^3$ where k is a constant for the rule.
I	A student has two small coils and notices that an alternating p.d. applied to one coil produces an alternating e.m.f. V in the other, even though they are not connected. There is a distance l between the two coils. He suggests that V is inversely proportional to l.

Table P2.1: For Question 6 (continued).

EXAM-STYLE QUESTIONS

1   A nail is placed vertically with its sharp end in contact with a piece of wood. When a mass falls a height h onto the flat end of the nail, the nail is driven into the wood. It is suggested that the distance d that the nail is driven into the wood depends on h according to the formula:

$d = kh^n$

where k and n are constants.

Design a laboratory experiment to investigate the relationship between d and h in order to find a value for n. You should draw a diagram showing the arrangement of your equipment. In your account you should pay particular attention to the:

   a   procedure to be followed   [2]

   b   measurements to be taken   [4]

   c   control of variables   [2]

   d   analysis of the data   [2]

   e   safety precautions to be taken.   [1]

   Remember also to give additional detail, state the graph you would plot and how it should be used.

                                                                    [Total: 11]

2   A mass M is suspended vertically from a spring with spring constant k. When the mass is displaced downwards it oscillates up and down. The time for ten complete oscillations T is measured.

   It is suggested that T, M and k are related by the equation:

$T = 20\pi\sqrt{\dfrac{M}{k}}$

CONTINUED

a   A graph is plotted of T^2 on the y-axis against M on the x-axis. Determine an expression for the gradient in terms of k.   [2]

b   Values of T and M are given in this table:

M / kg	T / s	T² / s²
0.075	10.8 ± 0.3	
0.125	13.7 ± 0.3	
0.175	16.8 ± 0.3	
0.225	19.0 ± 0.3	
0.275	20.6 ± 0.3	
0.325	22.5 ± 0.3	

Table P2.2

Calculate and record values of T^2 / s². Include the absolute uncertainties in T^2.   [2]

c   i   Plot a graph of T^2 / s² against M / kg. Include error bars for T^2.   [2]

   ii   Draw the straight line of best fit and a worst acceptable straight line on your graph.   [2]

   iii   Determine the gradient of the line of best fit. Include the uncertainty in your answer.   [2]

d   i   Determine a value for k. Include an appropriate unit in your answer.   [1]

   ii   Determine the percentage uncertainty in your value of k.   [1]

e   The experiment is repeated with $M = 0.200\,$kg. Determine the value of T. Include the percentage uncertainty in your answer.   [2]

[Total: 14]

> Glossary

Command words

Below are the Cambridge International definitions for Command words which appear in the syllabus and may be used in exams. The information in this section is taken from the Cambridge International syllabus for examination from 2022. You should always refer to the appropriate syllabus document for the year of your examination to confirm the details and for more information. The syllabus document is available on the Cambridge International website at www.cambridgeinternational.org.

Calculate   work out from given facts, figures or information

Comment   give an informed opinion

Compare   identify/comment on similarities and/or differences

Define   give precise meaning

Determine   establish an answer using the information available

Explain   set out purposes or reasons / make the relationships between things evident / provide why and/ or how and support with relevant evidence

Give   produce an answer from a given source or recall/ memory

Identify   name/select/recognise

Justify   support a case with evidence/argument

Predict   suggest what may happen based on available information

Show (that)   provide structured evidence that leads to a given result

Sketch   make a simple freehand drawing showing the key features

State   express in clear terms

Suggest   apply knowledge and understanding to situations where there are a range of valid responses in order to make proposals

Key words

absolute zero   the lowest possible temperature, zero kelvin, on the thermodynamic temperature scale

absorption line spectrum   a pattern of dark lines or discrete wavelengths in a continuous spectrum caused by the absorption of electromagnetic radiation

acceleration   rate of change of velocity of an object

accuracy   how close the value of a measured quantity is to the true value of the quantity

acoustic impedance   the product of the density of the substance and the speed of the ultrasound in the substance

activity   the number of nuclei in a sample that decay per unit time interval

alpha-particle   two protons and two neutrons ($^4_2\alpha$, the nucleus of a helium atom $^4_2$He) emitted from a nucleus during radioactive decay

amplitude   the maximum displacement of an oscillating particle from its equilibrium position

analogue display   a continuous display which represents the quantity being measured on a dial or scale

angular displacement   the angle through which an object moves in a circle

angular velocity   the rate at which the angular displacement changes

annihilation event   a positron annihilates on contact with an electron to produce two 500 keV photons travelling in opposite directions

antinode   a point on a stationary wave where the amplitude is a maximum

antineutrino   see **electron antineutrino**

antiparticle   a particle with the same mass and opposite charge as another particle, for example the antiparticle of the electron is the positively charged electron, or positron

atomic mass unit $\frac{1}{12}$ of the mass of a neutral atom of carbon-12, equal to 1.66×10^{-27} kg

attenuation (or absorption) coefficient   the fraction of a beam of X-rays that is absorbed per unit thickness of the absorber

baryon   a hadron made from three quarks or three antiquarks (an antibaryon)

beta-minus (β^-) decay   the emission of an electron (β^--particle, $^0_{-1}$e) from a nucleus as a neutron decays into a proton (proton number increases by 1 and an antineutrino is also emitted)

beta-plus (β⁺) decay the emission of a positron (β⁺-particle, $_{+1}^{0}e$) from a nucleus as a proton decays into a neutron (proton number decreases by 1 and a neutrino is also emitted)

Big Bang theory a model of the creation and evolution of the Universe from an extremely hot and dense state

binding energy the minimum external energy required to completely separate all the nucleons in a nucleus to infinity

black body an idealised object that absorbs all incident electromagnetic radiation falling on it; it has a characteristic emission spectrum and intensity that depends only on its thermodynamic temperature

Boyle's law the pressure exerted by a fixed mass of gas is inversely proportional to its volume, provided the temperature of the gas remains constant

braking radiation X-ray emissions produced by an electron as it collides successively with a series of atoms, giving up its kinetic energy. A whole range of different energy X-rays may be produced

capacitance (of a capacitor) the charge stored on one plate per unit potential difference between the plates

centre of gravity the point at which all the weight of the object seems to act

centre of mass the point at which we can consider the total mass of the object to be concentrated

centripetal acceleration the acceleration of an object towards the centre of its circular motion

characteristic radiation X-ray radiation produced when an inner electron is knocked out of its orbital by an incident electron. The X-ray is produced when another electron drops from a higher energy orbital. Each drop produces an X-ray of a specific energy

charge carrier a charged particle that contributes to an electric current; may be an electron, a proton or an ion

coherent two waves are coherent if they have a constant phase relationship

collimated beam a beam with parallel sides (this means that the beam does not spread out)

component the effect of a vector along a particular direction

component of a force the resolved part of a force in a particular direction

compression a region in a sound wave where the air pressure is greater than its mean value

conservation of charge electric charge can be neither created nor destroyed

conservation of momentum within a closed system the total momentum in any direction is constant

constructive interference when two waves arrive in phase and the resultant amplitude is the sum of the amplitudes of the two waves

normal contact force the force at right angles to a surface when two objects are in contact

contrast (of an image) the difference in brightness between the brightest and the darkest areas

control variable a quantity that has to be kept constant in an experiment, otherwise the relationship between the other variables is not tested fairly

Coulomb's law any two point charges exert an electrical force on each other that is proportional to the product of their charges and inversely proportional to the square of the distance between them

couple a pair of equal and opposite forces that act on an object at different points and produce rotation only

critical damping the minimum damping that causes the oscillating system to return to its equilibrium position in the minimum time without oscillating

CT scanning computerised axial tomography (CT or CAT) scanning, a technique in which X-rays are used to image the body, producing a 3D image of an internal structure

damped oscillation an oscillation in which resistive forces cause the energy of the system to be transferred to the surroundings

de Broglie wavelength the wavelength associated with a moving particle, given by the equation: $\lambda = \dfrac{h}{p}$

density the mass per unit volume of a material

dependent variable a physical quantity whose value changes as a result of the change in another quantity

destructive interference when two waves arrive 180° out of phase and the resultant amplitude is the difference in the amplitude of the two waves

diffraction the spreading of a wave at an edge or slit

digital display a display that gives the information in the form of characters (numbers or letters)

diode an electrical component that only conducts in one direction

dispersion the splitting of light into its component wavelengths

displacement the distance moved by an object in a particular direction (in a wave this is usually measured from the equilibrium position)

Doppler effect (also called Doppler shift) the change in frequency or wavelength of a wave when the source of the wave is moving towards or away from the observer (or when the observer is moving relative to the source)

drag a resistive force in air or a liquid

drift velocity see **mean drift velocity**

elastic potential energy the potential energy stored in a body due to a change in its shape (also called strain energy)

electric field a region in which an electrically charged particle experiences a force

electric field strength the force per unit positive charge at a point

electric potential at a point the work done per unit change in bringing a positive charge from infinity to that point

electromagnetic spectrum the family of waves that travel through a vacuum at a speed of $3.00 \times 10^8 \, \mathrm{m\,s^{-1}}$

electromotive force (e.m.f.) the amount of energy changed from other forms into electrical energy per unit charge produced by an electrical supply

electron antineutrino an antiparticle that is emitted in β^- decay, with virtually no rest mass and no charge

electron neutrino a lepton emitted in β^+ decay, having no charge and very small mass

electronvolt (eV) the energy gained by an electron travelling through a potential difference of 1 volt ($1\,\mathrm{eV} = 1.60 \times 10^{-19}\,\mathrm{J}$)

elementary charge the smallest unit of charge that a particle or an object can have, $e = 1.6 \times 10^{-19}\,\mathrm{C}$

emission line spectrum a series of discrete wavelengths emitted by an atom

energy level a quantised energy state, for example of an electron in an atom

equilibrium when the resultant force and the resultant moment on a body are both zero

exponential decay describes the decrease of a quantity where the rate of decrease is proportional to the value of the quantity

Faraday's law of electromagnetic induction the induced e.m.f. is proportional to the rate of change of magnetic flux linkage

Fleming's left-hand rule if the first finger of the left hand is pointed in the direction of the magnetic field and the second finger in the direction of the

conventional current, then the thumb points in the direction of the force or motion produced

free fall when an object accelerates due to gravity in the absence of any other forces such as air resistance

frequency the number of complete oscillations or waves that pass a point in unit time

friction a resistive force when two surfaces are in contact and tending to slide over one another

full-wave rectification the conversion of both halves of a cycle of an alternating current into a direct current, in only one direction

fundamental frequency the lowest-frequency stationary wave that can form in a system

fundamental particle an elementary particle that is not made from other particles, for example leptons and quarks

galvanometer an instrument which is used to measure or detect small electric currents

geostationary orbit an orbit of a satellite such that the satellite remains directly above the same point on the equator at all times

gravitational field a region where an object feels a force because of its mass

gravitational field strength the gravitational force exerted per unit mass on a small object placed at a point

gravitational potential the work done per unit mass in bringing a mass from infinity to a point in a gravitational field

gravitational potential energy (GPE) the energy of an object due to its position in a gravitational field

hadron any particle made from a quark

half-life the time taken for half the number of active nuclei in a radioactive sample to decay

half-wave rectification the conversion of one half of a cycle of an alternating current into a direct current, in only one direction

Hall effect the production of a potential difference across an electrical conductor when an external magnetic field is applied in a direction perpendicular to the direction of the current

Hall voltage the potential difference produced across the sides of a conductor when an external magnetic field is applied perpendicular to the direction of the current. The Hall voltage V_H is directly proportional to the magnetic flux density B

harmonic a mode of vibration with a frequency that is a multiple of the fundamental frequency

homogenous (or homogeneous) equations with the same base units on each side

Hooke's law provided the elastic limit is not exceeded, the extension of an object is proportional to the applied force

Hubble's law the recession speed of a star or galaxy is directly proportional to its distance from Earth

ideal gas a gas that behaves according to the equation $pV = nRT$

independent variable a physical quantity whose value is controlled or selected by the person performing an experiment

intensity power transmitted normally per unit cross-sectional area

interference the cancellation and reinforcement when two waves pass through each other

internal energy the sum of the random distribution of kinetic and potential energies of the atoms or molecules of a system

internal resistance the resistance inherent in a source of e.m.f. that reduces the terminal p.d. across the source when there is a current

ion an atom that has lost or gained one or more electrons, so that it is electrically charged

isotopes nuclei of the same element with different numbers of neutrons but the same number of protons

joule the work done (or energy transferred) when a force of 1 N moves a distance of 1 m in the direction of the force

kinetic energy (KE) the energy of an object due to its motion

Kirchhoff's first law the sum of currents entering any point is equal to the sum of the currents leaving that same point. This law represents the conservation of charge

Kirchhoff's second law the sum of the e.m.f.s around a closed loop is equal to the sum of the p.d.s in that same loop. This law represents the conservation of energy

Lenz's law an induced e.m.f. acts in such a direction so as to produce effects which oppose the change producing it

lepton a fundamental particle that is not affected by the strong nuclear force, for example an electron, positron and neutrino

light-dependent resistor (LDR) an electrical resistor whose resistance decreases as the brightness of the light falling on it increases

linear momentum the product of an object's mass and velocity

longitudinal wave a wave in which the points of the medium oscillate along the direction in which the wave travels

luminosity (of a star) the total radiant power emitted by a star

magnetic field a region in which a magnet, a wire carrying a current, or a moving charge experiences a force

magnetic flux the product of the magnetic flux density perpendicular to a circuit and the cross-sectional area of the circuit (magnetic flux has the unit weber, Wb)

magnetic flux density the force acting per unit current per unit length on a wire placed at right-angles to the magnetic field

magnetic flux linkage the product of magnetic flux through a coil and the number of turns in a coil (magnetic flux linkage has the unit weber-turns, Wb-turns)

Malus's law the intensity of plane polarised light transmitted by a polarising filter is directly proportional to the square of the cosine of the angle between the transmission axis of the filter and the plane of polarisation of the incident light

mass defect the difference between the total mass of the individual, separate nucleons and the mass of the nucleus

mean drift velocity the average speed of a collection of charged particles forming a current in a conductor

meson a hadron made from a quark and an antiquark

mole the amount of a substance that contains 6.02×10^{23} particles, the Avogadro constant N_A

moment the moment of a force about a point is the product of the force and perpendicular distance from the line of action of the force to the point

natural frequency the frequency at which a body vibrates when there is no (resultant external) resistive force acting on it OR when there is no driving force/ external force acting on it

neutrino see **electron neutrino**

Newton's first law of motion an object will remain at rest or keep travelling at constant velocity unless it is acted on by a resultant external force

Newton's law of gravitation any two point masses attract each other with a force that is directly proportional to the product of their mass and inversely proportional to the square of their separation

Newton's second law of motion   the net force acting on an object is equal to the rate of change of its momentum. The net force and the change in momentum are in the same direction

Newton's third law of motion   when two bodies interact, the forces they exert on each other are equal and opposite

node   a point on a stationary wave where the amplitude is zero

nuclear fission   the splitting of a nucleus into smaller nuclei

nuclear fusion   a nuclear reaction in which two light nuclei join together to form a heavier nucleus

nucleon   general term to describe a proton or a neutron

nucleon number   the total number of neutrons and protons in the nucleus of an atom

nucleus (of an atom)   the very small, but very dense, positively charged centre of an atom

nuclide   a particular nucleus with a specific combination of protons and neutron

null method   an experimental technique where a zero reading is sought

Ohm's law   the current in a metallic conductor is directly proportional to the potential difference across its ends provided physical conditions, such as temperature, remain constant

path difference   the extra distance travelled by one wave compared with an other; path difference is often given in terms of the wavelength λ of the waves.

period   the time taken to complete one cycle of an oscillation

PET scanning   positron emission tomography (PET) involves introducing a radioactive tracer into the body and produces images to show where the radioactive substance is concentrated

phase   the point that an oscillating particle has reached within the complete cycle of an oscillation

phase difference   a measure of the amount by which one oscillation leads or lags another, expressed as an angle, e.g. 360° if they are one whole oscillation out of step

photoelectric effect   the emission of an electron from the surface of a metal when light shines on the surface

photon   a quantum of electromagnetic energy

piezo-electric effect   the production of an e.m.f. across a crystal by putting the crystal under stress; the opposite effect is applying a p.d. across the crystal causing it to change shape

Planck constant (h)   a fundamental constant which links the energy of a photon E and its frequency f; $E = hf$

plane polarised   describes a transverse wave with oscillation in just one plane; only transverse waves can be polarised

polarisation   the process of restricting the oscillations of a transverse wave to be in one plane

positron   the antiparticle of the electron; it has the same mass as the electron but has a charge $+e$

potential difference (p.d.)   the energy transferred per unit charge as charge passes between two points

potential divider   a circuit in which two or more components are connected in series to a supply; the output voltage is taken across one of the components

potentiometer   a device used to compare potential difference or e.m.f.

power   the rate at which work is done (or energy is transferred) per unit time

precision   the smallest change in value that can be measured by an instrument or an operator or that is shown in a measurement; a precise measurement is one that, when made several times, gives the same or very similar values

pressure   the force acting normally in a fluid per unit area of a surface

principle of moments   the sum of the clockwise moments about a point is equal to the sum of the anticlockwise moments about the same point provided the body is in equilibrium

progressive wave   a wave that carries energy from one place to another

proton number   the number of protons in the nucleus of an atom

quantised   when a quantity has a definite minimum magnitude and always comes in multiples of that magnitude

quantum   the smallest amount of a quantity that exists independently, particularly the photon as the smallest amount of electromagnetic radiation that can be emitted or absorbed

quark   the fundamental particles of which hadrons are made; there are six types or flavours: up, down, strange, charge, top and bottom

radian   a unit of angle such that 2π radians = 360°

radiant flux intensity   the radiant power passing normally through a surface per unit area

radioactive decay constant the probability that an individual nucleus will decay per unit time interval

radioactive tracer a substance that consists of radioactive material attached to a natural chemical, such as glucose

random decay the decay of a nucleus that cannot be predicted, producing slightly different counts, above or below a mean value, in the same time interval

random error an error in a measurement that is unpredictable and which may vary from one measurement to the next

range the difference between the largest value and the smallest value of a measurement

rarefaction a region in a sound wave where the air pressure is less than its mean value

redshift the increase in the wavelength of electromagnetic waves due to recession of the source

resistance ratio of the potential difference across an electrical component to the current in the component

resistive force a force in the opposite direction to movement caused by friction or some other viscous force

resistivity a measure of electrical resistance, defined as resistance x cross-sectional area / length

resonance when the frequency of a driving force is equal to the natural frequency of the oscillating system, the system absorbs the maximum energy from the driver and has maximum amplitude

rest mass the mass of a particle when at rest

resultant force the single force acting on a body that has the same effect as the sum of all the forces acting on it

root-mean-square (r.m.s.) current or voltage the square root of the average value of the square of the current or voltage; numerically equal to the steady current or voltage that produces the same heating effect in a pure resistance

scalar a quantity with magnitude only

sharpness (of an image) the degree of resolution of an image, which determines the smallest item that can be seen

simple harmonic motion (s.h.m.) motion of an oscillator in which its acceleration is directly proportional to its displacement from its equilibrium position and is directed towards that position

specific heat capacity (of a substance) the energy required per unit mass to raise the temperature by 1 K (or 1 °C)

specific latent heat of fusion the amount of heat energy needed to convert unit mass of solid to liquid without change in temperature

specific latent heat of vaporisation the amount of heat energy needed to convert unit mass of liquid to gas without change in temperature

spontaneous decay the decay of a nucleus that is not affected by outside factors and occurs because of factors within itself

spring constant the force per unit extension of a spring

standard candle an astronomical object of known luminosity that is used to measure distance

stationary wave (also called standing wave) a wave pattern produced when two progressive waves of the same frequency travelling in opposite directions combine (there is no net transfer of energy)

Stefan's law $L = 4\pi \varepsilon r^2 T^4$, where σ is the Stefan–Boltzmann constant, L is the luminosity of an object, r is the radius of the object and T is its surface thermodynamic temperature

strain the extension per unit length produced by tensile or compressive forces

stress the force per unit cross-sectional area

superposition when two or more waves meet at a point the resultant displacement is the algebraic sum of the displacement of each wave

systematic error an error of measurement that differs from the true value by the same amount in each measurement

terminal potential difference the p.d. across an external resistor connected across a source of e.m.f.

terminal velocity the maximum velocity reached by an object falling under gravity or accelerated by a constant force

thermal energy energy transferred from a region of higher temperature to a region of lower temperature

thermal equilibrium a condition when two or more objects in contact are at the same temperature. They lose and receive the same amount of energy per unit time

thermistor an electrical resistor whose resistance decreases as temperature increases

thermodynamic temperature scale a temperature scale that does not depend on the properties of any particular substance

threshold frequency the minimum frequency of electromagnetic radiation that will eject electrons from the surface of a metal

threshold wavelength the maximum wavelength of electromagnetic radiation that will eject electrons from the surface of a metal

time constant the time taken for the charge (or current or voltage) of a capacitor to decay to $1/e$ of its initial value, where $e = 2.718$

torque of a couple the product of one of the two forces and the perpendicular distance between the forces

transition used to describe a jump made by an electron between two energy levels

transverse wave a wave in which the points of the medium oscillate at right angles to the direction in which the wave travels

ultrasound sound waves of frequencies higher than $20\,kHz$

uncertainty an estimate of the spread of values around a measured quantity within which the true value will be found

unified atomic mass unit the standard unit used for atomic masses; 1/12th of the mass of a carbon-12 atom, $1\,u = 1.66 \times 10^{-27}\,kg$

uniform acceleration when the change in velocity of an object is the same in the same time period; sometimes called constant acceleration

upthrust the force upwards in a liquid or gas caused by the pressure in the gas or liquid

vector a quantity with both magnitude and direction

wave a periodic disturbance travelling through space, characterised by a vibrating medium

wavelength the distance between two adjacent peaks or troughs in a wave or the distance between adjacent points having the same phase

Wien's displacement law $\lambda_{max}T = $ constant, where T is the thermodynamic temperature of the object and λ_{max} is the emitted wavelength at the peak intensity

work function the minimum energy required by a single electron to escape from a metal surface

Young modulus the ratio of stress to strain for a given material, provided Hooke's law is obeyed

zero error the measurement of a quantity when the true value is zero